Elections in Latin America

Elections in Latin America

Campaigns, Voters, and Institutions

Kevin Pallister

ROWMAN & LITTLEFIELD
Lanham • Boulder • New York • London

Published by Rowman & Littlefield
An imprint of The Rowman & Littlefield Publishing Group, Inc.
4501 Forbes Boulevard, Suite 200, Lanham, Maryland 20706
www.rowman.com

86-90 Paul Street, London EC2A 4NE

British Library Cataloguing in Publication Information Available

Library of Congress Cataloging-in-Publication Data

Names: Pallister, Kevin, author.
Title: Elections in Latin America : campaigns, voters, and institutions / Kevin Pallister.
Description: Lanham, Maryland : Rowman & Littlefield, [2024] | Includes
   bibliographical references and index.
Identifiers: LCCN 2023058568 (print) | LCCN 2023058569 (ebook) |
   ISBN 9781538189023 (cloth) | ISBN 9781538189030
   (paperback) | ISBN 9781538189047 (ebook) Subjects: LCSH:
Elections—Latin America—History. | Elections—
   Latin America—Public opinion. | Political parties—Latin America. |
   Political campaigns—Latin America. | Political candidates—Latin America.
Classification: LCC JL968 .P35 2024 (print) | LCC JL968 (ebook) |
   DDC 324.98—dc23/eng/20240131
LC record available at https://lccn.loc.gov/2023058568
LC ebook record available at https://lccn.loc.gov/2023058569

Contents

List of Tables, Figures, and Text Boxes

TABLES

FIGURES

TEXT BOXES

Chapter 1

Introduction

As dawn breaks across the country, voters begin to line up at their polling place, waiting patiently for voting to begin. Poll workers, who have been up since well before sunrise on this Sunday morning, are busy preparing the materials at their voting tables and readying themselves for the long day ahead. Poll watchers from political parties sit idly in the polling station as they wait for voting to begin. Nonpartisan election observers from international and domestic organizations arrive periodically throughout the day to monitor voting before driving off to the next polling station to visit.

At 7:00 a.m. the polls open, although some polling places open late. Once voting commences, voters in line proceed to the voting table to show their identification and receive their paper ballot, which they take to a separate table in the polling place with trifold cardboard erected to provide voters with privacy while they mark their ballot. Once completed, voters return their ballot to the polling table officials, who deposit it in the ballot box. At the end of an orderly day of voting, election workers begin the ballot counting process at each polling station, with party poll watchers scrutinizing the counting of each ballot. In all likelihood, citizens will know the election results by the late hours of the evening, as vote tallies are transmitted from polling stations to the central elections office in the capital city.

When the provisional results are announced, the winning parties kick off their celebrations. To promote an orderly environment on election day, alcohol sales are prohibited today—although a stroll past street vendors reveals that the prohibition is easy to circumvent. If the election results are close, the potential for conflict is high. If all goes well, any contested results or alleged irregularities will be adjudicated through the courts. If all does not go well, the election may be contested in the streets, through demonstrations and potentially even violence.

This is a typical election day in Latin America, a day of citizens fulfilling their civic duty at the culmination of an intense electoral campaign that has lasted several months. Politicians and party strategists have tried to mobilize their supporters and sway persuadable voters. In some cases they have tried to game the system, through both legal and illegal methods, to give themselves an advantage and to win or hold on to power. But on this day, it is ultimately the voters who decide who shall govern.

WHY ELECTIONS MATTER

Elections are the primary means by which citizens govern themselves. Elections provide voters with the ability to choose between different approaches to governing: whether governments will subsidize basic goods for the poor, devote more resources to health and education, reduce regulations on business, implement measures to protect the environment, raise or lower taxes, protect civil liberties or not, and so on. Elections also provide voters with the means to hold incumbent officeholders and their political parties accountable for their performance in office.

The outcome of elections can have enormous consequences. At the extreme, they can decide between democracy and dictatorship, as when voters elect as president someone who, once in office, refuses to give up power and turns increasingly authoritarian. The elections of Hugo Chávez in Venezuela in 1998 and Daniel Ortega in Nicaragua in 2006 are clear examples. Short of determining the fate of democracy, elections can also decide crucial issues of political economy, such as whether development will be pursued through free-market policies or state intervention in the market. Some elections also decide important value issues. In Costa Rica's 2018 election, for instance, cultural values surrounding religion and sexuality were front and center, with the electorate divided between conservative and progressive views on such issues as same-sex marriage. (Ultimately, the candidate espousing support for same-sex marriage defeated his opponent, an evangelical Christian pledged to support traditional family values.)[1]

Despite the significance of elections, many Latin Americans have grown distrustful of the electoral process as they have become frustrated with politicians, political parties, and poor governance. A common lament is that elections don't change anything. As a seamstress in Santiago, Chile, told a reporter prior to the country's election in 2021, "All the candidates come with the same message, that they're going to help people, that they're going to fix problems, that the economy will recover, that there will be jobs and that quality of life will improve. . . . But then they forget about all the promises; the faces change but everything remains the same."[2] Most Latin Americans express low levels of trust in elections, with younger people having less confidence in elections than older generations.[3]

In some instances, politicians have stoked distrust in election integrity for their own political gain when faced with the prospect of losing an election. The most notable case has been Brazilian president Jair Bolsonaro (discussed below), but other candidates have done so as well. Mexico's president Andrés Manuel López Obrador (AMLO) has consistently attacked his country's electoral agency, causing his supporters to be less trustful of the country's elections.[4] When losing presidential candidates dispute the outcome of an election—as AMLO did after losing Mexico's 2006 election, and as Peru's Keiko Fujimori did after losing the 2021 presidential election—their supporters' trust in elections declines.[5] After several decades of continuous democratic rule throughout much of Latin America, elections are both indispensable institutions of self-government and objects of popular skepticism.

There is, of course, more to democracy than just elections. But elections are at the heart of democracy in Latin America and even in the political life of countries in the region under nondemocratic rule. One cannot understand the politics or modern history of Latin America without understanding the institutions, behavior, and processes surrounding elections and voting. The aim of this book is to provide a thorough overview of elections throughout Latin America, including both formal electoral institutions, informal practices, and the behavior of voters and candidates. To this end, the book synthesizes a large body of scholarship on different facets of Latin American elections and draws on news sources, election observer reports, and original data to illustrate how elections work in modern Latin America.

INTRODUCING LATIN AMERICA

Latin America consists of nineteen countries with a total population size of approximately 630 million as of 2020.[6] The region has a long history of both democracy and authoritarianism, with periods of democratic rule punctuated by military coups and revolutionary upheaval. In the 1980s and 1990s, many countries in the region transitioned to democracy, part of a global wave of democratization commonly called the third wave of democracy.[7] By the end of the twentieth century, nearly all of Latin America was democratic by the minimal standard of holding free elections (see figure 1.1).

Since the third wave, some Latin American democracies have endured while others have given way to more authoritarian rule. In its 2023 report, the think tank Freedom House classified eight Latin American countries as *fully free*, eight as *partly free*, and three as *not free*.[8] The region's democracies and semi-democracies face myriad challenges: uneven economic growth,

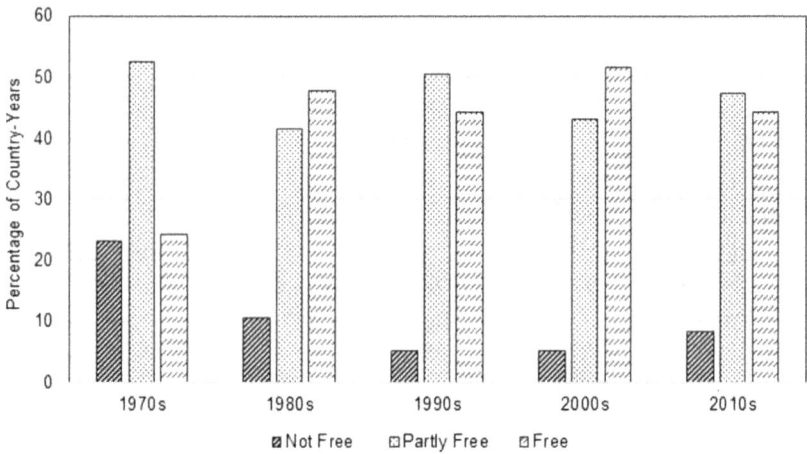

Figure 1.1   **Freedom House Scores in Latin America.** *Source*: Author's calculations based on data from Freedom House, Freedom in the World, https://freedomhouse.org /report/freedom-world#Data. Note: Bars show the percentage of all Latin American country-year scores in each Freedom House category (fully free, partly free, and not free).

high levels of economic inequality, political corruption, organized crime and citizen insecurity, and food insecurity, among others. Many governance challenges have been greatly exacerbated by the COVID-19 pandemic, which hit the region particularly hard.

In terms of constitutional structure, all Latin American countries today have presidential systems. There have been only limited experiments with alternatives to presidentialism, such as Chile's parliamentary period (1891–1925), a parliamentary system under a monarchy in Brazil during the nineteenth century, and a nine-member collegial executive adopted in 1952 in Uruguay.[9] Presidents in the region exercise a great deal of power relative to legislatures and courts. As a consequence, presidential coattails are important in legislative elections—the fortunes of political parties in winning legislative seats often rise and fall with the performance of their presidential candidates. The predominance of presidents and presidential candidates is reinforced by the prevalence of a personalistic style of politics in Latin America, where the will of leaders (often charismatic populists such as Juan Perón of Argentina, Hugo Chávez of Venezuela, and Alberto Fujimori of Peru) prevails over laws and institutions. At times some countries have fused presidential and legislative votes, so that voters selected just one party for both branches (e.g., Honduras before 1997), though this is no longer the case.

Since the start of the third wave of democracy, elections in Latin America have been hard-fought affairs. Although at times one political force dominates elections in a given country, control of the presidency and legislature is often up for grabs. Numerous political parties of different persuasions compete for votes. Candidates vie vigorously for voter support, as campaign professionals plan campaign strategy and advertisements blanket the airwaves and social media platforms. Voter participation levels tend to be high.

Historically this was not always the case. Electoral practices and institutions have evolved over time. While this book focuses on elections in modern Latin America (corresponding largely to the post-1980 period), the remainder of this chapter provides an overview of elections in Latin America before the third wave of democracy, along with case studies of several illustrative pivotal elections in the region since the third wave began. This history will hopefully serve as useful context to understand modern Latin American elections and provide familiarity with some of the most significant elections in the region's history.

ELECTIONS IN LATIN AMERICAN HISTORY

Elections were first introduced in Latin America at the very end of the colonial period, as new representative institutions at the municipal and provincial levels in the American colonies were established.[10] Following independence, republican institutions including constitutions and elections were maintained in much of the region, even though constitutional government was frequently interrupted by coups and civil wars. Mexico, for instance, saw sixteen presidents and thirty-three provisional governments between 1824 and 1857.[11] Many other countries experienced similar periods of political turmoil in the nineteenth century.

The greatest of the Latin American independence leaders, Simón Bolívar, came to favor less popular government as he witnessed the post-independence disorder in South America. He advocated a lifetime president in order to avoid "elections[,] which are the greatest scourge of republics and produce only anarchy, which . . . is the most immediate and most terrible danger of popular governments."[12] Bolívar's hopes would be disappointed: despite the political instability, the new Latin American nations returned to holding elections to allocate (or, in some cases, to demonstrate) power. Elections, with all their flaws and limitations, became "the indispensable symbols of popular sovereignty even when they failed to provide its real substance."[13]

There were periods when elections were not held in certain countries, such as during part of the rule of strongmen Getúlio Vargas in Brazil (1937–1945) and Tiburcio Carías in Honduras (1933–1949). But even some blatant dictatorships, such as the Somoza family dynasty in Nicaragua, did not do away with elections entirely. Almost every decade from the 1850s to the 1990s saw thirty-five to forty-five presidential elections.[14] Since the onset of the most recent wave of democratization in the 1980s, several hundred national-level elections have been held throughout Latin America. Moreover, more public offices became elected positions, as countries that had granted presidents the power to appoint governors and mayors now made those positions directly elected by voters. In Bolivia, for instance, mayors were appointed until 1985. In Colombia, the president appointed departmental governors who in turn named mayors; popular election of mayors started in 1988 and of governors in 1991.[15] In Venezuela, mayors and governors were not elected until 1989.[16] With some fifteen thousand municipalities in Latin America,[17] making local offices subject to direct election has dramatically opened new spaces for electoral competition.

The democratic quality of elections in the nineteenth and early twentieth centuries fell far short of today's standards. Suffrage was limited by gender and economic qualifications, although in some countries the income or property requirements for voting could be met by much of the adult male population.[18] Some Latin American countries such as Argentina, Colombia, Mexico, and Venezuela adopted principles of universal male suffrage before most Western democracies did.[19] In some cases, however, voting rights became more restricted over the course of the nineteenth century, with income and literacy requirements being adopted. Proponents of such restrictions justified them by pointing to the supposed lack of intelligence and autonomy of the illiterate, the peasantry, and the working class. As an influential Brazilian elite wrote in the 1870s, universal suffrage gave power to "the lowest segment of society, to the most ignorant and dependent," with voters nothing more than "a turbulent rabble, ignorant, undistinguished, and dependent."[20]

Further restricting the democratic nature of elections was the fact that some countries held indirect elections, whereby voters selected electors who in turn chose legislators and presidents. Argentina used such an electoral college to elect its presidents until 1994, while massive protests against indirect elections in Brazil were an important part of the country's democratic transition in the 1980s.[21] Voting was conducted verbally in the early years after independence, and the secret ballot was introduced throughout the region gradually from the mid-1800s to mid-1900s.[22] In some countries competition was limited by bans against particular political parties, especially socialist and communist parties in the twentieth century.

And not least of all, there was rampant election fraud and manipulation, including vote buying, voter intimidation, and ballot box stuffing. In many cases both governing parties and the opposition engaged in manipulative tactics,[23] and they devised many creative ways of cheating that shifted over time. Local officials that oversaw voter registration, typically partisan actors, could make arbitrary or biased decisions about who was qualified to vote.[24] In a context of severe economic inequality, patterns of clientelism were pervasive in many countries, such that large landowners (patrons) could mobilize their employees and tenant farmers on their estates (clients) for elections, controlling how they voted.[25] More short-term transactional forms of vote buying were also used. In Buenos Aires in the early twentieth century, "[b]arbecues, dances and cash were increasingly used to tempt the electorate into abandoning their political apathy on election day."[26] In Chile, campaigns "resorted to . . . cutting banknotes in half: the voter would only receive the second half after depositing the ballot in the urn."[27]

A typical example of election rigging is provided by historian David Rock, describing elections in Argentina in the 1930s in which the major reformist party, the Radical Civic Union, was banned:

> In various parts of the country the police confiscated the ballot tickets of known oppositions supporters. . . . [The winning candidate's] followers falsified voting registers, and in some jurisdictions the dead were resurrected in multitudes to cast their votes. Ballot rigging became a pandemic practice in the 1930s. A common trick of the time was to bribe voters into accepting sealed voting envelopes with pre-marked ballots. The complicit voter then smuggled the marked ballot into the voting booth and surrendered the legitimate blank ballot card as proof of having accomplished his mission.[28]

Elections could also be plagued by violence or threats of it. In Argentina in the 1860s and 1870s, violence was pervasive: "On election day, voters, who were generally armed either with guns or knives, were guided and guarded on their way to the poll stations by the members of the party clubs. Often the event ended in shootings and deaths which took place either at the time of voting, when opposition groups met at the polling tables, or when the votes were counted at the end of the election day."[29] Many elections were also followed by violence, as the losing side contested the results, claimed fraud, and sometimes revolted.[30]

Such electoral manipulation was common throughout Latin America. In some places, competing parties all bent or broke the rules seeking victory. In other cases, authoritarian regimes thoroughly controlled elections that were held merely to legitimize the dictatorship. Paraguay, for instance, held its first free presidential election only in 1928. The next free contest was sixty-one years later, in 1989.[31] During part of that period, dictator Alfredo Stroessner (in power from 1954 to 1989) was repeatedly reelected in sham contests. In yet other cases, competitive elections were overturned by the military when the results were not to the liking of the armed forces, as happened in Argentina and Guatemala. Even in Costa Rica, which would later become a bastion of liberal democracy, election fraud was pervasive in the late nineteenth and early twentieth centuries.[32]

Thus, most elections failed to meet democratic norms; the mere holding of elections did not mean that Latin American republics were democracies. But not all elections were shams, and even rigged elections meant that elites had to be somewhat attentive to the climate of public opinion. They had to mobilize the masses to ensure that voters went to the polls, and they had to build party infrastructure. Elections contributed to the creation of political clubs, partisan newspapers, and a norm of popular sovereignty. Elections were held so often that they "became a constant preoccupation in local life, and few could remain aloof from the process," as one historian wrote of nineteenth-century Brazil.[33] As Paul Drake argues in his history of Latin American democracy,

> [a]s they became routine and ritualized, elections engrained mores and customs that laid the foundation for more democratic rules and behavior in the future. From the beginning in the early nineteenth century, Latin Americans from most walks of life expressed their desire to vote, complained about grave defects in the process, and struggled to improve the implementation of elections. In the long haul, their electoral aspirations and efforts overcame formidable authoritarian obstacles to make their countries much more democratic.[34]

And indeed electoral practices became more democratic over time. Enfranchisement grew as economic and then gender and literacy barriers were removed. With the wave of democratization in the late twentieth century, independent electoral management bodies were established to administer elections and nonpartisan election observation became a widespread practice. Some routine election practices evolved to keep up with changing social norms: whereas men and women had voted separately in many countries (including Argentina, Chile, and Colombia),[35] such voter segregation had disappeared by the late twentieth century.

Electoral practices have not only reflected trends in democratization; elections themselves have at times played key roles in spurring democratization. Consider Costa Rica's contested 1948 election. After sitting out an interim term, former president Rafael Calderón Guardia was running for a second presidential term. While consecutive terms were prohibited, Calderón's party was still in power. The country's politics were polarized between Calderón's communist-supported coalition and the anti-communist opposition. Calderón's opponent, Otilio Ulate, apparently won the election, but Calderón's coalition kept a majority in the legislature. However, this official result was disputed, with both sides claiming fraud. Calderón's allies in the legislature annulled the presidential election and Ulate was arrested, setting off a brief civil war. The opposition to Calderón prevailed in the war, and opposition leader José Figueres took power. A new constitution was adopted (which included, among other reforms, the creation of a new independent electoral tribunal to administer elections and the adoption of universal adult suffrage) and elections resumed after a period of provisional government.[36] The outcome of this post-election fight set Costa Rica on a path to stable democratic government that was the envy of much of Latin America in the following decades of regional instability and authoritarianism.

PIVOTAL ELECTIONS IN MODERN LATIN AMERICA

As Costa Rica's 1948 election illustrates, some elections have been decisive turning points in the political trajectory of Latin American countries. Since the start of the most recent wave of democratization in Latin America, a number of elections have helped propel important political transitions, either pushing a country toward or away from democratic consolidation or helping to determine key aspects of a country's political economy. There are many candidates for inclusion in a list of pivotal elections: Venezuela's 1998 election that brought Hugo Chávez to the presidency, El Salvador's 1994 elections that marked the final transition from civil war to electoral democracy, Brazil's 2002 election that brought Luiz Inácio Lula da Silva to the presidency, and Colombia's elections since the 2000s that have helped decide the fate of that country's peace process with the FARC guerrillas.

This section selects five cases for readers to gain familiarity with pivotal elections in different countries in the region. Three of the cases marked clear turning points in their nations' histories: Mexico's 2000 election, Nicaragua's 1990 election, and a pair of elections in Chile in 1988 and 1989. The fourth case, Argentina's 2015 election, illustrates an election in "normal" political times: democracy was well established, and the country's institutional framework did not hinge on the election's outcome. Yet even here, in unfailingly unique Argentina, a "normal" election produced unprecedented results. The fifth case looks at Brazil's contentious 2022 election, which culminated in an insurrection strikingly similar to the January 6, 2021, riot in the United States. Taken together, the five cases illustrate a range of electoral practices and institutions that are explored in the thematic chapters to follow.

Chile 1988–1989: Saying No to a Dictator

With its long history of democracy, Chile's transition during the third wave was a re-democratization. By the late 1980s, Chile had been under military rule for a decade and a half. The country had become increasingly polarized in the 1960s, and in 1970 the socialist Salvador Allende was narrowly elected president (see chapter 2). Three years later the military, with U.S. support, overthrew Allende in a coup. General Augusto Pinochet came to dominate the military regime that replaced democracy, and the new government carried out large-scale repression against leftists and implemented drastic free-market reforms.

Under the 1980 constitution passed by the Pinochet regime, a plebiscite vote was required in 1988 to give voters a choice between another eight-year term for the government (the Yes option) or to hold elections the following year to elect a new president and legislature (the No option). The military regime conducted the campaign for the Yes vote, supported by right-wing political parties. The opposition faced the dilemma of participating and potentially legitimizing a rigged process or boycotting and conceding Pinochet's continuation in power. All segments of the opposition except for the most extreme elements on the left chose to participate, forming a coalition known as the Concertación.[37] The No campaign was at a disadvantage: its campaign workers faced intimidation and major media outlets provided progovernment coverage.[38] But Chile's Constitutional Tribunal ensured a fraud-free process by allowing opposition parties to field poll watchers on election day and mandating that vote counting be conducted in public. Pinochet's confidence in victory and U.S. pressure on the government to hold a fair election also contributed to a clean election process.[39]

The electorate was divided. A record of economic growth and public order made the regime popular with many, but authoritarianism and human rights abuses repelled a majority of Chileans. The No campaign worked diligently to get Chileans registered to vote, and ultimately over 90 percent of the eligible population registered.[40]

The campaigning was conducted through door-to-door canvassing, rallies, and especially television advertisements. Both sides received free airtime, with a thirty-minute television block divided equally between the two campaigns and airing simultaneously on all television channels. These campaign programs were widely watched and provided viewers with anti-regime messages that had been censored for fifteen years.[41] The Yes campaign praised the accomplishments of the Pinochet government while also instilling fear, portraying the plebiscite as a contest between freedom and communist tyranny, with provocative fearmongering messages in its advertisements portraying the opposition as radical.[42] For his part, Pinochet transformed from an intimidating dictator into "a smiling, grandfatherly candidate in business suits—bussing babies, waving at crowds, and donning miners' helmets and Indian blankets as he traveled the country promoting the government's good works and the importance of 'projecting' them into the future."[43]

The No campaign designed particularly effective messaging for its television programming. With the slogan "happiness is coming," the campaign "projected a positive, forward-looking message of national reconciliation."[44]

Its vision was a peaceful Chile that could move past dictatorship. One of its television ads included video footage of a police officer beating an unarmed protester with a baton. "As the camera alternated its focus between the protester and a baton-wielding officer, a voice repeated, for each one in turn, 'this man wants peace; this man is Chilean; this man fights for what he believes.' The spot concluded with the message 'Chile will be a great nation when everyone has a place in the homeland, so that this never happens again.'"[45]

On election day in October, rumors swirled of plots to overturn the election.[46] To Pinochet's surprise, the No campaign won a resounding victory of nearly twelve points. The No campaign's parallel vote count verifying the outcome, along with U.S. and business community support for respecting the result, contributed to the regime's acceptance of its defeat. As a result, a transition process began in anticipation of elections to be held in December 1989.

The 1989 election was essentially a rematch of the plebiscite the previous year, featuring many of the same players and campaign strategies. The seventeen-party Concertación coalition managed to stay united, with the largest parties—the Christian Democrats and Socialists—cooperating with each other and with smaller parties to select legislative candidates to appease all the parties in the coalition.[47] The Concertación ranged from left-wing to center-right, and its presidential candidate, seventy-one-year-old Patricio Aylwin, was a moderate Christian Democrat who had been a spokesman for the No campaign in 1988. Aylwin had opposed Allende's government in the 1970s, and his moderation helped reassure conservatives that he would not pursue significant economic reforms.

Opposing the Concertación was a right-wing coalition of the RN and UDI parties. Their presidential candidate, Hernan Büchi, had been finance minister from 1985 onward during a period of good economic performance. His successful stint as finance minister, along with his youth (he was forty years old) were appealing features, but the shy Büchi was a reluctant candidate who briefly withdrew his candidacy before reversing the decision.[48]

Aylwin led in the polls throughout the process. The Concertación continued to push a message of reconciliation, rather than retribution against those responsible for human rights abuses during the dictatorship. It also presented a moderate image on economic issues and avoided offering specific policy proposals.[49] Büchi made lavish promises of creating a million new jobs and providing housing and health care—offerings inconsistent with his previous policies as finance minister.[50] Pinochet himself mostly kept out of the 1989 campaign. But "[t]he central dilemma of the right, which was never resolved, was how to present itself in relation to the Pinochet government."[51] Ultimately the "effort to 'market' Büchi as the symbol of a modern, upwardly mobile society could not shake his image as a soulless protégé of dictatorship."[52]

The result was much the same as the previous year. With more than 90 percent of registered voters participating, Aylwin received 55 percent of the vote, while Büchi won only 29 percent (an independent populist candidate won 15 percent). The election process was well administered and fair, and the losing candidates graciously conceded on election night. The Concertación also won a majority in both houses of Congress, although the parties on the right won sufficient seats to block constitutional reforms.

Both the 1988 plebiscite and the 1989 general election were turning points in Chilean history. They returned the country to democracy, as Chileans ended a military dictatorship not through mass insurrection but through the ballot box, defeating the regime at its own game. The Concertación would go on to win the presidency in the next three elections, with two of those candidates coming from the Socialist Party. Elements of the military regime remained—some unelected figures from the regime served as senators for life, Pinochet remained for a time as commander of the armed forces, and the military retained extensive prerogatives for itself. But over time reforms would rid Chile's political system of these authoritarian holdovers, and Chile became one of Latin America's most democratic countries.

Nicaragua 1990: Voting for Peace and Ending a Revolution

Unlike Chile, Nicaragua had no sustained experience with democracy before the third wave of democratization. And rather than transitioning from a military regime as in Chile or a dominant-party regime as in Mexico, Nicaragua transitioned to democracy via a revolution that overthrew a personalist dictatorship and then an election that removed the revolutionary regime from power.

From 1937 to 1979, Nicaragua was ruled by the Somoza family, first under Anastasio Somoza García and subsequently under his sons. The Somozas at times ruled directly, at other times indirectly through puppet presidents. While elections were held periodically, they were controlled by the regime. Ballot box stuffing, multiple voting, translucent ballots that violated the secrecy of the vote, and censorship and intimidation were all common. In some cases, the National Guard (controlled by Somoza) distributed the ballots and counted the votes.[53] The Conservative Party served as token opposition to Somoza's Liberal Party, but when the Conservatives periodically boycotted elections, Somoza arranged for a different phony opposition party to run against him. Rather than real contests for power in which the outcome was uncertain, elections under the Somozas were facades to provide the regime with a veneer of legitimacy.

In 1979 a revolution overthrew the last Somoza ruler. The revolution, spearheaded by the leftist Sandinista Front of National Liberation (FSLN), initiated a left-wing regime. Throughout the 1980s, the United States worked to overthrow the Sandinistas from power. As the Reagan administration organized and funded anti-Sandinista insurgents (the counterrevolutionary forces, or Contras) and waged economic warfare against Nicaragua, the Sandinistas sought economic and diplomatic support from other countries, including democratic countries in Europe and Latin America. These pressures necessitated the holding of free elections to shore up the revolutionary regime's legitimacy both at home and abroad. To administer elections, a new Supreme Electoral Council (CSE) was established and new electoral laws were approved in consultation with opposition parties.

Competitive elections were held in 1984, but the U.S.-supported opposition boycotted. In 1990, however, all the opposition parties participated, with the FSLN facing a fourteen-party opposition coalition, the National Opposition Union (UNO).[54] For its presidential candidate, UNO ran Violeta Chamorro, the widow of journalist Pedro Joaquín Chamorro (who was murdered by the Somoza regime), publisher of a leading newspaper, and a member of one of Nicaragua's most prominent families. Chamorro faced off against the FSLN's Daniel Ortega, who had been elected president in 1984.

The election was marked by an extraordinary level of international involvement, drawing perhaps the largest international election observation effort in history, with the United Nations and various nongovernmental organizations such as the Carter Center fielding large observer missions. International organizations also provided financial and technical support to help administer the elections. While these forms of international involvement aimed to ensure a fair and efficient election, other types of foreign influence aimed to tilt the election's outcome. The UNO coalition's campaign was heavily funded by the United States, both through legal and covert channels. The Contra War hung over the election campaign, as voters understood that an UNO victory would bring an end to the war while a Sandinista victory might mean continued U.S. efforts to destabilize the country. Because of the U.S. role, "[t]he Sandinistas portrayed their domestic critics as puppets of U.S. imperialism and themselves as the true nationalists and the defenders of national sovereignty."[55]

The election was remarkably well administered by the CSE, which performed impartially and professionally. The CSE carried out a massive voter registration drive, encouraged voter participation, and employed safeguards against election fraud. With more than three-quarters of eligible voters participating, the results stunned the world. Proving the preelection polls wrong, Chamorro and the UNO defeated the Sandinistas, and Chamorro became the country's first female president. Exhaustion with a decade of war and economic crisis were decisive in the outcome, which ended the revolutionary period and transitioned Nicaragua toward more free-market economic policies. Although Daniel Ortega would return to the presidency after the 2006 election, he did so at the head of a profoundly transformed FSLN party that had shed much of its revolutionary ideology and was firmly controlled by Ortega and his inner circle. The 2006 contest that brought Ortega back to power would prove to be Nicaragua's last fair election (see chapter 2).

Mexico 2000: Ending Seven Decades of One-Party Hegemony

Mexico has a long history of holding elections, but before the 1990s little experience with fair elections. Nearly continuously from 1876 to 1910 the country was ruled by strongman Porfirio Díaz, elected seven times to the presidency. Elections during Díaz's reign (the Porfiriato) were tightly controlled, with every candidate for Congress being approved by Díaz.[56] Díaz's fraudulent reelection in 1910 precipitated the Mexican Revolution, one of the great social revolutions in modern history.

Since the Mexican Revolution, presidential elections have been held every six years and legislative elections every three years. After a decade of instability following the end of the revolution, Mexican politics came to be dominated by a single political party: the Institutional Revolutionary Party, or PRI.[57] The PRI combined genuine popular support with the use of clientelism, coercion, and election fraud (especially in rural and less developed areas) to maintain its grip over Mexican politics. As one scholar described vote buying under the PRI, "[p]articularistic material rewards—everything from minor kitchen appliances to land titles and public-sector jobs—were routinely and systematically used to purchase electoral support."[58] Until the 1990s the party controlled the machinery of election administration, allowing the party machine to engage in ballot box stuffing, vote buying, and other forms of manipulation known in Mexico as "electoral alchemy."[59] But the party also intensely mobilized its supporters and enjoyed a good deal of genuine support, and combined with electoral manipulation it racked up enormous margins of victory: from the 1930s through the 1970s the party "won" between 74 percent and 100 percent of the vote in presidential elections.[60] Such huge margins served to demonstrate the party's invincibility and thereby deter many ambitious office seekers from joining or forming opposition parties.[61]

By the 1980s, however, the PRI began to lose more municipal elections as economic crisis undermined the party's support. The most formidable opposition was the National Action Party (PAN), formed in 1939 as a Catholic-centered conservative party. For decades the PRI regime allowed the PAN to win only marginal numbers of legislative seats and local races, but as the end of the twentieth century approached, the PAN grew more competitive. Prior to the 1988 presidential election, the PRI suffered a split as some leftist members, led by Cuauhtémoc Cárdenas (son of famous Mexican president

Lázaro Cárdenas), left the party and went on to form the Party of the Democratic Revolution (PRD). Cárdenas ran for president in 1988 against the PRI's Carlos Salinas, and fraud in that contest may well have robbed Cárdenas of victory and kept the PRI in power.

Needing some opposition cooperation to implement economic reform policies following the contested 1988 election, the PRI agreed to electoral reforms that established a new election administration body (the Federal Electoral Institute, IFE). Subsequent reforms in the 1990s made IFE a truly independent body and instituted public campaign financing to help level the playing field. Although the PRI was able to win the 1994 presidential election, the party lost its majority in Congress for the first time in the 1997 midterm elections. The stage was set for a momentous presidential contest in 2000.

Prior to the election, the PRI held an open primary to select its presidential candidate for the first time, marking the end of the practice known as dedazo, by which the outgoing PRI president handpicked his party's candidate. The primary winner was Francisco Labastida, a former governor and cabinet member. Labastida faced two main challengers in the general election: Cárdenas, now mayor of Mexico City and running for the presidency for the third time with the PRD, and Vicente Fox, a former Coca Cola executive and governor of Guanajuato, running for the PAN.[62]

All three major candidates campaigned vigorously, flooding the airwaves with ads, holding rallies, participating in two widely watched debates, and generating extensive news media coverage. There was much attack messaging, especially with the Fox campaign attacking Labastida and the PRI regime throughout the campaign. Some of the mudslinging was personal, with Fox famously attacking Labastida for appearing unmanly.[63] As for the PRI, some local operatives threatened welfare program recipients that they would lose assistance if they didn't vote for the PRI.[64]

Vicente Fox's personality-centered campaign succeeded in framing the election around the theme of change, emphasizing the need to defeat the PRI after seventy years in power. Specific policy issues and ideological positions of the candidates mattered less than voters' views toward the PRI regime and the character traits of the candidates.[65] Fox successfully presented himself as the change candidate. As one analyst wrote, "Fox was change. Change was Fox. Everything else could be filled in by the voter as he or she wished."[66] For his part, Labastida failed to push back against the framing of the contest as a question of change.

Despite leading in the polls until the days before the election, the PRI went down to defeat. Fox won 43.4 percent of the vote, a robust victory over Labastida (who won 36.9 percent); Cárdenas trailed with just 17 percent. Many factors help explain the outcome. Vicente Fox was a charismatic candidate facing challengers who definitively lacked charisma. Some likely Cárdenas voters ended up voting for Fox as the candidate most likely to defeat the PRI. Labastida's campaign struggled to communicate how the candidate represented both change and continuity. Institutional changes made fraud much more difficult to perpetrate. And most fundamentally, many Mexican voters were ready for a change after seven decades of PRI rule.

Fox's victory and the PRI's defeat marked the culmination of a gradual transition from semi-authoritarianism under hegemonic party rule to electoral democracy. The alternation of parties in power continued in the years ahead, with PAN losing the presidency in 2012 to the PRI and the PRI losing it again in 2018. While Mexico's democracy remained saddled with problems related to crime, corruption, and economic vulnerability, the 2000 election was a watershed in the country's development of a truly competitive electoral system.

Argentina 2015: An Extraordinary Ordinary Election

The 1988–1989 elections in Chile, the 1990 contest in Nicaragua, and Mexico's 2000 election were all pivotal moments in modern Latin American history. Of course, most elections are less transformative, and as democratic competition becomes institutionalized, elections become quite routine affairs. This could be said of Argentina's 2015 presidential election. Even here, though, a routine election produced some notable outcomes.

The election pitted three competitive candidates against each other. Daniel Scioli, the governor of Buenos Aires province, ran under the banner of the Peronist movement (the Front for Victory coalition), the country's long-standing populist movement and the party of the outgoing president Cristina Fernández de Kirchner. Businessman and Buenos Aires mayor Mauricio Macri ran under the Cambiemos (Let's Change) coalition, which included his own center-right party and the Radical Civic Union, a traditional centrist party. Dissident Peronist Sergio Massa was also on the ballot and trailed Macri and Scioli in the primary election.

Outgoing two-term president Cristina Fernández de Kirchner (often referred to as CFK) was constitutionally barred from running for an additional term and offered lukewarm support to the Peronist candidate Scioli.[67] Although both Scioli and CFK were Peronists, Scioli wasn't a Kirchner loyalist, and his candidacy aimed to win over some moderate voters who liked Kirchnerist policies but not her combative style.[68]

The campaigns of both Macri and Scioli spent heavily on advertising—Macri's campaign produced three hundred spots for television and social media—and hired international campaign consultants, with Scioli hiring the famed American campaign consultant James Carville.[69] Both campaigns made extensive use of social media platforms. Macri employed a large communications team that managed the campaign's social media accounts.[70] Scioli's campaign used a full array of platforms (Facebook, Twitter, Instagram, YouTube, Vine), sent followers digital materials and hashtags to post on their social media accounts, and distributed information about upcoming campaign events via WhatsApp.[71]

The election took place in the context of a stagnant economy and high inflation. According to surveys, the economy and public safety were the biggest issues for voters. The candidates emphasized the economy and governability, and the economy was the main issue of the presidential debate held before the runoff.[72]

Yet while issues mattered, the discourse of the campaigns was short on specific policy proposals, and instead focused on themes of continuity or change, pessimism and optimism, along with an emphasis on valence issues like the economy.[73] After two terms of CFK in office (2007–2015), which were preceded by a presidential term of her late husband Néstor Kirchner (2003–2007), the central theme of the campaign was continuity versus change. Macri avoided taking positions on difficult issues like the national debt and inflation and "portrayed himself as a pragmatist who could manage bureaucrats and get things done," while "his campaign radiated optimism, hope, teamwork, and (of course) 'change.'"[74]

While the candidates avoided offering detailed policy proposals in favor of emphasizing themes of continuity or change, they attempted to diminish their opponent in the eyes of voters. Scioli's campaign attacked Macri as an out-of-touch businessman who would bring back unpopular neoliberal economic policies that Argentina implemented in the 1990s.[75] Macri effectively countered these attacks with a campaign heavy on developing an empathetic image. Key to this strategy were visits that Macri made to the households of ordinary Argentinians. The campaign filmed these visits and used footage in campaign spots showing Macri sitting around the kitchen table having conversations with ordinary people.[76]

For his part, Macri tried to tie Scioli to the shortcomings of the Kirchner government. This put Scioli in the difficult spot of emphasizing continuity with the outgoing government to maintain the support of Kirchner loyalists while also indicating that his presidency would bring change.[77] (The PRI candidate in Mexico's 2000 race had faced a similar dilemma.) Similarly, Scioli alternated between aligning himself with Cristina Fernández and her aggressive rhetoric and distancing himself from CFK's attacks against Macri.[78]

Analyses of vote choice in the election found that voters' assessments of incumbent performance on the economy drove vote choice, with ideology and specific issue positions having little impact. Voters with a positive view of the economy tended to vote for Scioli, of the incumbent Peronists, while those with a negative view of the economy voted for Macri.[79] The election outcome thus illustrated the classic dynamic of retrospective voting (see chapter 9).

Argentina's presidential elections include an open primary round that determines which candidates make it to the general election and a runoff election if no candidate wins 45 percent of the vote (or 40 percent plus a ten-point margin over the second place candidate) in the general election. After coming in second in the open primary, Mauricio Macri went on to win the presidency in the runoff round. The 2015 election marked the first time a runoff election was held in Argentina and the first time since 1946 that a candidate not from the Peronists or Radical Civic Union was elected to the presidency.[80] Macri would also go on to become the first non-Peronist president to complete his term in office, with other non-Peronists having resigned from office early or been removed in military coups.

Macri's election led many observers of Latin America to suggest that the region was shifting to the right of the political spectrum after years of leftist dominance in Argentina and many other countries in the region. The turn to more conservative government did not last long in Argentina, however. After governing over a difficult economic situation, Macri lost his bid for reelection in 2019 to his Peronist opponents. In the wake of economic troubles and the COVID-19 pandemic, many other Latin American countries followed suit and elected left-of-center presidential candidates. Argentina's 2015 and 2019 elections were thus something of a bellwether for the entire region.

Brazil 2022: A Polarized Democracy on the Brink

Brazil's 2022 general election was the most consequential since the country returned to democracy in the 1980s after two decades under a military regime. The presidential contest pitted the right-wing incumbent Jair Bolsonaro against former two-term president Luiz Inácio Lula da Silva (widely known as Lula) of the left-wing Workers' Party (PT). The campaign was polarized and divisive, and the aftermath of the election brought about the gravest threat to Brazil's democracy since the 1964 coup that had ushered in military rule.

Lula served two terms as president from 2003 to 2010. Lula benefited from strong economic growth during his presidency, and he implemented popular social programs. His successor, Dilma Rousseff (also from the PT), won election in 2010 and again in 2014, but was impeached and removed from office in 2016 amid a severe economic recession and a massive corruption scandal that implicated politicians across the political spectrum. Lula himself was convicted in a corruption case in 2017 and sentenced to twelve years in prison, but his conviction was overturned in 2019 after revelations that the judge in the case had improperly colluded with prosecutors.

Lula's conviction had prevented him from running for president again in the 2018 election. That year, right-wing populist Jair Bolsonaro—a crass, charismatic candidate who presented himself as an outsider—rode a wave of anger over corruption and economic malaise to the presidency, easily defeating the PT's candidate in the runoff round. Bolsonaro's term was marked by controversies and accusations of corruption, and during the COVID-19 pandemic Bolsonaro downplayed the seriousness of the threat and discouraged Brazilians from taking public health precautions. With approval ratings below 50 percent and facing off against Lula, Bolsonaro's prospects in the 2022 election looked dim.

However, Brazil in 2022 was much more polarized than it had been a decade earlier. Although Lula had left office with sky-high approval ratings, corruption scandals and recession in the intervening years had left Brazilians discontent and angry at the PT, and many had become radicalized as they increasingly consumed news via social media. Voters faced clearly differentiated options in terms of government policy. For instance, deforestation had increased drastically during Bolsonaro's term, as his administration allowed agricultural and mining operations to clear Amazon rainforest. His government also loosened restrictions on gun ownership. But voters also faced a polarized choice in terms of cultural values. "Bolsonaro stood for hard-right nationalism, law and order, and a conservative discourse in 'defense of the family,' which extended to vocal support for figures such as Vladimir Putin and Viktor Orbán. Lula promoted progressive social values, strong support for minoritized populations, and concern with restoring Brazil's voice in the international community."[81]

Polls showed Lula comfortably ahead before the first round of voting, but the results were much closer than polling had anticipated: Lula won 48.2 percent of the vote to Bolsonaro's 43.2 percent, pushing the election to a runoff round. In the lead up to both rounds of voting, Bolsonaro pulled out all the stops. He boosted social welfare spending to try to win over voters.[82] Networks of his supporters on social media "relentlessly tarred Lula as a godless communist intent on shuttering all Christian churches in the country."[83] And on the day of the runoff vote, highway police—headed by a staunch Bolsonaro ally—stopped buses carrying voters to polling places in Lula strongholds in an attempt to disenfranchise Lula voters.[84] Nevertheless, Lula won the second round vote, 50.9 percent to 49.1 percent, in what was the narrowest margin in a presidential election in Brazil's history.

Many Bolsonaro supporters refused to accept the results. In fact, just as Donald Trump had promoted baseless conspiracy theories about election fraud in the United States, Bolsonaro had for years spread misinformation about election fraud in Brazil.[85] Bolsonaro's conspiracy theories centered on claims that Brazil's electronic voting machines were vulnerable to manipulation, despite overwhelming evidence to the contrary. Misinformation about election integrity was ubiquitous in right-wing circles on social media and messaging services like Telegram.[86]

When the results were announced on election night, Brazil's political leaders—including pro-Bolsonaro lawmakers—and countries around the world quickly recognized Lula as the winner. But many Bolsonaro supporters, awash in misinformation and fearful of what another Lula presidency would bring, were primed to believe that the election had been stolen. In the days after the election, Bolsonaro supporters blocked highways around the country in protest. Bolsonaro made no public statements for days after the election, and he never conceded that he had lost. For the following two months, thousands of his supporters camped outside military bases calling for a coup. They hoped the military would prevent Lula from taking office and overturn the election results. There was no coup, and Lula was duly sworn into office on January 1, 2023. Rather than attend the inauguration, Bolsonaro had left the country days earlier, traveling to Florida for a months-long stay.

In another stunning parallel to the United States, on January 8, 2023, Bolsonaro supporters invaded and ransacked the presidential, congressional, and Supreme Court buildings. Elected officials were not in the buildings at the time—the insurrection occurred on a Sunday—but scenes of the destruction left behind by the rioters shook Brazil and garnered worldwide media coverage. Motivated by beliefs that the election had been stolen and that another Lula term would destroy the country, Bolsonaro supporters had tried to overturn the election and spark a military coup. Brazil's democracy appeared more tenuous than it had been since the height of the Cold War, and Lula began his third term facing the daunting challenge of unifying a deeply divided country.

CONCLUSION

Elections are central to contemporary politics in Latin America. Outside of Cuba, every country in the region elects their national and local officials through electoral processes of varying quality. Most countries in the region have a history of electing national leaders that goes back to the earliest days of independence. As this chapter has shown, elections throughout the nineteenth and twentieth centuries were often exclusionary, violent, manipulated, and rigged—yet nevertheless meaningful for developing a norm that governments are ultimately elected by the people.

Beginning with the third wave of democratization in the late twentieth century, elections have become an even more central part of the region's political landscape. Some elections have been pivotal in their nation's political history, helping to launch democratization, settle violent political conflicts, and elect transformational leaders. Yet after several decades of sustained electoral competition, many Latin Americans are dissatisfied with their political systems and the lack of responsiveness of elected governments to citizens' needs. This shouldn't be surprising; as political scientist Adam Przeworski observes, "[i]t is only natural that when people participate in successive elections, see governments change, and discover that their lives remain the same, they find something wrong with 'the system' or 'the establishment.'"[87]

The aim of this book is to allow readers to make knowledgeable assessments of Latin American elections, with all of their promise and shortcomings. The following chapters reveal the many noteworthy and often admirable developments of electoral practices over time. Countries in the region have made great strides in election administration, successfully registering voters, conducting orderly voting on election day, and transmitting results in a timely fashion. Voting rights have been expanded, extending even to citizens living outside their country of citizenship. Gender quotas have increased the presence of women on candidate lists for legislatures. Latin American countries have been laboratories for institutional innovations in the areas of legislative electoral systems (tinkering with many variations of proportional representation), presidential election rules (becoming a world leader in adopting majority runoff systems), compulsory voting, the use of referenda, regulations aimed at the influence of money in campaigns, and the use of primary elections.

Alongside these advances, Latin American elections also all too often leave much to be desired. Some incumbent parties rig elections to stay in power. Clientelism and vote buying are common. Campaigns are centered much more on personalities and empty promises than on concrete and realistic policy proposals. Political party systems in many countries present voters with a bewildering array of indistinguishable options. Campaign finance regulations are frequently subverted, allowing criminal groups to buy influence with candidates.

This book examines all these facets of elections in modern Latin America. It benefits from the enormous body of scholarly research that has developed over the past several decades, along with the reports and data that are available from international organizations that work on elections. The following chapters examine the legal framework of elections, including the degree to which elections meet international standards of electoral integrity (chapter 2); the electoral systems used and the rules surrounding the right to vote (chapter 3); the rules and processes pertaining to running for national office (chapter 4); political party systems and their relevance for electoral processes (chapter 5); campaigning strategies and methods (chapter 6); the challenges of regulating campaign finance (chapter 7); and voter behavior, including the factors that influence whether people vote (chapter 8) and who they vote for (chapter 9).

NOTES

1. "Costa Rica Election: Carlos Alvarado Set to Be President," BBC News, April 2, 2018, https://www.bbc.com/news/world-latin-america-43614744.

2. Pascale Bonnefoy and Ernesto Londoño, "José Antonio Kast, Far-Right Candidate, Leads after First Round of Chile's Presidential Election," *New York Times*, November 21, 2021, https://www.nytimes.com/2021/11/21/world/americas/chile-election-boric-kast.html.

3. Ehab Alhosaini and Oscar Castorena, "Trust in Elections and Electoral Integrity," in *Pulse of Democracy*, ed. Noam Lupu, Mariana Rodríguez, and Elizabeth J. Zechmeister (Nashville, TN: LAPOP, 2021), 34–49, https://www.vanderbilt.edu/lapop/ab2021/2021_LAPOP_AmericasBarometer_2021_Pulse_of_Democracy.pdf.

4. Alejandro Monsiváis-Carrillo, "Happy Winners, Sore Partisans? Political Trust, Partisanship, and the Populist Assault on Electoral Integrity in Mexico," *Journal of Politics in Latin America* 15, no. 1 (2022), https://doi.org/10.1177/1866802X221136147.

5. Victor Hernández-Huerta and Francisco Cantú, "Public Distrust in Disputed Elections: Evidence from Latin America," *British Journal of Political Science* 52, no. 4 (2022), doi:10.1017/S0007123421000399.

6. The countries included in this book are Argentina, Bolivia, Brazil, Chile, Colombia, Costa Rica, Dominican Republic, Ecuador, El Salvador, Guatemala, Honduras, Mexico, Nicaragua, Panama, Paraguay, Peru, Uruguay, and Venezuela. Because of its lack of competitive elections, Cuba is excluded. These countries constitute "Latin America" through their shared heritage of colonial rule by Iberian powers from the sixteenth to nineteenth centuries—with Portugal colonizing modern-day Brazil and Spain colonizing what became the other countries of the region. Population is calculated from World Bank data at https://data.worldbank.org/indicator/SP.POP.TOTL?locations=ZJ.

7. Samuel P. Huntington, *The Third Wave: Democratization in the Late Twentieth Century* (Norman, OK: University of Oklahoma Press, 1991).

8. Sarah Repucci and Amy Slipowitz, *Freedom in the World 2023: Marking 50 Years in the Struggle for Democracy*, Freedom House, 2023, https://freedomhouse.org/report/freedom-world/2023/marking-50-years. The *fully free* countries are Argentina, Brazil, Chile, Colombia, Costa Rica, Ecuador, Panama, and Uruguay. Classified as *partly free* are Bolivia, the Dominican Republic, El Salvador, Guatemala, Honduras, Mexico, Peru, and Paraguay. The *not free* are Cuba, Nicaragua, and Venezuela.

9. On Uruguay, see Ronald H. McDonald, *Party Systems and Elections in Latin America* (Chicago: Markham Publishers, 1971), 201.

10. Jaime E. Rodríguez O., *The Independence of Spanish America* (New York: Cambridge University Press, 1998), 94.

11. Jay Kinsbruner, *Independence in Spanish America* (Albuquerque: University of New Mexico Press, 1994), 128.

12. Rodríguez O., *Independence*, 234.

13. John Charles Chasteen, *Americanos: Latin America's Struggle for Independence* (New York: Oxford University Press, 2008), 186.

14. Paul W. Drake, *Between Tyranny and Anarchy: A History of Democracy in Latin America, 1800–2006* (Stanford: Stanford University Press, 2009), 40.

15. Eduardo A. Gamarra, "Municipal Elections in Bolivia," in *Urban Elections in Democratic Latin America*, ed. Henry A. Dietz and Gil Shidlo (Wilmington, DE: Scholarly Resources, 1998), 21–22; Gary Hoskin, "Urban Electoral Behavior in Colombia," in *Urban Elections in Democratic Latin America*, ed. Henry A. Dietz and Gil Shidlo (Wilmington, DE: Scholarly Resources, 1998), 92.

16. Cynthia McClintock, *Electoral Rules and Democracy in Latin America* (New York: Oxford University Press, 2018), 67.

17. Salvador Romero Ballivián, *Elecciones en América Latina* (Tribunal Supremo Electoral and Instituto Internacional para la Democracia y Asistencia Electoral, 2020), 265.

18. This was the case in Chile and Brazil in the nineteenth century. J. Samuel Valenzuela, "Building Aspects of Democracy before Democracy: Electoral Practices in Nineteenth Century Chile," in *Elections before Democracy: The History of Elections in Europe and Latin America*, ed. Eduardo Posada-Carbó (New York: St. Martin's Press, 1996); Richard Graham, *Patronage and Politics in Nineteenth-Century Brazil* (Stanford: Stanford University Press, 1990), 103–8.

19. Eduardo Posada-Carbó, "Electoral Juggling: A Comparative History of the Corruption of Suffrage in Latin America, 1830–1930," *Journal of Latin American Studies* 32, no. 3 (2000): 616, doi:10.1017/S0022216X00005782.

20. Graham, *Patronage and Politics*, 190.

21. Argentina held some direct presidential elections in the twentieth century, but repeatedly returned to using an electoral college until 1994. In Brazil, the 1985 election that transferred power from the military to civilians employed an electoral college, but the incoming civilian government quickly amended the constitution to institute direct presidential elections.

22. Drake, *Between Tyranny and Anarchy*, 44, 86.

23. Posada-Carbó, "Electoral Juggling," 634.

24. This was the case in Brazil, for instance. Graham, *Patronage and Politics*, 106–7.

25. Graham, *Patronage and Politics*.

26. Paula Alonso, "Voting in Buenos Aires (Argentina) Before 1912," in *Elections before Democracy: The History of Elections in Europe and Latin America*, ed. Eduardo Posada-Carbó (New York: St. Martin's Press, 1996), 194.

27. Posada-Carbó, "Electoral Juggling," 639.

28. David Rock, *Argentina, 1516–1987: From Spanish Colonization to Alfonsín* (Berkeley: University of California Press, 1987), 217.

29. Alonso, "Voting in Buenos Aires," 191.

30. Posada-Carbó, "Electoral Juggling," 636. On post-election violence in Bolivia, see Herbert S. Klein, "Bolivia from the War of the Pacific to the Chaco War, 1880–1932," in *The Cambridge History of Latin America*, v. 5, ed. Leslie Bethell (New York: Cambridge University Press, 1986), 564.

31. Marta León-Roesch and Richard Ortiz Ortiz, "Paraguay," in *Elections in the Americas: A Data Handbook, vol. 2, South America*, ed. Dieter Nohlen (New York: Oxford University Press, 2005), 412.

32. Fabrice E. Lehoucq and Iván Molina, *Stuffing the Ballot Box: Fraud, Electoral Reform, and Democratization in Costa Rica* (Cambridge University Press, 2002); Deborah J. Yashar, *Demanding Democracy: Reform and Reaction in Costa Rica and Guatemala, 1870s–1950s* (Stanford: Stanford University Press, 1997), 53–55.

33. Graham, *Patronage and Politics*, 103.

34. Drake, *Between Tyranny and Anarchy*, 41.

35. McDonald, *Party Systems and Elections*, 102, 128, 186.

36. Ralph Lee Woodward, Jr., *Central America: A Nation Divided* (New York: Oxford University Press, 1999), 225–27; James Mahoney, *The Legacies of Liberalism: Path Dependence and Political Regimes in Central America* (Baltimore: Johns Hopkins University Press, 2001), 222–24.

37. Pamela Constable and Arturo Valenzuela, *A Nation of Enemies: Chile under Pinochet* (New York: W.W. Norton, 1991), 300–302.

38. Ibid., 303; Taylor C. Boas, "Voting for Democracy: Campaign Effects in Chile's Democratic Transition," *Latin American Politics and Society* 57, no. 2 (2015): 73, doi:10.1111/j.1548-2456.2015.00267.x.

39. Constable and Valenzuela, *Nation of Enemies*, 303–5.

40. Ibid., 305–6.

41. Boas, "Voting for Democracy," 73–74.

42. Taylor C. Boas, *Presidential Campaigns in Latin America: Electoral Strategies and Success Contagion* (New York: Cambridge University Press, 2016), 55–56; Constable and Valenzuela, *Nation of Enemies*, 305.

43. Constable and Valenzuela, *Nation of Enemies*, 298.

44. Boas, "Voting for Democracy," 74.

45. Boas, *Presidential Campaigns in Latin America*, 53. Video of this advertisement can be found at https://www.youtube.com/watch?v=HSsvZ5SsSpw.

46. Constable and Valenzuela, *Nation of Enemies*, 307–8.

47. Ibid., 313–14.

48. Alan Angell and Benny Pollack, "The Chilean Elections of 1989 and the Politics of the Transition to Democracy," *Bulletin of Latin American Research* 9, no. 1 (1990): 8, https://www.jstor.org/stable/i275696.

49. Ibid., 5; Boas, *Presidential Campaigns in Latin America*, 59.

50. Constable and Valenzuela, *Nation of Enemies*, 315.

51. Angell and Pollack, "The Chilean Elections of 1989," 9.

52. Constable and Valenzuela, *Nation of Enemies*, 316.

53. Richard Millett, *Guardians of the Dynasty: A History of the U.S.-Created Guardia Nacional de Nicaragua and the Somoza Family* (Maryknoll, NY: Orbis Books, 1977), 181; Knut Walter, *The Regime of Anastasio Somoza, 1936–1956* (Chapel Hill: University of North Carolina Press, 1993), 92.

54. Much has been written about the 1990 election. Among other sources, I draw on reports from the United Nations election observation mission and the Carter Center's election observer report, *Observing Nicaragua's Elections, 1989–1990*.

55. Dario Moreno, "Respectable Intervention: The United States and the Central American Elections," in *Elections and Democracy in Central America Revisited*, ed. Mitchell A. Seligson and John A. Booth (Chapel Hill: University of North Carolina Press, 1995), 239. The 1990 election was not the first time the United States was deeply involved in a Nicaraguan election. Presidential elections in 1928 and 1932 had been directly supervised by the United States.

56. Friederich Katz, "Mexico: Restored Republic and Porfiriato, 1867–1910," in *The Cambridge History of Latin America*, v. 5, ed. Leslie Bethell (New York: Cambridge University Press, 1986), 35.

57. The party, formed in 1929, went by different names before settling on PRI.

58. Wayne A. Cornelius, "Mobilized Voting in the 2000 Elections: The Changing Efficacy of Vote Buying and Coercion in Mexican Electoral Politics," in *Mexico's Pivotal Democratic Election: Candidates, Voters, and the Presidential Campaign of 2000*, ed. Jorge I. Dominguez and Chappell Lawson (Stanford/La Jolla, CA: Stanford University Press and Center for U.S.-Mexican Studies, University of California at San Diego, 2004), 48.

59. Paul Gillingham, "Mexican Elections, 1910–1994: Voters, Violence, and Veto Power," in *The Oxford Handbook of Mexican Politics*, ed. Roderic Ai Camp (New York: Oxford University Press, 2012), 55.

60. Ibid., 54.

61. Beatriz Magaloni, *Voting for Autocracy: Hegemonic Party Survival and Its Demise in Mexico* (New York: Cambridge University Press, 2006).

62. Much has been written about the 2000 Mexican elections. In addition to the sources cited in this section, I draw on James A. McCann, "Changing Dimensions of National Elections in Mexico," in *The Oxford Handbook of Mexican Politics*, ed. Roderic Ai Camp (New York: Oxford University Press, 2012); Jorge I. Domínguez, "Mexico's Campaigns and the Benchmark Elections of 2000 and 2006," in *The Oxford Handbook of Mexican Politics*, ed. Roderic Ai Camp (New York: Oxford University Press, 2012); and Jorge I. Dominguez and Chappell Lawson (eds.), *Mexico's Pivotal Democratic Election: Candidates, Voters, and the Presidential Campaign of 2000* (Stanford/La Jolla, CA: Stanford University Press and Center for U.S.-Mexican Studies, University of California at San Diego, 2004).

63. See Alejandro Moreno, "The Effects of Negative Campaigns on Mexican Voters," in *Mexico's Pivotal Democratic Election: Candidates, Voters, and the Presidential Campaign of 2000*, ed. Jorge I. Dominguez and Chappell Lawson (Stanford/La Jolla, CA: Stanford University Press and Center for U.S.-Mexican Studies, University of California at San Diego, 2004).

64. Chappell Lawson, "Introduction," in *Mexico's Pivotal Democratic Election: Candidates, Voters, and the Presidential Campaign of 2000*, ed. Jorge I. Dominguez and Chappell Lawson (Stanford/La Jolla, CA: Stanford University Press and Center for U.S.-Mexican Studies, University of California at San Diego, 2004), 5.

65. Joseph L. Klesner, "The Structure of the Mexican Electorate: Social, Attitudinal, and Partisan Bases of Vicente Fox's Victory," in *Mexico's Pivotal Democratic Election: Candidates, Voters, and the Presidential Campaign of 2000*, ed. Jorge I. Dominguez and Chappell Lawson (Stanford/La Jolla, CA: Stanford University Press

and Center for U.S.-Mexican Studies, University of California at San Diego, 2004); Beatriz Magaloni and Alejandor Poiré, "The Issues, the Vote, and the Mandate for Change," in *Mexico's Pivotal Democratic Election: Candidates, Voters, and the Presidential Campaign of 2000*, ed. Jorge I. Dominguez and Chappell Lawson (Stanford/La Jolla, CA: Stanford University Press and Center for U.S.-Mexican Studies, University of California at San Diego, 2004).

66. Kathleen Bruhn, "The Making of the Mexican President, 2000: Parties, Candidates, and Campaign Strategy," in *Mexico's Pivotal Democratic Election: Candidates, Voters, and the Presidential Campaign of 2000*, ed. Jorge I. Dominguez and Chappell Lawson (Stanford/La Jolla, CA: Stanford University Press and Center for U.S.-Mexican Studies, University of California at San Diego, 2004), 142.

67. María Victoria Murillo and Steven Levitsky, "Economic Shocks and Partisan Realignment in Argentina," in *Campaigns and Voters in Developing Democracies: Argentina in Comparative Perspective*, ed. Noam Lupu, Virginia Oliveros, and Luis Schiumerini (Ann Arbor: University of Michigan Press, 2019), 40.

68. Noam Lupu, "The End of the Kirchner Era," *Journal of Democracy* 27, no. 2 (2016): 37–38, doi:10.1353/jod.2016.0033.

69. Kenneth F. Greene, "Dealigning Campaign Effects in Argentina in Comparative Perspective," in *Campaigns and Voters in Developing Democracies: Argentina in Comparative Perspective*, ed. Noam Lupu, Virginia Oliveros, and Luis Schiumerini (Ann Arbor: University of Michigan Press, 2019), 171.

70. Pablo Sirvén, "Macri Camina . . . por las Redes Sociales," *La Nación*, December 14, 2014, https://www.lanacion.com.ar/opinion/macri-camina-por-las-redes-sociales-nid1752269.

71. Rosario Ayerdi, "Un Batallón de 10 Mil Cibermilitantes en la Ola Naranja," *Perfil*, June 28, 2015, https://www.perfil.com/noticias/politica/Un-batallon-de-10-mil-cibermilitantes-en-la-ola-naranja-20150628-0026.phtml.

72. Luis Schiumerini, "Macri's Mandate: Structural Reform or Better Performance?" in *Campaigns and Voters in Developing Democracies: Argentina in Comparative Perspective*, ed. Noam Lupu, Virginia Oliveros, and Luis Schiumerini (Ann Arbor: University of Michigan Press, 2019), 139.

73. Noam Lupu, Virginia Oliveros, and Luis Schiumerini, "Toward a Theory of Campaigns and Voters in Developing Democracies," in *Campaigns and Voters in Developing Democracies: Argentina in Comparative Perspective*, ed. Noam Lupu, Virginia Oliveros, and Luis Schiumerini (Ann Arbor: University of Michigan Press, 2019), 1, 20–21.

74. Lupu, "End of the Kirchner Era," 39.

75. Ibid.; Greene, "Dealigning Campaign Effects," 173.

76. Ana Slimovich, "La Ruta Digital a la Presidencia Argentina: Un Análisis Político e Hipermediático de los Discursos de Mauricio Macri en las Redes Sociales," *Dixit* 26 (2017): 37.

77. Lupu, "End of the Kirchner Era," 39.

78. Greene, "Dealigning Campaign Effects," 173; Carlos Gervasoni and María Laura Tagina, "Explaining Support for the Incumbent in Presidential Elections," in *Campaigns and Voters in Developing Democracies: Argentina in Comparative*

Perspective, ed. Noam Lupu, Virginia Oliveros, and Luis Schiumerini (Ann Arbor: University of Michigan, 2019), 129.

79. Schiumerini, "Macri's Mandate."

80. Lupu, "End of the Kirchner Era," 37.

81. Wendy Hunter and Timothy J. Power, "Lula's Second Act," *Journal of Democracy* 34, no. 1 (2023): 127, http://doi.org/10.1353/jod.2023.0008.

82. Ibid., 133.

83. Ibid., 134.

84. Ana Ionova, André Spigariol, Laís Martins, and Jack Nicas, "Brazil's Election Officials Demand Answers for Police Stops of Buses Carrying Voters," *New York Times*, October 30, 2022, https://www.nytimes.com/2022/10/30/world/americas/brazil-voters-police-elections.html.

85. Jack Nicas, Flávia Milhorance, and Ana Ionova, "How Bolsonaro Built the Myth of Stolen Elections in Brazil," *New York Times*, October 25, 2022, https://www.nytimes.com/interactive/2022/10/25/world/americas/brazil-bolsonaro-misinformation.html.

86. Elizabeth Dwoskin, "Come to the 'War Cry Party': How Social Media Helped Drive Mayhem in Brazil," *Washington Post*, January 8, 2023, https://www.washingtonpost.com/technology/2023/01/08/brazil-bolsanaro-twitter-facebook/.

87. Adam Przeworski, *Why Bother with Elections?* (Cambridge, UK: Polity, 2018), 133.

Chapter 2

Electoral Integrity

Almost all countries around the world hold regular elections. In authoritarian regimes, elections are tools of autocratic control. Rigged contests help authoritarian leaders divide their opposition, signal their invincibility to potential opponents, and perhaps acquire a degree of legitimacy by appearing to be chosen by the people.[1] Only where electoral processes are open and fair are elections a tool of democracy. Yet even in democratic systems, the quality of electoral processes can vary greatly.

Scholars use the concept of electoral integrity to refer to the degree to which an electoral process conforms to widely agreed-upon international norms of conduct.[2] In democratic elections marked by high integrity, the country's most powerful officeholders are elected by universal adult suffrage in elections where diverse parties and candidates can run, people are free to express their preferences at the ballot box, and votes are counted fairly and weighed equally.[3] Myriad problems can undermine electoral integrity, from intimidation and disenfranchisement of voters to illegitimate campaign advantages enjoyed by a ruling party and the corruption of the vote count.

The integrity of electoral processes matters for ensuring that election results accurately reflect the will of the voters. Election fraud and manipulation—or widespread perceptions of them—can undermine popular confidence in the legitimacy of elections and elected officials and feed polarization and conflict. In the extreme, perceptions of election fraud can lead to violence and threaten democracy, as we saw in the case of Brazil in chapter 1.

In this chapter we focus on a broad array of practices that undermine electoral integrity. The chapter speaks to a number of pressing questions in contemporary Latin American politics: How well do elections in the region meet democratic standards? In what ways is the democratic quality of elections subverted across Latin America? How do some candidates attempt to buy votes? What challenges do new media forms pose to electoral integrity? And what are the dangers posed by public perceptions of election rigging?

METHODS OF MANIPULATION

Around the world, political actors find myriad ways of subverting electoral integrity. Prior to election day, ruling parties might find ways of excluding opposition candidates and parties from the ballot, while opposition voters might face intimidation and bureaucratic obstacles to registering to vote. Opposition campaigning can be hindered by unequal access to media and campaign finance. On election day, ballot boxes might be stuffed with fraudulent ballots and some voters may be turned away from the polling place without being able to vote. After the vote is concluded, vote tallies might be altered to change the outcome or pad the winning party's margin of victory.[4]

Measuring the quality of electoral processes—that is, how well they avoid these manipulative tactics—is difficult. But the evidence shows that overall, Latin American elections stack up well against other regions of the world. Most elections in the region are free of serious intentional manipulation. Most electoral management bodies perform efficiently. Voting on election day is usually calm and orderly, and in most cases the vote count and tabulation process is transparent. According to one research project that quantifies expert opinions on elections across a wide range of variables related to electoral integrity, the average summary electoral integrity score for Latin American elections is slightly higher than the world average.[5]

But shortcomings are common. Poll workers are not always adequately trained. There is often insufficient enforcement of rules regarding electoral offenses. And sometimes serious violations of electoral integrity undermine the democratic quality of the process and cast doubt on the legitimacy of the winning parties. Across the region, citizen confidence in elections tends to be low, as it does for many public institutions.[6] In some cases disputed election outcomes lead to post-election protests and clashes in the streets, as happened in Peru in 2000, Mexico in 2006, and Honduras in 2017.

Naturally there is a large degree of variation in election quality from country to country. Latin America's most consistently democratic countries—Costa Rica, Uruguay, and Chile—hold clean and transparent elections. At the other extreme are cases like Venezuela and Nicaragua, where elections are rigged at the behest of autocratic governments. Most countries in the region fall between these two poles. In the sections below we look at some of the common types of election manipulation in contemporary Latin America.

Erasing the Competition

One of the most extreme methods of election rigging is to simply disqualify the opposition from running. This tactic is rare in Latin America but has been used in authoritarian contexts. In Nicaragua under Daniel Ortega, opposition parties have faced threats to their legal status. Prior to the 2016 elections, several political parties lost their legal registration and the Supreme Court barred opposition leader Eduardo Montealegre, Ortega's most formidable opponent, from running for president, handing leadership of his party to a less popular figure.[7] In 2021, Ortega won a fourth consecutive presidential term in an election that was preceded by the arrest of all prominent opposition figures that might have run for president against Ortega, including Cristiana Chamorro, the daughter of a former president.[8] These steps followed the passage of a vaguely worded law in 2020 that barred people labeled as "traitors" from running for office.[9] In a broader context of government surveillance and harassment of government critics, new laws that limit free speech, and a divided opposition, Ortega's reelection was assured.

Many opposition candidates and parties have also been barred from competing in authoritarian Venezuela. After opposition parties boycotted the 2017 municipal elections, authorities announced that they would not be allowed to participate in the 2018 presidential election.[10] Major opposition leaders like Henrique Capriles and Leopoldo López were already barred from running because of dubious legal charges against them. López had been banned from running for office in 2004 over corruption allegations when he challenged then-president Hugo Chávez.[11] In 2015, López was sentenced to over thirteen years in prison following an unfair trial after he had called for demonstrations against President Maduro.[12] Capriles, who Maduro had narrowly defeated in the 2013 presidential election, was barred from politics for fifteen years in 2017 based on accusations of "administrative irregularities" during his term as governor.[13] In the lead up to legislative elections in 2020, the Supreme Court suspended the leadership of three opposition parties and appointed Maduro loyalists in their place.[14] The opposition called on voters to boycott the election, which Maduro's coalition won with a two-thirds majority in an election marked by extraordinarily low voter turnout. Through its control of the courts, the regime had eliminated all but token opposition to Maduro and his socialist party.

While authoritarian Nicaragua and Venezuela have seen the most brazen instances of erasing the opposition, dubious candidate disqualifications have also occurred in slightly less authoritarian contexts. In Bolivia, election authorities suspended a political party during 2015 regional elections in one department "on grounds that it disseminated an unauthorized poll," resulting in the party's candidates not appearing on the ballot.[15] In Guatemala, politically motivated court rulings prevented several anti-corruption presidential candidates from running in 2019 and 2023 as part of a broader pattern of democratic erosion in the country.

Illegal Voter Registration

Subtler forms of manipulation involve the exploitation of the voter registration system. Political parties that control the electoral body responsible for compiling the voter registry may intentionally remove known opposition supporters from the voter rolls to prevent them from voting. This was the case in the 1994 presidential election in the Dominican Republic, which is thought to have been stolen by the incumbent through deletion of thousands of names from the voter rolls.[16]

More common is the use of fraudulent voter registrations to influence local elections. This involves local candidates organizing the registration of voters to vote in a locality where they do not live. Fraudulent changes of residence for voting purposes are observed in countries as diverse as Honduras, Guatemala, and Brazil.[17] An illustrative case is a municipal council candidate in Brazil who was convicted in 2010 of bringing voters into his district and providing them with a cash payment and other inducements to vote for him.[18] Elections in Guatemala routinely see accusations of residence fraud in municipal races, where it is known as traslado (transfer). The scope of the problem is not known, but it is common for election officials to detect a small number of such cases in each election cycle.[19]

Partly to combat registration fraud, most Latin American countries have early voter registration closing dates that prevent voters from updating their address immediately before an election. While making registration fraud more difficult, these measures impose a burden on voters who move in the months before an election, who may need to travel to the precinct of their previous residence to vote.

Abuse of State Resources

Another common violation of electoral integrity is the use of state resources by incumbent candidates and parties. This entails the use of public resources such as government vehicles, buildings, equipment, and social programs for partisan campaigning purposes. For example, a party in power that uses government vehicles to transport supporters to campaign rallies is abusing state resources.

Perhaps the most notorious abuse of state resources occurred in Mexico during the long reign of the PRI party (1929–2000), where the PRI blurred the line between state and party and routinely used state resources for campaigning. But this problem has been common elsewhere as well. In Peru's presidential election in 2000, in which strongman Alberto Fujimori was running for a second reelection, observers noted that local welfare officials threatened the loss of food aid to areas that didn't vote for Fujimori.[20] The abuse of state resources has also been among the tools of manipulation in Venezuela, where public buildings and government vehicles are used for campaign activities, public officials participate in the ruling party's campaign events, and state workers are pressured to vote.[21] This tactic can also occur in less authoritarian settings: in Paraguay's 2018 general election, for example, international observers reported the use of public resources including social programs and medicines used for campaigning, "and undue influence on public employees to financially contribute to and attend campaign events of the ruling party during working hours."[22]

Electoral Violence

In some Latin American countries, high levels of crime and violence have deleterious effects on election integrity. In countries where drug cartels, street gangs, and armed guerrilla groups are prevalent, criminal violence often taints electoral processes.

A case in point is Mexico, where dozens of drug-trafficking organizations and related criminal groups vie for territorial control. The widespread criminal violence in Mexico subverts electoral integrity as drug cartels try to co-opt candidates to ensure they protect cartel interests once in office, threaten or kill candidates they oppose, and intimidate voters.[23] Grisly statistics show the human consequences: in Mexico's 2018 general election, forty-eight candidates were murdered.[24] In the lead up to midterm and local elections in 2021, at least thirty-four candidates were murdered and hundreds more received threats, and parties couldn't campaign in some areas that were deemed too dangerous.[25]

A similar dynamic is found in remote areas of Colombia, where competing armed groups involved in drug trafficking and other illicit activities operate largely outside the reach of the state. Candidates running for office in these areas face threats and occasional attacks from criminal groups.[26] During the campaign for local elections in 2019, seven candidates were murdered.[27]

Electoral violence routinely disrupts campaigning and voting in Guatemala as well. The 2019 general election saw at least seven election-related murders; the public prosecutor for electoral crimes fled the country after receiving threats; and voting could not be held in one municipality after local election officials resigned after receiving death threats.[28] Threats affect voters as well as candidates and election officials: a survey conducted during Guatemala's 2011 general election estimated that "about 18% of respondents were targets of violent intimidation."[29]

While violence typically affects municipal races as criminal groups attempt to influence local officials, occasionally national-level candidates are victims. This was the case most recently in Ecuador, where in 2023 presidential candidate Fernando Villavicencio was assassinated after a campaign rally. Such pervasive electoral violence and intimidation violate core principles of democratic elections, including the ability of candidates to freely campaign for support and of voters to freely choose their representatives.

Clientelism and Vote Buying

Of all the forms of electoral manipulation in Latin America, perhaps the most pervasive is vote buying. This involves candidates and political parties giving voters money, goods, or services in exchange for their votes. Vote buying is one form of clientelism, or the distribution of targeted benefits to individuals contingent on their political support.[30]

Campaign operatives can hand out a staggering array of goods to try to buy votes. In addition to money, campaigns have been reported to hand out "food, clothing, gift cards, and even sheep" in Mexico.[31] A 2001 survey in Argentina found that food was the most common campaign handout, but vote buying also included "clothing, mattresses, medicine, milk, corrugated metal, construction materials, blankets, hangers, utility bill payments, money, eyeglasses, chickens, trees, and magnets."[32] And in Ecuador, legislative candidates have been observed distributing "soccer balls, meat, rice, beer, cane alcohol, wine, and cigarettes," as well as providing entertainment with disc jockeys or bands.[33] More creatively, one candidate handed out baby chicks to families to win their votes, while another distributed cans of tuna with the manufacturer label replaced with a label featuring the candidate and party names on it.[34] The political scientist that observed these practices in indigenous communities noted that one campaign worker "joked that in the Amazon, the campaign season was deemed the Navidad de los Indios, the Indians' Christmas."[35]

Vote buying is widely seen as a violation of democratic norms. Democratic theory emphasizes the ability of autonomous citizens to vote for their true preferences in elections. To the extent that voters cast their ballot for someone who is not their preferred choice because they have been paid to do so, election results no longer reflect the will of the people. If politicians can gain votes simply by paying voters, they won't need to consider voters' policy views in order to win elections or improve public services once in office. Especially if vote-buying parties attempt to violate the secrecy of the ballot to ensure that people they paid fulfilled their end of the bargain, voters become accountable to politicians for their votes rather than politicians being held accountable by voters.

Not everyone views vote buying as purely negative. Some recipients of campaign handouts might view the transaction positively or may view the receipt of payments as one way of recovering money from corrupt politicians. People also may not attach a stigma to accepting payments for their votes if they were already going to vote for the party making the payment or if they really need the goods being distributed. However, surveys from five Latin American countries have found that when presented with hypothetical scenarios of someone accepting a payment in exchange for their vote, the share of people saying the payment is acceptable never reaches 10 percent.[36] Thus while views of vote buying may vary from person to person, Latin Americans seem to overwhelmingly view it as an undesirable electoral practice.

How Common Is Vote Buying?

Measuring the prevalence of vote buying is difficult, but there is no doubt that it is common in Latin America despite widespread disapproval of the practice. When asked directly in surveys conducted in 2010 whether they have been offered something in exchange for their vote, nearly 19 percent of people in Bolivia, 18 percent in Argentina, and over 16 percent in Mexico and Brazil said that they had. In contrast, only 5.6 percent in Uruguay, 6.4 percent in Chile, and 8.5 percent in Costa Rica reported being offered something for their vote.[37]

But because vote buying is almost always illegal, and accepting a handout from a campaign might be perceived by some as inappropriate, survey respondents may not answer truthfully when asked whether they have received goods or favors in exchange for their vote. This challenge—known as social desirability bias (when survey respondents underreport socially undesirable behavior or beliefs)—is expected to result in an underestimation of the true scope of vote buying. One way of trying to overcome the problem is to ask survey respondents about their perceptions of vote buying in their community, rather than whether they personally were offered or accepted a gift. For example, an influential study of vote buying in Argentina found that while 7 percent of survey respondents reported receiving a campaign handout in a recent election, 44 percent said parties handed out goods in their neighborhoods during the election campaign.[38] Other studies find similar results in Argentina and elsewhere.[39]

Another method of overcoming social desirability bias is the list experiment, in which surveyors present respondents with a list of items and ask them how many of the items they have experienced (but without asking which ones). The survey group is randomly divided in two: a control group and a treatment group. The two groups are presented with an identical list of items, except that the treatment group's list adds the sensitive item (such as receiving a gift from a campaign). By comparing the average number of things that the treatment group reports to the average of the control group, researchers can estimate how many people participated in the sensitive activity.

TEXT BOX 2.1: MEASURING VOTE BUYING THROUGH LIST EXPERIMENTS

List experiments are conducted as part of surveys. A typical list experiment involves the interviewer presenting the survey respondent a list of campaign activities and asking the respondent to report how many of the activities candidates or political parties carried out during the most recent campaign.

The control group's list might look like this:[a]

1. They put up campaign posters/signs in your neighborhood.
2. They visited your home.
3. They placed campaign advertisements on television or radio.
4. They threatened you to vote for them.

The treatment group's list would add the sensitive item.

1. They put up campaign posters/signs in your neighborhood.
2. They visited your home.
3. They gave you a gift or did you a favor.
4. They placed campaign advertisements on television or radio.
5. They threatened you to vote for them.

Researchers can then compare the average number of items reported by respondents in each group. If the average number for the treatment group is higher, researchers can infer that there is some vote buying. If responses from the treatment group average, say, 2.5, and the average for the control group is 2.25, we can estimate that the proportion of people receiving a gift or favor is (2.5-2.25) = 0.25, or 25 percent.

Researchers can make this inference because survey respondents are randomly assigned to be in either the control group or treatment group, so there should be no systematic differences between the two groups. If they were presented with the same list of items, the average response would be about the same between the groups. But because the treatment group's list contains an extra item, the average response for that group should be higher—and *how much* higher it is tells us how many people received a gift or favor from a party.

Some argue that list experiments may actually underestimate the prevalence of vote buying because more educated survey respondents are more likely to understand the complicated question structure. This could account for why some list experiments find that more educated people are more likely to report being offered something in exchange for their vote—exactly the opposite that we would expect (and what is evident in direct survey questions about vote buying).[b] Proponents of list experiments argue, in contrast, that more educated people are more aware of democratic norms against vote buying, and thus are the most likely to underreport receiving something in exchange for their vote; thus list experiments are the best way of getting a true measure of how widespread vote buying really is.[c] This methodological debate is ongoing, but suffice it to say that all survey methods used to measure vote buying suggest that the practice is widespread in many Latin American countries.

[a] This example is taken from Rodrigo Castro Cornejo and Ulises Beltrán, "List Experiments, Political Sophistication, and Vote Buying: Experimental Evidence from Mexico," *Journal of Politics in Latin America* 12, no. 2 (2020): 222, https://doi.org/10.1177/1866802X20937713.
[b] Castro Cornejo and Beltrán, "List Experiments."
[c] Chad P. Kiewiet de Jonge, "Who Lies about Electoral Gifts? Experimental Evidence from Latin America," *Public Opinion Quarterly* 79, no. 3 (2015), https://doi.org/10.1093/poq/nfv024.

A study in Nicaragua found that while only 2 percent of respondents indicated being offered something in exchange for their vote when directly asked, a list experiment found that 24 percent of voters were offered a gift or service in exchange for their vote.[40] In a 2011 survey in Guatemala, only 4 percent of survey respondents said that they received gifts in exchange for their votes, but a list experiment estimated a 10 percent rate of vote buying.[41] List experiments in El Salvador in 2014 and Argentina in 2015 have found results similar to the Guatemala survey.[42]

How Does Vote Buying Work and Why Does It Persist?

While vote buying is widespread, there is much debate about exactly how it works. In particular, scholars have offered differing explanations for who is targeted for payoffs in exchange for votes, and why. Logic dictates that parties should pay swing voters—voters who don't strongly support the party (since their votes are already assured) or strongly oppose the party (since a small payoff won't prompt them to vote for the party). Yet the evidence suggests that parties tend to give campaign handouts to their supporters more than to swing voters.[43]

Scholars have proposed several theories to explain this anomaly. Parties may target payoffs to their supporters who are unlikely to turn out to vote, with the expectation that receiving a payoff increases their chances of voting (what is known as turnout buying).[44] Alternately, the fact that parties rely on lower-level operatives, sometimes known as brokers,[45] to hand out goods in exchange for votes may account for the fact that party loyalists receive most handouts. Parties depend on the detailed knowledge that local operatives have about the voters in their neighborhoods. In order to demonstrate their usefulness to the party—and thereby assure the continued flow of payments to the broker—brokers will try to maximize the size of their network of voters. Susan Stokes and her colleagues argue that the simplest way for brokers to do so is to provide goods and favors to loyal voters. Thus campaign payoffs go to loyal voters because of the incentives facing the local brokers who decide who to pay for their votes, rather than the incentives of party leaders who might prefer to pay swing voters.[46] Yet another theory posits that party operatives pay people who actively engage in political discussion and persuasion within their social networks, so that their campaign payments can win the vote not only of the recipient but also people in their social network who the recipient might persuade to vote for the party.[47]

The relationship between voters' party loyalty and their chances of receiving payment for their vote is still far from settled. What seems more certain is that the poor are more often the targets of vote buying than are middle class and wealthy voters.[48] Presumably, people in precarious economic circumstances will prefer immediate delivery of concrete benefits compared to promises of future policies. Buying the votes of more affluent voters becomes expensive, and more affluent and educated voters may be more aware of how clientelist practices divert funds from public goods and violate democratic values.[49]

Whether poor or not, many recipients of election payoffs do not just receive one handout at election time. Rather, they are embedded in ongoing clientelist relations in which they turn to trusted brokers or politicians for assistance in times of need in a context of poorly developed social safety nets. In this sense, at least some (and possibly most) vote buying involves voters requesting payment, and brokers' responsiveness to this request signals their credibility to continue providing support after receiving clients' votes.[50]

Underlying the issue of who is targeted for vote buying is the question of whether it really affects how people vote. Vote buying raises questions of compliance. How do parties know that voters who receive a payment in exchange for their votes follow through by voting for the party? Since every Latin American country has a secret ballot, we might expect vote buying to be an ineffective electoral strategy. Indeed, in Mexico's 2006 election, the PAN party sought to undermine the effectiveness of the rival PRI party's vote buying by telling voters to "take the dough and vote for PAN"—in other words, feel free to accept handouts and then vote your conscience.[51]

Of course, it is possible that many voters will not trust the secrecy of their ballot. They might believe that local party operatives will be able to make good guesses about how individual people voted, and might fear losing future benefits if they don't vote for the broker's party.[52] In fact some surveys have found high proportions of citizens who doubt that their votes are entirely secret, from 33 percent in Uruguay to 52 percent in Honduras.[53] Certainly parties sometimes make efforts to monitor how people vote in order to enforce a vote buying agreement. Historically in Mexico, for instance, a party broker might have a child accompany a voter into the voting booth to observe how he or she marked their ballot. More recently brokers have asked voters to take a photo of their completed ballot with their cell phone to show the broker as evidence of how they voted.[54] But despite such efforts, ballot secrecy is generally well protected.

An alternative explanation for why vote buying might be effective is that voters feel a norm of reciprocity to vote for the party that gives them something.[55] Thus even if they do not fear being punished for voting against the party making the payment, many voters will feel a normative sense that they should reciprocate a gift by voting for the gift-giving party. This might especially be the case where vote buying is not a one-off exchange but instead part of a broader clientelist relationship between voters and party officials where a sense of obligation can develop over time. Norms of reciprocity could help explain the persistence of vote buying and clientelism even in countries with weak parties that lack the ability to monitor voter behavior.

A final theory is that campaigns distribute goods to potential voters to attract them to campaign rallies. Drawing large crowds to campaign events signals to voters, campaign donors, and activists that the candidate or party is a viable contender, thus drawing more attention and ultimately more donations and votes.[56] No doubt it is a combination of these factors—attempts to monitor people's votes, voters' sense of reciprocal obligation, and attracting attendance at campaign rallies—that explains the persistence of vote buying across Latin America.

Given the pervasiveness of vote buying, many countries have stepped up the enforcement of laws banning the practice. In Brazil, enforcement of rules against campaign handouts began increasing after 1999, when a citizen petition led to the enactment of a law increasing penalties. A later 2010 law barred people from running for office for eight years if they are convicted of certain crimes, including vote buying.[57] In Mexico, offering payment or gifts in exchange for votes can result in prison terms of six months to three years.[58] In El Salvador, vote buying can be punished with four to six years in prison, although enforcement of the law is lacking.[59]

Moreover, electoral management bodies routinely carry out public education campaigns that assure people of the secrecy of the vote and encourage people to avoid vote selling. In Mexico's pivotal 2000 election, for example, the electoral commission undertook a campaign to inform people that the vote was secret and "enclos[ed] voting booths with curtains emblazoned with the statement, 'Your vote is free and secret.'"[60] More recently, election officials in some countries encourage voters to not bring their cell phones with them to vote, since one way of enforcing a vote buying agreement is to require that the voter show a photo of their completed ballot.

Election Misinformation: Bots, Trolls, and Fake News

Vote buying, like many other forms of election manipulation, is an old practice. New technologies and modes of communication are giving rise to new tools to tilt the electoral playing field—above all the use of misinformation to sway voters and to discredit electoral processes when one's side loses. This new challenge for electoral integrity in Latin America has received the most attention in Mexico and Brazil.

The use of social media bots and trolls has become common in Mexican elections. In the 2012 presidential election, the campaign of Enrique Peña Nieto hired some one thousand people to influence discussions on social media, with at least 350 fake accounts that posted hundreds of times per day in favor of Peña Nieto. In 2018 fake news was widespread on social media, and the presidential campaigns accused each other of using trolls and bots to flood social media platforms. One fake story claimed that the Pope had criticized Andrés Manuel López Obrador, the eventual winner of the election, while another story claimed that López Obrador had murdered his own brother. In response to the flood of fake news, media companies joined with nongovernmental organizations and universities to form a fact-checking group. Individuals could send stories to the group with the hashtag #QuieroQueVerifiquen ("I want you to verify this"). The effort was supported by Facebook, Google, and Twitter, which took steps to prioritize verified news stories in users' feeds.[61]

Fake accounts and fake news have also been common in Brazil. The 2010 presidential campaign of Dilma Rousseff and her Workers' Party allegedly ran a network of fake accounts that helped spread disinformation, including the untrue claim that Rousseff's opponent supported abortion and might be excommunicated by the Catholic Church. In this case the fake accounts were operated manually rather than being automated. "Profile photos were taken from various corners of the internet: from pages and blogs outside Brazil, and from dating sites. Most 'ectos' [fake profiles] were women with attractive profile pictures, deliberately chosen to hook in men."[62]

Since the 2010 election, the use of fake profiles to spread electoral content has become illegal in Brazil. Nevertheless, so-called cyborg accounts (humans operating networks of fake profiles) were common in the 2014 Brazil elections.[63] Since then the messaging service WhatsApp has become a main forum for the spread of election misinformation. Because the app provides encrypted messaging between users, it is difficult for outside fact checkers to rebut misinformation that is spread between private groups of users. Misinformation on WhatsApp in the 2018 election particularly benefited Jair Bolsonaro's candidacy. Fake stories echoed conspiracy theories about election fraud, contained doctored photos of members of the Workers' Party, and spread fabricated polling results.[64] One study of a hundred thousand widely shared WhatsApp images "found that more than half contained misleading or flatly false information."[65] One of the most widely shared stories on social media falsely claimed that Fernando Haddad, Bolsonaro's election opponent, was a pedophile who would make the government choose children's gender if he were elected.[66] As in Mexico, media companies in Brazil started a fact-checking effort to debunk false stories circulating on WhatsApp, although the effort's effectiveness is unknown.[67]

Misinformation on WhatsApp is particularly problematic in Brazil and other countries because of the large number of app users in the country, with an estimated 44 percent of Brazilians using the app to get political information.[68] In response to the role of misinformation in the 2018 elections, Brazil's Supreme Electoral Tribunal launched an effort to fight disinformation and partnered with major social media platforms to increase content moderation. During the 2022 general election, the chief justice of the electoral tribunal took drastic, and controversial, action against rampant online misinformation by ordering social media companies to remove specific content immediately or risk a shutdown of their service in the country.[69]

Fake news, misinformation, and social media trolls are not limited to Mexico and Brazil. In Colombia's 2018 presidential election, a viral Facebook post falsely claimed that one candidate had an illegitimate daughter who supported her father's opponent.[70] In Guatemala, journalists have found troll farms (locally known as "net centers") where employees make fake social media profiles and post on topics like sports and religion to appear like real people. When hired by a campaign, they turn to posting in support of that candidate and attacking the candidate's opponents.[71]

Election misinformation on social media and WhatsApp groups presents many challenges for electoral integrity. Increasingly large segments of the electorate get their political news from social media. Fact checkers struggle to keep up with the scale and pace of misinformation, and viral social media stories often come to dominate the news coverage of traditional media.[72] It is difficult to discern the effects of misinformation on election outcomes, but there is little doubt that it will continue to shape electoral processes in Latin America as more people consume news from nontraditional sources.

PROTECTING ELECTORAL INTEGRITY:
ELECTION OBSERVATION

While the methods of electoral manipulation are wide ranging, safeguards have been developed to protect electoral integrity. These include poll watchers from political parties that observe voting and vote counting; the use of indelible ink on voters' fingers to prevent people from voting more than once;[73] and the transparent publication of the vote tally for each polling place.

An important element in the struggle to improve the quality of elections around the world has been international election observation. In the 1980s and 1990s, international election monitoring became an international norm, as developing countries invited observers to signal their commitment to democratization.[74] Teams of observers from intergovernmental organizations such as the Organization of American States (OAS) and the European Union (EU), and nongovernment organizations such as the Carter Center, arrive in the country in advance of election day and monitor all aspects of the electoral process. They issue periodic public reports and offer recommendations to the host country to improve the quality of their elections.

Many Latin American elections are monitored by teams of international election observers, often from several organizations, as well as domestic civic groups that observe elections. Some of the innovations in election monitoring have occurred in Latin America, including the parallel vote tabulation (or quick count), by which observers report the vote tally from a sample of polling stations to arrive at an estimate of the election's full results. Official results that differ drastically from the quick-count projection suggest manipulation in the results. This method uncovered election fraud in Panama in 1989, and its use in Nicaragua in 1990 confirmed that the incumbent Sandinista government had lost the election, encouraging a peaceful transition of power.[75]

Election monitors may help improve election quality by deterring cheating (by increasing the chance that cheating will be detected) and by offering recommendations for improvement to electoral officials. And indeed, some research finds that the presence of credible international observers improves the quality of elections.[76] Election observation has its limits, however. Recommendations for improvement are often not implemented: one study finds that about half of the recommendations from OAS observer missions from 1999 to 2015 were implemented.[77] Additionally, as election observation became common, some governments have sought subtler methods of manipulation that are less likely to draw condemnation from observers, such as influencing media coverage and abusing state resources.[78]

This arms race between those attempting to manipulate elections and their opponents continues, and election observers are now adapting to the challenges posed by misinformation and widespread distrust of political institutions.

CASE STUDIES

As the preceding sections show, violations of electoral integrity come in many forms. The case studies below present overviews of some electoral processes that illustrate not only the subversion of electoral integrity (Nicaragua and Venezuela) but also the stark consequences of widespread perceptions of election fraud (Honduras and Bolivia).

Elections under Authoritarianism: Nicaragua and Venezuela

The most severe electoral problems in Latin America since the turn of the century have occurred in Venezuela and Nicaragua as part of broader patterns of growing authoritarianism. The elimination of opposition in both countries was described above, but electoral manipulation has taken other forms as well.

In Nicaragua, after serving a term as president in the 1980s, Daniel Ortega was elected again in 2006. He chipped away at democratic institutions, and over the years he and his Sandinista party (FSLN) came to monopolize political power by stacking the courts and the electoral commission with loyalists and exerting control over the media and opposition parties.[79] After widespread protests in 2018, Ortega's government grew more repressive, arresting and sometimes killing protesters and shutting down remaining independent media outlets.

Electoral manipulation was part of this erosion of democracy. With Ortega up for reelection in 2011, Nicaragua experienced a highly flawed election. The Sandinista party dominated electoral administration from the top election commission to the polling stations. Civic groups were barred from fielding election observation teams. The distribution of identity documents needed to vote was marred by partisan bias, likely preventing some people from voting.[80] Some opposition party poll watchers and international observers were kicked out of polling stations before ballots were counted and the final tally of the votes lacked transparency (with the electoral commission not following the standard practice of publishing disaggregated results by polling station).[81] Ortega won handily in 2011 and again in 2016, when the opposition boycotted the election. While Ortega was genuinely more popular than the opposition thanks to solid economic growth and low crime rates, the 2016 race was also slanted by the disqualification of Ortega's main opponent and the failure to invite international election observers.[82]

In Venezuela elections became less competitive during the presidency of Hugo Chávez (1999–2013). Under his successor, Nicolás Maduro, elections were marked by the disqualification of key opposition candidates, abuse of state resources by the incumbent party, slanted media coverage, and threats to withdraw food aid from people who don't vote for the ruling party. Maduro's party controls the electoral commission and the courts, and from 2017 onward elections occurred in a context of violent repression and politically motivated arrests of dissidents.

In both these cases, elections continued to be held as each country transitioned from democracy to dictatorship. Rather than competitive contests that allow voters to meaningfully participate in self-government, Nicaraguan and Venezuelan elections have become demonstrations of these regimes' repressive authoritarianism.

Honduras 2017

In 2017 Honduran president Juan Orlando Hernández was running for reelection two years after a controversial Supreme Court ruling that effectively struck down the presidential term limits found in the country's constitution. Hernández's National Party had been in power since 2010, and since that time had eroded checks and balances, including replacing four Supreme Court justices in 2012.[83]

Controversy erupted on election night. The Supreme Electoral Tribunal (TSE) released preliminary results from 57 percent of polling stations, showing that Hernández's main opponent, Salvador Nasralla, was leading by five points. Vote tallies from many of the remaining polling stations, mostly from rural areas, were slower to be transmitted to the TSE. As these results came in, Nasralla's lead shrunk. Then a computer server failure led the TSE to halt the processing of results for hours, raising questions about the integrity of the vote tally. Tensions were exacerbated by the fact that both Hernández and Nasralla declared victory before the full election results were announced.

Once all votes were tallied, the TSE announced that Hernández had narrowly beat Nasralla by fifty thousand votes, 42.9 percent to 41.4 percent. While the United States accepted the results of the election, the OAS—which had observed the elections—called for a new election to be held. Conflict over the election outcome led to clashes in the streets. Human rights investigators documented at least twelve people killed by security forces during subsequent demonstrations.[84] Hernández was ultimately sworn in to a second term amid a cloud of uncertainty about the integrity of the election.

But was the election outcome rigged? The OAS observer mission concluded that "[t]he abundance of irregularities and deficiencies is such as to preclude full certainty regarding the outcome."[85] The EU's observer mission issued a more positive report. Certainly there were some problems in the conduct of the election. Poll workers were sometimes poorly trained, since in Honduras political parties are responsible for training the poll workers that represent their parties. Some parties also sold the credentials for their poll workers to other parties, so that poll workers ostensibly representing one political party were actually from a different party. Juan Orlando Hernández and his National Party were advantaged with more resources than other parties, and sometimes politicized the distribution of state social programs by blurring the distinction between the government and the National Party.[86]

But the opposition parties' allegations of fraud centered on the tally of votes. For its part, the OAS observers identified technical anomalies in the TSE's computer system and commissioned a statistical analysis of election results that found that some late-counted votes disproportionately favored the National Party. However, the EU observers confirmed that the TSE's server malfunction was not the result of manipulation. They also stressed that the TSE gave all parties full access to all stages of the electoral process, and the larger parties had representatives at nearly all polling stations, who received copies of the official tally sheets. The polling station tally sheets in the possession of the political parties matched the results published by the TSE. Recounts of the vote from thousands of polling stations also turned up no significant discrepancies. Two major opposition parties called for the presidential election results to be annulled, but they presented no evidence to support their challenge.[87]

Bolivia 2019

The 2019 presidential race in Bolivia in many ways parallels the Honduran election two years prior. Incumbent president Evo Morales was running for reelection in a context of growing polarization. First elected president in 2005, Morales was reelected in 2009 and 2014. In 2016 he put a referendum before Bolivian voters to decide whether to eliminate presidential term limits found in the constitution. When voters narrowly defeated the proposal, Morales and his MAS party turned to the courts to overcome the constitutional impediment to Morales remaining in power. A constitutional court ruling in 2017 nullified presidential term limits. Just as the Honduran court had done, the Bolivian tribunal argued that presidential term limits were a violation of the rights of the president and voters.

The 2019 electoral process was marred by problems. Public confidence in the impartiality of the Supreme Electoral Tribunal (TSE) was low. The MAS party abused state resources for campaigning purposes, with government ministers launching public works projects close to the election, "blurring the distinction between the MAS campaign and the delivery of government projects."[88] Many vote tally sheets from polling stations contained mistakes that should have led to the votes from those stations being annulled, and some polling stations reported 100 percent of the vote going to Morales. The TSE failed to give explanations for anomalies such as electoral materials being found at people's homes.[89]

Despite all of these problems, there was no doubt that Morales led his closest opponent, Carlos Mesa, in the first round of voting. What was unclear was whether Morales would win the first round by at least ten percentage points, which under Bolivia's electoral rules would hand him the presidency without needing a runoff round. On election night TSE's preliminary results system reported that Morales led Mesa by just less than eight points with nearly 84 percent of the votes counted. Mesa announced that the election would go to a second round, "while Morales declared victory in the first round, arguing that the missing votes were mainly from rural areas in which support for the MAS was traditionally very high."[90]

When reporting of the provisional vote count resumed the following day, Morales had extended his lead to over ten points. Suspicions flared. The OAS observer mission called the surge of votes for Morales "inexplicable" and cast doubt on the legitimacy of the vote count.[91] Anti-Morales protests spread across the country, and several election offices were burned. As the vote count concluded, the TSE announced Morales the winner of the election. But in response to street protests and international pressure, Morales invited the OAS to conduct an audit of the vote count.

Following its audit, the OAS reported that it had found a lack of security controls in the TSE's computer systems, inadequate controls over the chain of custody of election materials, anomalies in some vote tally sheets from polling places, and a statistically anomalous pattern in the final 5 percent of the election results reported.[92] The OAS recommended holding new elections with new members of the TSE, to which Morales agreed. But by this time the country's conflict had begun to spin out of control. The police mutinied against the Morales government, pro- and anti-MAS demonstrators clashed in the streets, and ultimately the head of the armed forces publicly suggested that Morales should resign as president—which he promptly did.[93]

Subsequent analyses of the election results have cast a cloud over the OAS audit. While the OAS concluded that the final share of vote tallies were suspiciously favorable to Morales, several statistical analyses have cast doubt on that claim.[94] It seems plausible that the final results to be reported came from rural areas where Morales was highly popular. Thus while the electoral process was far from perfect and Morales and MAS benefited from state resources, the evidence supporting claims of fraud in the final vote count is murky.

The consequences for Bolivia were profound. The climate of distrust and the shoddy administration of the election by the TSE led to violent street clashes, more polarization between pro- and anti-MAS Bolivians, and the removal of Morales as president in what some people consider a coup.[95] Both the Bolivian and Honduran cases highlight how the evidence of electoral manipulation can be ambiguous, and how critically important public perceptions and confidence in the electoral process are for democratic legitimacy.

NOTES

1. Carl Henrik Knutsen, Håvard Mokleiv Nygård, and Tore Wig, "Autocratic Elections: Stabilizing Tool or Force for Change?" *World Politics* 69, no. 1 (2017), doi: 10.1017/s0043887116000149.

2. See, for example, Pippa Norris, Richard W. Frank, and Ferran Martínez i Coma, "Assessing the Quality of Elections," *Journal of Democracy* 24, no. 4 (2013), http://doi.org/10.1353/jod.2013.0063.

3. Andreas Schedler, "Elections without Democracy: The Menu of Manipulation," *Journal of Democracy* 13, no. 2 (2002), http://doi.org/10.1353/jod.2002.0031.

4. Daniel Calingaert, "Election Rigging and How to Fight It," *Journal of Democracy* 17, no. 3 (2006), doi:10.1353/jod.2006.0043.

5. Pippa Norris and Max Grömping, "Perceptions of Electoral Integrity," (PEI-7.0), version 2, 2019. Harvard Dataverse. This dataset covers national legislative and presidential elections from July 1, 2012, to December 31, 2018. The Latin American average is 56.2, compared to 54.9 for the world.

6. Miguel Carreras and Yasemin Irepoglu, "Trust in Elections, Vote Buying, and Turnout in Latin America," *Electoral Studies* 32, no. 4 (2013): 610, https://doi.org /10.1016/j.electstud.2013.07.012; Agustina Haime, "What Explains Voter Turnout in Latin America? A Test of the Effect of Citizens' Attitudes Towards the Electoral Process," *Revista de Ciencia Política* 37, no. 1 (2017): 77, http://dx.doi.org/10.4067/ S0718-090X2017000100004.

7. Oliver Della Costa Stuenkel and Andreas E. Feldman, "The Unchecked Demise of Nicaraguan Democracy," Carnegie Endowment for International Peace, 2017, https://carnegieendowment.org/2017/11/16/unchecked-demise-of-nicaraguan -democracy-pub-74761.

8. Associated Press, "Nicaragua Arrests 5 More Opposition Leaders in Crackdown," June 13, 2021, https://apnews.com/article/caribbean-nicaragua-religion -arrests-0e67d619db76deece2bc0decad6d64dd.

9. Human Rights Watch, "Nicaragua: Law Threatens Free, Fair Elections," December 22, 2020, https://www.hrw.org/news/2020/12/22/nicaragua-law-threatens -free-fair-elections#.

10. BBC News, "Venezuela Opposition Banned from Running in 2018 Election," December 11, 2017, https://www.bbc.com/news/world-latin-america-42304594. In

any event, the opposition parties called for a general boycott of the 2018 election on the grounds that conditions for a fair election were not in place.

11. Wil S. Hylton, "Can Venezuela Be Saved?" *The New York Times Magazine*, March 1, 2018, https://www.nytimes.com/2018/03/01/magazine/can-venezuela-be -saved.html.

12. Juan Cristóbal Nagel, "Venezuela's Most Famous Dissident Gets 13 Years," *Foreign Policy*, September 11, 2015, https://foreignpolicy.com/2015/09/11/venezu-elas-most-famous-dissident-gets-13-years-leopoldo-lopez-maduro/.

13. BBC News, "Venezuela Opposition Leader Capriles Banned from Politics," April 8, 2017, https://www.bbc.com/news/world-latin-america-39534732.

14. The court argued that the party leaders had violated regulations concerning the selection of party authorities. Human Rights Watch, "Venezuela: Rulings Threaten Free and Fair Elections," July 7, 2020, https://www.hrw.org/news/2020/07/07/ven-ezuela-rulings-threaten-free-and-fair-elections.

15. Omar Sánchez-Sibony, "Competitive Authoritarianism in Morales's Bolivia: Skewing Arenas of Competition," *Latin American Politics and Society* 63, no. 1 (2021): 123, doi:10.1017/lap.2020.35.

16. NDI, Interim Report on the May 16, 1994, Elections in the Dominican Republic, https://www.ndi.org/sites/default/files/263_do_94elections.pdf.

17. On Honduras, see European Union Election Observation Mission, Honduras, Final Report, General Elections 2017, p. 16.

18. Simeon Nichter, *Votes for Survival: Relational Clientelism in Latin America* (New York: Cambridge University Press, 2018), 29.

19. Kevin Pallister, *Election Administration and the Politics of Voter Access* (New York: Routledge, 2017), 97, 117 note 4.

20. NDI and Carter Center, Peru Elections 2000: Final Report of the National Democratic Institute/Carter Center Joint Election Monitoring Project, 20.

21. Carter Center, Study Mission of The Carter Center 2013 Presidential Elections in Venezuela, Final Report (2013), 7, 39; Girish Gupta, "Venezuelan Vote Data Casts Doubt on Turnout at Sunday Poll," Reuters, Aug. 2, 2017, https://www.reuters.com/article/venezuela-politics-vote-idINKBN1AI0B0.

22. European Union Election Observation Mission, Republic of Paraguay, Final Report, General Elections, 22 April 2018, 16.

23. Andreas Schedler, "The Criminal Subversion of Mexican Democracy," *Journal of Democracy* 25, no. 1 (2014), http://doi.org/10.1353/jod.2014.0016.

24. Maria Fernanda Pérez Argüello and Donara Barojan, "Disinformation in the 2018 Elections: Mexico," in Luiza Bandeira et al., *Disinformation in Democracies: Strengthening Digital Resilience in Latin America* (Washington, DC: Atlantic Council, 2019), 20.

25. David Agren, "'Huge Incentives to Kill': Mexico Crime Groups Target Election Candidates," *The Guardian*, May 31, 2021, https://www.theguardian.com/global -development/2021/may/31/mexico-election-candidates-violence-assassinations.

26. Elizabeth Dickinson, "Local Polls in Colombia Put Peace to the Test," International Crisis Group, 2019, https://www.crisisgroup.org/latin-america-caribbean/andes /colombia/local-polls-colombia-put-peace-test.

27. Organization of American States, Electoral Observation Mission, Elections of Local Authorities, Republic of Colombia, October 27, 2019, Final Report, 3.

28. OAS, Electoral Observation Mission, Republic of Guatemala, Final Report, 2020, 35.

29. Ezequiel Gonzalez-Ocantos, Chad Kiewiet de Jonge, Carlos Meléndez, David Nickerson, and Javier Osorio, "Carrots and Sticks: Experimental Evidence of Vote-Buying and Voter Intimidation in Guatemala," *Journal of Peace Research* 57, no. 1 (2020): 53, https://doi.org/10.1177/0022343319884998.

30. This contrasts with programmatic politics, where parties offer voters competing packages of policy ideas and public resources are distributed according to clear rules, and with pork barrel politics, where benefits are targeted at specific groups or geographic areas without being contingent on political support for the party distributing the benefits. See Susan Stokes, Thad Dunning, Marcelo Nazareno, and Valeria Brusco, *Brokers, Voters, and Clientelism: The Puzzle of Distributive Politics* (New York: Cambridge University Press, 2013).

31. Simeon Nichter and Brian Palmer-Rubin, "Clientelism, Declared Support, and Mexico's 2012 Campaign," in *Mexico's Evolving Democracy: A Comparative Study of the 2012 Elections*, ed. Jorge I. Domínguez, Kenneth F. Greene, Chappell H. Lawson, and Alejandro Moreno (Baltimore: Johns Hopkins University Press, 2015), 201.

32. Stokes et al., *Brokers, Voters, and Clientelism*, 38.

33. Karleen Jones West, *Candidate Matters: A Study of Ethnic Parties, Campaigns, and Elections in Latin America* (New York: Oxford University Press, 2020), 120.

34. Ibid., 169.

35. Ibid., 143.

36. Ezequiel Gonzalez Ocantos, Chad Kiewiet de Jonge, and David W. Nickerson, "The Conditionality of Vote-Buying Norms: Experimental Evidence from Latin America," *American Journal of Political Science* 58, no. 1 (2014), https://doi.org/10.1111/ajps.12047.

37. Data from the Latin American Public Opinion Project, reported in West, *Candidate Matters*, 190.

38. Valeria Brusco, Marcelo Nazareno, and Susan Carol Stokes, "Vote Buying in Argentina," *Latin American Research Review* 39, no. 2 (2004), http://www.jstor.org/stable/1555401.

39. For Argentina's 2015 election, very few survey respondents said that they received anything from a campaign operative, but over 30 percent reported that parties distributed goods in their neighborhood before the first round of voting. Virginia Oliveros, "Perceptions of Ballot Integrity and Clientelism," in *Campaigns and Voters in Developing Democracies: Argentina in Comparative Perspective*, ed. Noam Lupu, Virginia Oliveros, and Luis Schiumerini (Ann Arbor: University of Michigan Press, 2019), 223–24. For similar results in El Salvador, see Ezequiel González-Ocantos, Chad Kiewiet de Jonge, and Covadonga Meseguer, "Remittances and Vote Buying," *Latin American Research Review* 53, no. 4 (2018), doi:10.25222/larr.396.

40. Ezequiel Gonzalez-Ocantos et al., "Vote Buying and Social Desirability Bias: Experimental Evidence from Nicaragua," *American Journal of Political Science* 56, no. 1 (2012), https://doi.org/10.1111/j.1540-5907.2011.00540.x.

41. Gonzalez-Ocantos et al., "Carrots and Sticks," 53.

42. González-Ocantos, Kiewiet de Jonge, and Meseguer, "Remittances and Vote Buying"; Oliveros, "Perceptions of Ballot Integrity," 225.

43. Stokes et al., *Brokers, Voters, and Clientelism*.

44. Simeon Nichter, "Vote Buying or Turnout Buying? Machine Politics and the Secret Ballot," *American Political Science Review* 102, no. 1 (2008), doi:10.1017/S0003055408080106.

45. In the words of Susan Stokes and colleagues, "Brokers are local intermediaries who provide targeted benefits and solve problems for their followers; in exchange, they request followers' participation in political activities such as rallies—and often demand their votes." Stokes et al., *Brokers, Voters, and Clientelism*, 75.

46. Stokes et al., *Brokers, Voters, and Clientelism*.

47. Joby Schafer and Andy Baker, "Clientelism as Persuasion-Buying: Evidence from Latin America," *Comparative Political Studies* 48, no. 9 (2015), https://doi.org/10.1177/0010414015574881.

48. Brusco, Nazareno, and Stokes, "Vote Buying in Argentina"; Herbert Kitschelt and Melina Altamirano, "Clientelism in Latin America: Effort and Effectiveness," in *The Latin American Voter: Pursuing Representation and Accountability in Challenging Contexts*, ed. Ryan E. Carlin, Matthew M. Singer, and Elizabeth J. Zechmeister (Ann Arbor: University of Michigan Press, 2015).

49. Kitschelt and Altamirano, "Clientelism," 254; Rebecca Weitz-Shapiro, "What Wins Votes: Why Some Politicians Opt Out of Clientelism," *American Journal of Political Science* 56, no. 3 (2012), https://doi.org/10.1111/j.1540-5907.2011.00578.x.

50. Nichter, *Votes for Survival*. This type of relational clientelism has been documented in Paraguay; see Tomás Dosek, "El Clientelismo en Paraguay: Compra de Votos o Compra de Participación Electoral?" *Latin American Research Review* 58, no. 3 (2023), doi:10.1017/lar.2023.8.

51. Nichter, *Votes for Survival*, 181–82.

52. Brusco, Nazareno, and Stokes, "Vote Buying in Argentina." In a survey of over seven hundred vote brokers in Argentina, almost 80 percent answered that they would know if someone with whom they had a lot of dealings voted for a different party's candidate. See Stokes et al., *Brokers, Voters, and Clientelism*, 100–101.

53. Oliveros, "Perceptions of Ballot Integrity," 218.

54. Gilles Serra, "Vote Buying with Illegal Resources: Manifestation of a Weak Rule of Law in Mexico," *Journal of Politics in Latin America* 8, no. 1 (2016): 135, 141, https://doi.org/10.1177/1866802X1600800105.

55. Chappell Lawson and Kenneth F. Greene, "Making Clientelism Work: How Norms of Reciprocity Increase Voter Compliance," *Comparative Politics* 47, no. 1 (2014), https://www.jstor.org/stable/43664343.

56. Paula Muñoz, *Buying Audiences: Clientelism and Electoral Campaigns When Parties Are Weak* (New York: Oxford University Press, 2020).

57. Nichter, *Votes for Survival*, 19, 63.

58. Serra, "Vote Buying with Illegal Resources," 141.

59. European Union Election Observation Mission, El Salvador 2019 Final Report, 16.

60. Nichter, *Votes for Survival*, 181.

61. Kirk Semple and Marina Franco, "Bots and Trolls Elbow into Mexico's Crowded Electoral Field," *New York Times*, May 1, 2018, https://www.nytimes.com/2018/05/01/world/americas/mexico-election-fake-news.html; Carmen Beatriz Fernández, "Ciberpolítica 2018: Tendencias En Latinoamérica," in *Nuevas Campañas Electorales en América Latina*, ed. Ángel Arellano (Montevideo, Uruguay: Konrad-Adenauer-Stiftung, 2018), 153–55; Maria Fernanda Pérez Argüello and Donara Barojan, "Disinformation in the 2018 Elections: Mexico," in *Disinformation in Democracies: Strengthening Digital Resilience in Latin America*, ed. Luiza Bandeira et al. (Washington, DC: Atlantic Council, 2019), 24; Marcos Martinez, "Mexico Election: Concerns about Election Bots, Trolls and Fakes," BBC News, May 30, 2018, https://www.bbc.com/news/blogs-trending-44252995.

62. Juliana Gragnani, "Fake Profiles Boosted Brazilian Ex-President Dilma," BBC News, March 21, 2018, https://www.bbc.com/news/blogs-trending-43371212.

63. Juliana Gragnani, "Inside the World of Brazil's Social Media Cyborgs," BBC News, December 13, 2017, https://www.bbc.com/news/world-latin-america-42322064.

64. Daniel Avelar, "WhatsApp Fake News during Brazil Election 'Favoured Bolsonaro,'" *The Guardian*, October 30, 2019, https://www.theguardian.com/world/2019/oct/30/whatsapp-fake-news-brazil-election-favoured-jair-bolsonaro-analysis-suggests; Luca Belli, "WhatsApp Skewed Brazilian Election, Proving Social Media's Danger to Democracy," *The Conversation*, December 5, 2018, http://theconversation.com/whatsapp-skewed-brazilian-election-proving-social-medias-danger-to-democracy-106476.

65. Mike Isaac and Kevin Roose, "Disinformation Spreads on WhatsApp Ahead of Brazilian Election," *New York Times*, October 19, 2018, https://www.nytimes.com/2018/10/19/technology/whatsapp-brazil-presidential-election.html.

66. Luiza Bandeira and Roberta Braga, "Disinformation in the 2018 Elections: Brazil," in *Disinformation in Democracies: Strengthening Digital Resilience in Latin America*, ed. Luiza Bandeira et al. (Washington, DC: Atlantic Council, 2019), 13–14.

67. Ibid, 18.

68. Isaac and Roose, "Disinformation Spreads on WhatsApp."

69. Jack Nicas, "To Fight Lies, Brazil Gives One Man Power over Online Speech," *New York Times*, October 21, 2022, https://www.nytimes.com/2022/10/21/world/americas/brazil-online-content-misinformation.html.

70. Jose Luis Peñarredonda and Roberta Braga, "Disinformation in the 2018 Elections: Colombia," in *Disinformation in Democracies: Strengthening Digital Resilience in Latin America*, ed. Luiza Bandeira et al. (Washington, DC: Atlantic Council, 2019), 39.

71. Cora Currier and Danielle Mackey, "The Rise of the Net Center," *The Intercept*, April 7, 2018. https://theintercept.com/2018/04/07/guatemala-anti-corruption-trolls-smear-campaign/.

72. Bandeira and Braga, "Disinformation in the 2018 Elections: Brazil," 15.

73. Poll workers check voters' fingers before allowing them to vote to ensure that they have not already voted.

74. Susan Hyde, *The Pseudo-Democrat's Dilemma: Why Election Observation Became an International Norm* (Ithaca and London: Cornell University Press, 2011).

75. Eric C. Bjornlund, *Beyond Free and Fair: Monitoring Elections and Building Democracy* (Baltimore: Johns Hopkins University Press, 2004), 85.

76. Judith G. Kelley, *Monitoring Democracy: When International Election Observation Works, and Why It Often Fails* (Princeton: Princeton University Press, 2012).

77. Ferran Martínez i Coma, "Electoral Reform," in *Election Watchdogs: Transparency, Accountability and Integrity*, ed. Pippa Norris and Alessandro Nai (New York: Oxford University Press, 2017).

78. Alberto Simpser and Daniela Donno, "Can International Election Monitoring Harm Governance?" *Journal of Politics* 74, no. 2 (2012), https://doi.org/10.1017/S002238161100168X.

79. Kai M. Thaler, "Nicaragua: A Return to Caudillismo," *Journal of Democracy* 28, no. 2 (2017), http://doi.org/10.1353/jod.2017.0032.

80. EU Election Observation Mission, Nicaragua 2011, Final Report on the General Elections and Parlacen Elections; Carter Center, Las Elecciones de 2011 en Nicaragua: Informe de una Misión de Estudio; Pallister, *Election Administration*, 152–53.

81. Carter Center, Las Elecciones de 2011, 9; Organization of American States, Final Report of the OAS Mission of Electoral Accompaniment to Nicaragua for the General Elections, November 6, 2011, 11.

82. BBC News, "Nicaragua Leader Daniel Ortega Wins Third Consecutive Term," November 7, 2016, https://www.bbc.com/news/world-latin-america-37892477.

83. Peter J. Meyer, "Honduras: Background and U.S. Relations," Congressional Research Service, April 27, 2020, https://fas.org/sgp/crs/row/RL34027.pdf.

84. Elisabeth Malkin, "U.S. Backs Honduran President's Victory in Disputed Election," *New York Times*, December 22, 2017, https://www.nytimes.com/2017/12/22/world/americas/us-honduras-president-hernandez.html.

85. Organization of American States, Electoral Observation Mission, General Election, Honduras, November 26, 2017, Final Report, 4.

86. Organization of American States, Electoral Observation Mission, 9; European Union Election Observation Mission, Honduras Final Report, General Elections 2017, 4.

87. European Union Election Observation Mission, 4–6.

88. European Union, Election Expert Mission, Bolivia 2019, Final Report, 18.

89. Ibid., 4, 31, 33.

90. Jonas Wolff, "The Turbulent End of an Era in Bolivia: Contested Elections, the Ouster of Evo Morales, and the Beginning of a Transition Towards an Uncertain Future," *Revista de Ciencia Política* 40, no. 2 (2020): 166, http://dx.doi.org/10.4067/S0718-090X2020005000105.

91. Anatoly Kurmanaev and María Silvia Trigo, "A Bitter Election. Accusations of Fraud. And Now Second Thoughts," *New York Times*, November 9, 2020, https://www.nytimes.com/2020/06/07/world/americas/bolivia-election-evo-morales.html.

92. Organización de Estados Americanos, Análisis de Integridad Electoral: Elecciones Generales en el Estado Plurinacional de Bolivia, October 20, 2019, http://www

.oas.org/documents/spa/press/Informe-Auditoria-Bolivia-2019.pdf; European Union, Election Expert Mission, 35–36.

93. Wolff, "The Turbulent End," 168.

94. Jack Johnston and David Rosnick, "Observing the Observers: The OAS in the 2019 Bolivian Elections," CEPR, 2020, https://www.cepr.net/wp-content/uploads /2020/03/bolivia-2020-3.pdf; John Curiel and Jack R. Williams, "Bolivia Dismissed Its October Elections as Fraudulent. Our Research Found No Evidence of Fraud," *Washington Post: Monkey Cage*, February 27, 2020, https://www.washingtonpost. com/politics/2020/02/26/bolivia-dismissed-its-october-elections-fraudulent-our-research-found-no-reason-suspect-fraud/.

95. Max Fisher, "Bolivia Crisis Shows the Blurry Line between Coup and Uprising," *New York Times*, November 12, 2019, https://www.nytimes.com/2019/11/12/ world/americas/bolivia-evo-morales-coup.html.

Chapter 3

The Legal Framework of Elections

In 1970, socialist candidate Salvador Allende won the presidential election in Chile with 36.3 percent of the vote. At the time, Congress decided the winner of the presidential election if no candidate won a majority of the vote, and Congress traditionally selected the candidate with the most votes. Allende had eked out a lead of about one percentage point over the second-place candidate, the conservative Jorge Alessandri, while the third-place candidate garnered 28 percent of the vote. Allende's presidency was marked by growing polarization between the left and right, growing economic crisis, and a campaign by the United States to undermine his government. This culminated in a military coup in 1973 that ended decades of Chilean democracy and ushered in a sixteen-year military dictatorship under General Augusto Pinochet.

One remarkable feature of this episode is the role that electoral institutions played in the death of Chile's democracy. Although Allende won a plurality of the vote, he was likely the least preferred of the three candidates among a majority of the electorate. If Chile had required a runoff election between Allende and Alessandri, rather than granting Congress the power to select the winner, Allende most likely would have lost. While an Alessandri presidency may have also coincided with troubled times politically, we can be sure that the military would not have overthrown the government to remove a president seen as a radical Marxist.

Chile's experience in the early 1970s illustrates how crucially important electoral rules can be. In this case, even without changing the preferences of voters, a different rule for electing the president (in this case, majority runoff rather than plurality) would have changed the outcome of the election—and the course of Chilean history.

Elections are structured by rules and institutions that determine who can vote, how they vote, and how their votes are translated into control of public offices. While some rules are straightforward, such as the voting age, others are complex, and the myriad combinations of rules produce a wide variety of electoral systems. Electoral rules determine whether voters can select only a political party on the ballot or individual candidates from party lists of candidates; whether voters can select only one candidate for the legislature or more than one, and whether voters choose only district-level representatives, only national-level representatives, or both; how votes are added together to determine who wins legislative seats; and many other features of electoral competition.

Latin American countries exhibit a diversity of electoral system rules, although with some common threads. Historically the region has experimented with many electoral rules, with electoral reforms adopted with staggering frequency throughout the nineteenth and twentieth centuries. Hundreds of constitutions and the nearly constant drafting of new electoral laws or amending old laws have produced frequent changes to term lengths, term limits, the number of members of the legislature, the size of legislative districts, and the methods used to elect representatives.[1] Illustrative is the varying term length for presidents in Brazil: starting with four years (from 1889 to 1930), then five years (1946–1979), to six years (1979–1985), back down to five years (1985–1994), and then four years (since 1995).[2] Other countries have seen similar rollercoaster patterns for many electoral rules.

This chapter provides an overview of contemporary electoral rules and institutions in Latin America. It covers voting rights, voting procedures, the electoral systems used for electing presidents and legislatures, the timing of elections (whether or not presidential and legislative elections are held simultaneously), mechanisms of direct democracy such as referenda and recall elections, and the electoral management bodies that administer elections.

Because the legal framework of elections shapes the democratic quality of electoral competition and of elected governments, the study of electoral institutions covered in this chapter speaks to enduring questions in political science. How do rules for electing presidents and legislators affect electoral competition and the types of candidates that get elected? What types of electoral rules and institutions best promote democratic values such as citizen participation, representation, and accountability? Are there particular institutions that best embody democratic principles, or do all institutional arrangements pose trade-offs between competing democratic values?

VOTING RIGHTS

One of the most fundamental aspects of election law pertains to who has the right to participate. Today all Latin American countries grant nearly all their adult citizens the right to vote. It was not always so: suffrage experienced periods of expansion and contraction throughout the nineteenth and early twentieth centuries. As one historical study notes, "Only from the 1930s onward would there develop a general, persistent pattern of suffrage expansion."[3]

Most Latin American countries today set their voting age at eighteen; the exceptions are Argentina, Brazil, Ecuador, and Nicaragua, which allow people to vote beginning at age sixteen. Uruguay was the first in the region to set a voting age of eighteen for all voters in 1918. Many countries lowered their voting age to eighteen only in the 1970s, typically setting the age at twenty-one before then.[4] Historically some countries set varying voting ages depending on whether a citizen was married. For instance, before 1994 Bolivia set the voting age at eighteen for married citizens but twenty-one for those who were not married.[5]

While universal adult suffrage is well established, it arrived just a few generations ago. While most countries had fully enfranchised their male citizens by the early twentieth century (Bolivia was the last, in 1952), women generally were not enfranchised until the middle of the century; Ecuador was the first to do so in 1929. Before universal suffrage, countries historically disenfranchised citizens based on varying criteria such as income, property ownership, and tax payments, in addition to gender. As a typical example, Peru's 1896 electoral law limited the vote to literate, tax-paying men over the age of twenty-one.[6] In a few countries, a significant barrier to enfranchisement was not removed until after women won the right to vote: literacy. Illiterate citizens were not enfranchised until 1970 in Chile, 1978 in Ecuador, 1979 in Peru, and 1988 in Brazil.[7]

Despite formal universal suffrage, some groups remain excluded from voting. Most common are those who are mentally incapacitated and those who are imprisoned, whether after being convicted of a crime or while being held on criminal charges. This latter provision can result in many thousands of adults being disenfranchised. In El Salvador, for instance, over twelve thousand detainees awaiting trial were unable to vote in the 2019 election.[8] A number of other countries similarly strip the right to vote not only from convicts but from those in pre-trial detention, whether explicitly by law or de facto by not providing for absentee voting or polling stations in prisons.

Less common today (although widespread historically) is the disenfranchisement of police officers and members of the armed services. For example, active-duty members of the military cannot vote in Colombia, Guatemala, Honduras, Paraguay, and the Dominican Republic.[9] Armed service members were enfranchised in Venezuela with the 1999 constitution.[10] In Peru, members of the armed forces and the police were barred from voting prior to a 2005 reform to the constitution, while in Ecuador soldiers and police were granted the right to vote in the 2008 constitution (with voting for them being optional, not compulsory as it is for civilians).[11] Although intended to keep the security services from interfering in politics and to prevent enlisted soldiers' votes from being coerced by their superior officers, the disenfranchisement of soldiers and police officers raises serious normative concerns.

The laws of several countries also provide additional grounds for disenfranchisement, including "notoriously vicious" conduct (El Salvador) and habitual dishonorable conduct or being part of an organization that aims to destroy the fundamental basis of the nation (Uruguay).[12] Such potentially arbitrary grounds for disenfranchisement seem to be rarely if ever applied.

While some Latin American citizens lose their voting rights for certain periods, a few countries in the region grant the right to vote to some resident non-citizens. Foreign residents in Bolivia can vote in municipal elections after two years of residence.[13] In Chile and Ecuador, foreigners with five years of residence may vote. Foreign residents in Venezuela can vote in municipal and regional elections after ten years of residence, while Uruguay grants the right to vote after fifteen years of residence.[14]

The most common recent extension of voting rights has been to citizens who are temporarily or permanently living outside their home country. Most countries around the world have reformed their laws to allow their citizens living abroad to vote (known as external voting or out-of-country voting), although countries differ as to which offices external voters may elect and what voting methods are used.

In Latin America, all but two countries—Nicaragua and Uruguay—allow expatriates to vote in presidential elections. Many also allow them to vote in legislative elections and in national referenda. In the case of Ecuador, citizens abroad directly elect six members of the National Assembly who serve as representatives of the expatriate community.

Implementing voting from abroad can be costly, as mechanisms must be put in place to register emigrant voters and securely receive and count their votes. The norm for Latin American countries is in-person voting at the country's consulates in large cities abroad, while in a few cases (El Salvador, Mexico, Panama) expatriates can vote by mail.

External voting has been an important reform considering the large size of emigrant populations from some Latin American countries and their home countries' reliance on economic remittances from migrants living abroad. Advocacy from emigrants themselves has sometimes contributed to the adoption of external voting, while in some cases political parties in power adopt external voting in the hopes of benefiting electorally from migrant votes. The implementation of external voting has in some cases led parties to campaign for votes in the United States. For instance, vice presidential candidates for the major parties in El Salvador visited the

Table 3.1   External Voting in Latin America

	Year Implemented[a]	Types of Elections	Voting Method
Argentina	1993	Presidential, Legislative	In-Person
Bolivia	2009	Presidential, Referenda, Recalls	In-Person
Brazil	1989	Presidential	In-Person
Chile	2017	Presidential, Referenda	In-Person
Colombia	1962	Presidential, Legislative	In-Person
Costa Rica	2014	Presidential, Referenda	In-Person
Dominican Republic	2004	Presidential, Legislative	In-Person
Ecuador	2006	Presidential, Legislative	In-Person
El Salvador	2014	Presidential, Legislative, Municipal	Postal
Guatemala	2019	Presidential	In-Person
Honduras	2001	Presidential	In-Person
Mexico	2006	Presidential, Senatorial, Referenda	Postal
Nicaragua	*No external voting*	-	-
Panama	2009	Presidential	Postal, Electronic
Paraguay	2013	Presidential, Senatorial	In-Person
Peru	1980	Presidential, Legislative, Referenda	In-Person
Uruguay	*No external voting*	-	-
Venezuela	1998	Presidential	In-Person

Source: Data from International IDEA, Voting from Abroad Database, https://www.idea.int/data-tools/data/voting-abroad.

[a] In some cases, reforms extended voting abroad from presidential to legislative, local, or referenda elections. Dates of those reforms are not shown.

United States to meet with groups of Salvadorans in 2014. In the lead-up to the 2019 election, the winning candidate, Nayib Bukele, campaigned in the United States and won 86 percent of the external vote, although more important than the votes was "the fact that Salvadorans abroad provided financial support for his in-country campaign."[15]

The results of implementing external voting have been disappointing. Voter participation among migrants is extremely low, as many migrants may lack interest in the politics of their home country and procedural hurdles to registering and voting may be high. In El Salvador's 2019 election, fewer than four thousand Salvadorans living abroad voted out of a population of over one million.[16] In Honduras, the first election with external voting was in 2001, and voting was held in six large U.S. cities. Fewer than 4,500 valid ballots were cast by Honduran migrants. By 2013, the number of external votes was nearly identical despite an estimated population of 1.2 million Hondurans living in the United States.[17] With such low turnout, the administrative costs for external voting in Honduras average five times more for each vote from abroad than for each vote cast in the country.[18]

VOTING PROCEDURES

A citizen's ability to exercise the right to vote is affected by the procedural requirements put in place to ensure that only eligible voters cast ballots, that each voter casts only one ballot, and that the voting process proceeds smoothly. Throughout Latin America the procedures for registering to vote and casting a ballot facilitate participation in some ways and raise obstacles to voting in others.[19]

Most Latin American countries have automatic voter registration. When a citizen obtains an identification card, which is needed for a wide array of transactions such as opening a bank account and receiving government services, they are automatically added to the voter rolls. The voter register is typically highly inclusive. For example, a 2017 audit of the voter register in Bolivia found that nearly 99 percent of eligible citizens were registered to vote.[20] Nevertheless, there are some obstacles to getting registered or updating one's registration before an election. Countries close the voter register to new additions or revisions (other than citizens just turning eighteen) months before election day as a precaution against voter registration fraud.

Voters cast ballots almost entirely at polling places on election day, which is always a Sunday in every country. Early voting and mail voting is almost never used, and absentee voting is mostly limited to in-person voting at an alternative polling place for voters who are away from their home precinct. Voters show their ID card when voting, but it is the same ID that automatically registers them to vote, so registered voters rarely lack the required ID.

Voters in Brazil, Venezuela, and (as of 2023) Paraguay cast their votes on electronic machines. In Brazil, voters type in a number corresponding to their preferred candidate or party, and the candidate or party list appears on the screen. The voter then confirms or cancels their choice.[21] In other countries voters use paper ballots (although some local jurisdictions in Argentina and elsewhere have begun to experiment with electronic voting). To facilitate voting by those who cannot read, ballots include political party symbols and in many cases candidate photographs, at least for presidential races. One of the achievements of Latin American democracies since the third wave has been to implement effective voting procedures that are generally efficient and inclusive.

ELECTORAL SYSTEMS FOR
PRESIDENTIAL ELECTIONS

While voting rights and procedures determine who can vote, other rules determine the choices that voters face and how their choices are translated into control of government offices. These include rules for presidential elections.

Latin America has always been home to various methods of electing presidents. From the early twentieth century until 1996, Uruguay used the "double simultaneous vote," whereby voters selected a candidate from one of the factions within a political party. The winner was determined by which party won the most overall votes, then which faction within that party won the most votes. The candidate from that faction won the election. "In effect, Uruguay was holding primaries at the same time as the election."[22] In Honduras until 1997, voters simply chose a political party rather than casting separate votes for president and Congress.[23] This fused vote was also used in Bolivia and in Brazil's 1982 election under its military regime.[24] In Bolivia before 2009, if no candidate won a majority of the vote, the legislature chose from among the top candidates.[25]

Today Latin American presidents are all directly elected to terms ranging from four to six years. Three types of electoral system are used: plurality, majority runoff, and qualified runoff (see table 3.2). In plurality systems the candidate with the most votes wins, even if that candidate receives less than a majority of the vote. If three or more candidates split the vote, the winner might receive notably less than 50 percent yet still win the presidency. In Mexico, for example, many presidential elections have seen the vote divided between three parties. In 2012, Enrique Peña Nieto won the presidency with 38 percent of the vote, compared to just under 32 percent for the runner up.

Majority runoff systems use two rounds of voting (when needed) to ensure that the winner receives over 50 percent of the vote. If no candidate receives a majority of the vote in the first round, a second round of voting is held between the top two candidates from the first round. In some cases a candidate wins a majority in the first round and no runoff is needed; this has commonly been the case in El Salvador. Typically, though, countries with majority runoff hold two rounds of voting.[26] In Guatemala, for instance, all ten presidential elections from 1985 to 2023 went to a runoff. (In four cases the winner had been the runner up in the previous election's second round.)

In majority systems it is common for the candidate who leads in the first round to go on to win the runoff. In Brazil's 2018 election, for example, Jair Bolsonaro handily led the first round of voting, but fell four points shy of a majority. He went on to win the runoff by ten points. But it is not unusual for the second-place finisher to go on to win the runoff by capturing the majority of votes from voters who had supported one of the candidates eliminated in

Table 3.2   Presidential Election Methods

	Threshold
Majority Runoff	
Brazil	50%
Chile	50%
Colombia	50%
Dominican Republic	50%
El Salvador	50%
Guatemala	50%
Peru	50%
Uruguay	50%
Qualified Runoff	
Argentina	45% or 40% plus 10-point lead
Bolivia	40% plus 10-point lead
Costa Rica	40%
Ecuador	40% plus 10-point lead
Plurality	
Honduras	-
Mexico	-
Nicaragua	-
Panama	-
Paraguay	-
Venezuela	-

Source: Data from Cynthia McClintock, *Electoral Rules and Democracy in Latin America* (New York: Oxford University Press, 2018), 16, updated by author.

the first round. This was the case in Colombia in 2014, Argentina in 2015, and Peru in 2016, for example. Some countries also use majority runoff for subnational executive elections—governors and mayors. The first-place finisher in the first round typically wins the runoff in these races.[27]

Four countries currently use qualified runoff, which is a middle ground between plurality and majority runoff. In these systems a runoff vote is held only if the leading candidate falls short of a threshold that is lower than 50 percent. In Costa Rica, a first-place candidate wins in the first round if she reaches 40 percent of the vote. In the other three cases (Argentina, Bolivia, and Ecuador), a leading candidate must win 40 percent of the vote and enjoy a ten-point lead over the runner up to avoid a runoff vote. Argentina waives the ten-point lead requirement if the leader wins 45 percent in the first round.

The trend during the third wave of democratization in Latin America has been to adopt majority or qualified plurality rules.[28] Nicaragua is an exception. After having a qualified runoff system that required a leading candidate to win 45 percent of the vote to win the election in the first round, a reform in 2000 reduced the threshold to 40 percent or 35 percent plus at least a five-point lead over the second-place candidate. A further reform in 2014 adopted a pure plurality rule. The move from qualified runoff to plurality benefited (and was initiated by) Daniel Ortega, who consistently enjoyed reliable support from about 35 percent of the population but struggled to reach majority support in several elections before returning to power in 2006.

Scholars and reformers have been interested in whether one of these systems is better than the others. Many scholars have argued for the benefits of plurality. In their view, plurality encourages a two-party (or two-coalition) system, because smaller parties with no shot at winning a plurality will tend to join larger parties. In contrast, majority runoff systems encourage small parties to compete in the first round because if they do reasonably well, they will then have some bargaining power before the second round, trading their support for one of the candidates for post-election benefits such as cabinet appointments. If legislative elections are held concurrently with the first round of presidential voting, many parties might win seats in the legislature—leading to a situation where the congress is fragmented and no party holds a majority of seats, making governing difficult. This is notoriously the case in Brazil and Peru, where the president's party typically holds only a minority of seats in the legislature and executive-legislative gridlock is the norm. In contrast, plurality elections are thought to be more likely to produce unified majority government.[29]

Proponents of majority runoff argue that it ensures that the winner has legitimacy by being the choice of a majority of voters. Runoff also is argued to promote ideological moderation, as candidates in the second round have to appeal to swing voters in the center to win over a majority of the electorate. Runoff also encourages the emergence of new parties, as voters don't feel compelled to vote strategically for a leading party in the first round and can vote their genuine preference, knowing that they can choose the lesser of two evils if their top choice doesn't make it to the runoff.[30]

Electing presidents by majority certainly seems to give the president a greater sense of legitimacy. A number of presidents elected via plurality or under qualified runoff likely would have lost a runoff election if one had been required, such as Paraguay's 1993 election and Nicaragua's 2006 election, in which Daniel Ortega won the presidency with just 38 percent of the vote.[31] The most notorious case is Chile's 1970 election won by the socialist Salvador Allende, as discussed in this chapter's introduction. Similarly, some presidential candidates in runoff systems who lead in the first round go on to lose in the second round; if they were to win the presidency through plurality they would suffer a legitimacy deficit.[32]

Majority runoff systems also promote more political parties, as seen by the typically higher number of parties competing in majority presidential elections than in plurality elections. Whether the runoff system encourages ideological moderation among candidates in the second round is more debatable.

Certainly not all candidates pivot to the center in the runoff round, as evident from Jair Bolsonaro's right-wing campaigns in Brazil in 2018 and 2022.

Peru illustrates both the strengths and weaknesses of the majority runoff system. In the 2016 election, Keiko Fujimori led Pedro Pablo Kuczynski in the first round, 39.9 percent to 21.1 percent. If elected with such a plurality, Fujimori, a polarizing daughter of former dictator Alberto Fujimori, would no doubt have been viewed as an illegitimate president by much of the population. As it turned out, Kuczynski went on to win the runoff by a razor-thin margin. Fujimori again made it to the runoff in the next election in 2021 after coming in second place in the first round. The first-place finisher, Pedro Castillo, went on to win the runoff narrowly. But with just 19 percent of the vote in the first round, in which eighteen candidates participated, Castillo's majority in the runoff no doubt gave his presidential victory greater legitimacy (although this was tarnished by Fujimori's baseless allegations of fraud). Castillo, a socialist, also moderated his campaign discourse after the first round of voting as he sought to assuage centrist voters.

While the majority runoff system thus gave winning candidates greater legitimacy and encouraged some moderation, it also contributed to executive-legislative gridlock. In 2016, although Fujimori ultimately lost the presidential election, her political party won a majority of seats in Congress (the legislative elections were held concurrently with the first round of presidential voting).[33] Thus the incoming president faced a hostile Congress dominated by the opposition; Kuczynski was ultimately impeached and removed from office. Similarly in 2021, Castillo's party won only 37 of 130 seats in Congress, assuring that he would struggle to govern effectively. His presidency likewise ended in impeachment after he attempted to shut down Congress in 2022, resulting in his immediate removal from office and arrest.

ELECTORAL SYSTEMS FOR LEGISLATIVE ELECTIONS

While Latin American countries use plurality, majority runoff, and qualified runoff to elect presidents, there is also a fair amount of diversity in the electoral systems used to elect legislatures. Nine Latin American countries have bicameral legislatures, consisting of a lower house (often called the chamber of deputies) and an upper house (senate): Argentina, Bolivia, Brazil, Chile, Colombia, Dominican Republic, Mexico, Paraguay, and Uruguay. The remaining countries have a unicameral legislature.[34] Legislators in the region's lower chambers serve terms ranging from three to five years, while senators sometimes serve longer terms.[35] Senators in Chile, for instance, serve eight-year terms, with half the seats up for election every four years.

There are many electoral systems used around the world to elect legislatures, but the most common general types are single-member district plurality and proportional representation. Under single-member district plurality, a country is divided into districts, and each district elects one representative. Whichever candidate wins a plurality of the vote—meaning more votes than any other candidate, even if it's not a majority of the vote (above 50 percent)—wins the seat. This system is used to elect the U.S. House of Representatives, but no Latin American country exclusively uses single-member districts to elect its legislature.

Instead, Latin American countries employ at least some element of proportional representation (PR). PR systems use electoral districts that elect more than one representative each; in political science terminology, district magnitude (the number of representatives per district) is greater than one. The legislative seats for each district are then allocated to political parties in rough proportion to their share of the vote in that district. For example, in a district that elects ten representatives (district magnitude of ten), a party that wins 30 percent of the vote will win about three of the ten seats, depending on the exact mathematical formula used to calculate the allocation of seats.[36] The larger the district magnitude, the more proportional the allocation of seats in the legislature can be to the share of the vote that parties receive.

In Latin America, electoral districts normally correspond to administrative boundaries within countries (states, departments, or provinces), and district magnitude tends to be low, although there is variation across countries and across individual districts.[37] A district in a large metropolitan area will have a large district magnitude, while more sparsely populated districts will elect only a small number of representatives. For example, in Argentina's Chamber of Deputies, the province of Buenos Aires elects seventy representatives, while other districts range from five to twenty-five representatives each. Additionally, a few countries use more than one tier of proportional representation: in addition to electing a set number of representatives for their district, voters also vote for a national list of candidates. In Guatemala and Nicaragua, approximately one-fifth of legislators are chosen from a national list.

Latin American countries adopted proportional representation in the early to mid-1900s, beginning with Costa Rica in 1913.[38] While all countries in the region use PR to elect at least part of their legislatures, several countries combine PR with single-member districts. These mixed systems take two main forms, illustrated by Mexico and Bolivia.

In Mexico's 500-member Chamber of Deputies, 300 seats are elected via plurality vote in single-member districts, while the other 200 seats are elected by proportional representation in five 40-seat districts. The two systems—single-member districts and PR—operate separately: the election results in the 40-seat districts do not affect the results in the single-member districts (giving this electoral system its name: parallel). Panama and Venezuela use similar mixed systems.

In contrast, Bolivia employs what is known as a mixed member proportional system. In this system, the seats elected via proportional representation are used to compensate for disproportionality produced by the single-member district elections. The seats in the lower chamber of the legislature are divided nearly evenly between those elected from single-member districts and those elected via proportional representation. The PR portion is tied to the presidential vote: each party wins approximately the percentage of legislative seats that its candidate receives in the presidential election. Thus, in addition to the seats that a party wins in single-member districts, it is awarded a certain number of additional seats to bring its total number of seats into line with the proportional results.

Adding further variety is the fact that proportional representation comes in two main varieties: closed list and open list. In both cases, parties put forward a list of candidates in each district; typically, the number of candidates equals the number of representatives for that district. Under closed list, voters select only a political party on their ballots. If that party wins any seats in a district, those seats are filled by the candidates at the top of the party's candidate list.

In open-list systems, voters can choose one or more individual candidates from a party's list. All votes for a party's candidates are added together for purposes of calculating how many seats in the district the party wins; the most voted-for candidates on that party list then win those seats. Figure 3.1 shows a ballot in El Salvador for a district electing six representatives, with eight parties each putting forward a list of six candidates. Unlike in most open-list PR systems, where voters choose only one candidate, in El Salvador voters can select as many candidates as there are seats to be filled in their district (a system known as panachage). Honduras also uses this system.[39]

Open-list voting entails not only competition between parties, but also competition between candidates of the same party who vie against each other for votes. Closed list is slightly more common in Latin America, although open-list PR has been increasingly prevalent in recent years. Colombia allows parties to choose whether their candidate lists are open or closed, with most parties opting for open lists.

A well-known open-list PR system is Brazil. With large district magnitudes (the average district magnitude for the lower house is nineteen) and many political parties, voters are faced with an overwhelming choice of candidates for congress. A voter in São Paulo, with its seventy congressional seats, is faced with choosing one candidate out of perhaps a thousand choices.[40] With so much competition, candidates have to stand out from a

Figure 3.1 Legislative Ballot, San Miguel, El Salvador. *Source*: Tribunal Supremo Electoral de El Salvador, https://www.tse.gob.sv/elecciones-2021/inicio.

crowd to win votes. They attempt to do this in part by running zany ads on television, with some dressing up as superheroes or celebrities.[41] They also often resort to buying votes, which requires raising a lot of money from contributors that expect something in return if the candidate is elected (thereby fueling corruption).[42]

The systems used for the upper house add even more complexity. Several countries use nationwide PR rather than employing subnational electoral districts. Brazil and the Dominican Republic use single-member district plurality rather than PR. In Argentina, two Senate seats are awarded to the most voted-for party in each district, and one seat is awarded to the second-place party. Mexico also does this to fill three-quarters of the seats in the Senate, but also elects one-fourth of the Senate via nationwide PR. Table 3.3 includes the basic elements of each country's legislative electoral system.

Scholars of electoral systems have long debated the effects of different institutional designs. The most famous hypothesis regarding the effects of electoral systems is Duverger's Law, which holds that single-member district plurality systems tend to produce two-party systems, whereas proportional

Table 3.3   Electoral Systems for Legislatures

	Electoral System for Lower House	Average District Magnitude, Lower House	Electoral System for Upper House
Argentina	Closed-list PR	10.8	3-seat districts. Two seats for most-voted party; one seat for second-place party
Bolivia	Mixed (MMP), closed-list	5.9	Closed-list PR (tied to presidential vote)
Brazil	Open-list PR	19	Plurality (three seats per state, elected on rotating schedule by plurality)
Chile	Open-list PR	5.5	Open-list PR
Colombia	List PR	4.8	List PR (100-seat nationwide district, plus 2 seats reserved for indigenous Colombians)
Costa Rica	Closed-list PR	8.1	-
Dominican Republic	Open-list PR	5.5	Single Member District Plurality
Ecuador	Closed-list PR	3.6	-
El Salvador	Open-list PR	6	-
Guatemala	Closed-list PR	5.7	-
Honduras	Open-list PR	7.1	-
Mexico	Mixed (Parallel), closed-list	40	Mixed (combination of closed-list PR and 3-seat districts with two seats for most-voted party and one seat for second-place party)
Nicaragua	Closed-list PR	4.1	-
Panama	Mixed (Parallel), open-list	5.9	-
Paraguay	Open-list PR	4.7	Closed-list PR (45-seat nationwide district)
Peru	Open-list PR	5	-
Uruguay	Closed-list PR	5.2	Closed-list PR (30-seat nationwide district)
Venezuela	Mixed (Parallel), closed-list	6.8	-

Source: International IDEA, Electoral System Design Database, https://www.idea.int/data-tools/continent-view/Americas/44; Dieter Nohlen, Elections in the Americas: A Data Handbook, vol. 2 South America (New York: Oxford University Press, 2005), 31–33, 48; updates by author. Note: For countries that use mixed systems or more than one tier of proportional representation, average district magnitude excludes single-member districts and the nationwide tier.

representation tends to produce multiparty systems.[43] Under plurality rules, small parties will be unable to win seats (larger parties will always win a plurality), and many voters will avoid "wasting" their vote on a party with no shot at winning in the district. PR, in contrast, provides smaller parties with greater chances of winning legislative seats.

While many Latin American countries have more than two major political parties along with proportional representation, research finds that reality is much more complicated than Duverger's Law suggests.[44] The number of political parties in a country is also influenced by societal cleavages and other institutional factors. One such institutional rule is an electoral threshold—a minimum share of the vote that a party must win in order to obtain seats in the legislature. Several countries employ thresholds, such as Peru (5 percent), Argentina (3 percent), and Mexico (2 percent), while others have no threshold for representation in the legislature. Thresholds attempt to limit the fragmentation of the legislature into many parties and prevent small extremist parties from winning seats.

There is much debate about the pros and cons of various electoral system features. While PR provides more equitable representation to political parties and is generally associated with higher voter turnout and the election of more of women and ethnic minorities, single-member district plurality is argued to provide stronger links between representatives and their constituents (since each voter has one clearly identifiable representative in the legislature) and be more likely to produce majority government (especially when executive and legislative elections are held concurrently). Among PR systems, open-list voting gives more choice to voters and can forge a personal connection between voter and candidate, but it also gives politicians incentives to focus on inefficient pork-barrel spending or vote buying to maintain popular support. Closed-list voting simplifies voters' choices and can contribute to more coherent political parties, but it can make politicians more beholden to party leaders who control their placement on the party list than to their constituents.

While different electoral systems have their advantages and disadvantages, one clear problem in some Latin American countries is malapportionment, or the "discrepancy between the share of legislative seats and the share of population held by electoral districts."[45] Where some districts have more seats than their population warrants, and others have fewer seats, the votes of citizens in the overrepresented districts effectively weigh more than the votes of citizens in other districts. A handful of Latin American countries have some of the highest levels of malapportionment in the world, with sparsely populated rural regions overrepresented and densely populated urban areas underrepresented. In Argentina, for example, the least populated provinces containing less than 30 percent of the population account for over half of the seats in the Chamber of Deputies and 80 percent of seats in the Senate.[46] Bolivia, Brazil, Chile, and Ecuador have historically had high levels of malapportionment as well.[47]

TEXT BOX 3.1: CHILE'S BINOMIAL SYSTEM

From 1989 to 2015 Chile employed a unique electoral system for its legislature, known as the binomial system.[a] All members of the Chamber of
Deputies and the Senate were elected from two-member districts. Each
coalition of parties ran a list of two candidates in each district, and each
coalition's list was open, meaning voters could choose an individual candidate on the ballot. The coalition with the most votes for their list won
one seat (and the most voted-for candidate on that coalition's list would
get the seat). In order to win the second seat, that same coalition had to
win more than double the number of votes of the runner-up coalition.
Otherwise, the leading candidate for the second-place coalition would win
the second seat.

This system benefited the second-place coalition by giving it equal
representation to the first-place coalition if it could win just more than
one-third of the vote. For instance, a coalition could win just 34 percent of
the vote in a district and win the same number of seats (one) as a coalition
that won 66 percent of the vote.

The binomial system was adopted by the outgoing military regime of
Augusto Pinochet in the late 1980s. In part the military regime aimed to
design an electoral system that encouraged a two-party system.[b] But the
system's designers also aimed to benefit right-wing parties associated with
the military regime and prevent the opposition from winning the legislative
majorities needed to change the country's military-imposed constitution.[c]
Anticipating that the center-left Concertación coalition would win majorities (though not two-to-one majorities) in future elections, the binomial
system would produce a draw between the Concertación and the right in
most districts. Right-wing parties were additionally boosted by the severe
malapportionment of legislative districts which gave extra weight to rural
areas that were more conservative than urban areas.

The binomial system was finally scrapped in 2015. In the new electoral
system, the number of electoral districts for the Chamber of Deputies was
reduced from 60 to 28, with each electing between 3 and 8 seats. The number of districts for the Senate was reduced to 15, each electing between 2
and 5 seats. Malapportionment was also reduced somewhat for the Chamber of Deputies, although not for the Senate.

The binomial system had been much criticized for many years, but perhaps the biggest impetus for eliminating it was the challenge it posed for
the center-left coalition. Because each coalition could run only two candidates in each district, and the center-left coalition was made up of seven
political parties, the parties had to negotiate over which parties' candidates

would be on the ballot in each district. The reform not only increased district magnitude but also allowed coalitions to run one candidate more than the number of seats in each district, which effectively allows more parties to get their own candidates on the ballot as part of a coalition.[d]

The binomial system and its reform illustrate how electoral systems can be designed with the intent of benefiting some parties over others and how electoral institutions shape incentives for parties to form coalitions with each other. While the binomial system didn't lead Chile to have just two main political parties, it did contribute to the persistence of two coalitions of parties, one including center and left parties and the other bringing together conservative parties. The stability and dominance of those coalitions was disrupted in the years after the binomial system was eliminated.

---

[a] For a concise overview of the binomial system and the 2015 reform that did away with it, see John Carey, "Chile's Electoral Reform," *Global Americans*, May 27, 2015, https://theglobalamericans.org/2015/05/chiles-electoral-reform/.

[b] Peter Siavelis, "Continuity and Change in the Chilean Party System: On the Transformational Effects of Electoral Reform," *Comparative Political Studies* 30, no. 6 (1997): 656, https://doi.org/10.1177/0010414097030006001.

[c] Daniel Pastor, "Origins of the Chilean Binominal Election System," *Revista de Ciencia Política* 24, no. 1 (2004), http://dx.doi.org/10.4067/S0718-090X2004000100002.

[d] Ricardo Gamboa and Mauricio Morales, "Chile's 2015 Electoral Reform: Changing the Rules of the Game," *Latin American Politics and Society* 58, no. 4 (2016), https://doi.org/10.1111/laps.12005.

ELECTORAL CALENDARS

Beyond the many questions of how electoral systems will be designed, countries must also decide when elections will be held. Most Latin American countries have fully concurrent elections, meaning presidential and legislative voting occurs on the same day. In other words, they only hold general elections; there are no midterm elections for the legislature. For countries with a majority runoff system for presidential elections, the legislative elections are held concurrently with the first round of voting for president.

Three countries hold non-concurrent elections: Colombia, El Salvador, and Venezuela. While presidential and legislative elections may be held in the same year, they occur on different days. For instance, Colombia's 2022 congressional elections took place in March, while the first round of the presidential election occurred in May. In two countries, Argentina and Mexico, elections are partly concurrent. Presidential elections are held simultaneously with some legislative elections, but additional legislative elections are held at other times as well (similar to the U.S. system of general and midterm elections).[48] In both countries, state and local elections are only sometimes concurrent with national elections. Argentina is an interesting case: in each election year, provincial governments can decide whether to hold provincial elections on the same day as that year's national elections or on a different date. Governors choose strategically based on whether they think their party will benefit from the coattails effect of their party's presidential candidate.

DIRECT DEMOCRACY: REFERENDA, INITIATIVES, AND RECALLS

The election of legislators and chief executives is a hallmark of representative democracy. But many countries have adopted mechanisms of direct democracy to complement the election of representatives to make policy. Modern-day direct democracy takes several forms, including referenda, initiatives, and recall elections. Referenda involve citizens voting directly on ballot questions to approve or reject particular laws. They are put forward by the executive and/or legislative branch for voters to decide. Initiatives are similar, but they originate with citizens organizing support for a question to be put up for a popular vote. (An alternative type of initiative, indirect or "agenda" initiatives, entail citizens petitioning to get a bill to be voted on by the legislature.) Recall elections give voters the chance to vote an elected official out of office before their term expires.

Most Latin American countries adopted mechanisms of direct democracy in the 1980s and 1990s.[49] Mexico was a latecomer, adopting direct democracy measures in 2014. Table 3.4 reports the availability of each mechanism for every Latin American country.

All Latin American countries have some provision for government-initiated referenda. Most countries allow for both mandatory and optional referenda. A mandatory referendum is required by the constitution when certain issues are decided, such as constitutional amendments. Panama's constitution, for example, "requires that the government consult citizens whenever the Panama Canal is to be modified or if a new canal is to be built."[50] Costa Rica's constitution requires that the creation of new provinces be approved by referendum.[51] An optional referendum is one that the legislature or the executive decides to refer to voters, even though it is not constitutionally required to do so. A president or congress might prefer to put an issue to a popular vote if the issue is particularly controversial or if one branch of government hopes to approve a policy that the other branch would otherwise block.[52] The rules for optional referenda vary from country to country, and some countries require a minimum threshold of voter participation in order for the referendum results to be binding.

Most countries also have provisions for citizens to put questions on the ballot. However, in practice many obstacles make the use of this mechanism

Table 3.4 National-Level Mechanisms of Direct Democracy

	Initiative	*Referendum*	*Recall*
Argentina		✓	
Bolivia	✓	✓	✓
Brazil	✓	✓	
Chile		✓	
Colombia	✓	✓	
Costa Rica	✓	✓	
Dominican Republic	✓	✓	
Ecuador	✓	✓	✓
El Salvador		✓	
Guatemala		✓	
Honduras	✓	✓	
Mexico	✓	✓	
Nicaragua	✓	✓	
Panama		✓	✓
Paraguay	(unclear)	✓	
Peru	✓	✓	
Uruguay	✓	✓	
Venezuela	✓	✓	✓

Source: Juve Cortés, "Self-Governance in Latin America: To What Extent Can Citizens Make Policy via Direct Democracy?" *Latin American Policy* 9, no. 1 (2018); ACE Electoral Knowledge Network, Comparative Data, https://aceproject.org/epic-en/.

rare. Some countries place certain issues (most commonly taxes) off limits for citizen initiatives. Getting a question on the ballot requires a large number of signatures, commonly 2 or 5 percent of all eligible voters. Moreover, citizen initiatives are not always binding even if they are approved by voters.[53] Given these obstacles, it is not surprising that the overwhelming majority of referenda held in Latin America are government initiated.[54]

Some countries also provide for a legislative initiative process that allows citizens to propose bills to the legislature, but with the legislature rather than voters ultimately approving or rejecting the bill. In Brazil, for example, citizens can introduce legislation with signatures equal to 1 percent of the national electorate.[55]

Finally, a few Latin American countries allow for recall elections at the national level, although this is the least common mechanism of direct democracy in the region. A recall allows a specified number of citizens to petition for an election to be held to decide whether an elected official can serve out the rest of their term. In Ecuador, for example, 15 percent of the country's registered voters can petition for a recall election for the president in between the first and last year of their term (for other officials, the threshold is 10 percent of registered voters). Because of the high bar to meet, recall elections for national office are exceedingly rare; the most famous has been the 2004 recall election in Venezuela, which failed to oust Hugo Chávez from office.[56]

Some countries, such as Colombia and Peru, allow for recall elections at the state and local level, where they are used more frequently.[57]

Despite the widespread adoption of direct democracy mechanisms in recent decades, their use is not especially common. Only ten referenda were held from 2010 through 2020 (with some referenda including more than one ballot question); ten countries held no referenda during that period, and Ecuador was the only country with more than one referendum election.[58] Several countries—El Salvador, Honduras, Mexico, and Nicaragua—have never made use of their direct democracy mechanisms.

Nevertheless, some significant issues have been decided via referenda. Costa Rican voters approved their country's entry into the Central American Free Trade Agreement in 2007. Paraguayans approved the extension of voting rights to citizens living abroad, and Uruguayans voted to approve the adoption of a qualified plurality rule for electing the president. In a 2016 referendum, Colombians narrowly rejected a government peace deal with the FARC guerrillas (although the government ultimately implemented a revised peace deal without subjecting it to a referendum). And in a referendum in 2020, 78 percent of Chilean voters supported the drafting of a new constitution. The subsequent election of delegates to the constituent assembly produced an assembly dominated by independents and nontraditional parties, and the first such assembly in the world with an equal balance of female and male members. However, the constitution produced by that assembly was rejected by voters in its own referendum in 2022.

ELECTORAL MANAGEMENT BODIES

A final set of institutions that are critical to elections consists of the agencies that organize and administer electoral processes. These agencies are known as electoral management bodies (EMBs) and are typically responsible for conducting most of the nuts and bolts of elections: maintaining the voter register, choosing the location of polling places, recruiting and training poll workers, preparing ballots, registering candidates and political parties, conducting public information campaigns to inform voters of when and where to vote, and monitoring compliance with laws pertaining to campaigning and campaign finance. Some EMBs are also responsible for issuing national ID cards to citizens, and many have the legal authority to propose election-related laws to the legislature.

EMBs typically consist of a handful of commissioners or magistrates at the national level, along with a technical staff, and a corresponding commission in each province and/or municipality that is under the authority of the national EMB. At the lowest level of this hierarchy are poll workers, who in many Latin American countries are chosen by lottery from the voter register (serving as a poll worker is thus similar to jury duty). In a few countries, such as Paraguay, poll workers are representatives of the political parties.[59] Some countries divide responsibilities for administering elections between two EMB bodies. In Colombia, for example, the National Registry of Civil Status issues ID cards, maintains the voter register, and plans the logistics of voting, while the National Electoral Council exercises oversight over the electoral process and has authority over infractions of electoral rules. In Peru, one agency issues ID cards and maintains the voter registry, while a second agency administers the electoral process.

Because of the critical role that EMBs play in carrying out elections, the professionalism and impartiality of EMB officials are important not only to the efficiency and integrity of the electoral process but also to perceptions of fairness. Many countries require EMB commissioners to meet professional requirements, in some cases the same requirements that must be met to serve on the country's highest courts. When it comes to ensuring impartiality and keeping partisan interests from influencing the administration of elections, Latin American countries vary in their institutional designs. In some cases the EMB is designed to give representation to multiple political parties so that no one party dominates the institution. This was the case in El Salvador following its democratic transition, where three of the five magistrates on the Supreme Electoral Tribunal were nominated by the three largest political parties (with the other two nominated by the Supreme Court).

Most countries formally try to keep partisan operatives off the EMB, including legal requirements that magistrates cannot have held leadership positions in a political party in the years before being nominated. But in practice the role of legislatures and presidents in nominating EMB magistrates can undermine such formal legal provisions. In Bolivia, six of the seven magistrates are elected by two-thirds vote of the legislature, and one magistrate is named by the president. Magistrates cannot be party members and cannot have been a party leader or candidate in the preceding five years.[60] Nevertheless, the political party of President Evo Morales appointed magistrates perceived as close to the party.[61] Even more egregious cooptation of the EMB by ruling parties has been at the heart of the corruption of elections in Venezuela and Nicaragua. In Venezuela's 2012 election, for instance, four of the five top election officials were aligned with president Hugo Chávez.[62] The key factor in these cases is that one political party was able to monopolize control over the EMB; with no other parties to check its power, the ruling party was able to bias the administration of elections in its own favor.

Despite the partisan bias of some EMBs, most electoral bodies in Latin America display a high degree of professionalism and integrity. Costa Rica's highly regarded Supreme Electoral Tribunal is headed by three magistrates (increasing to five during election season) selected by a two-thirds vote of the Supreme Court with no interference from political parties.[63] Like many of the region's EMBs, it oversees efficient and transparent electoral processes. Mexico's National Electoral Institute (INE), formerly the Federal Electoral Institute (IFE), is also an internationally respected EMB. Its leadership consists of an eleven-member general council elected by two-thirds vote of the lower chamber of the legislature. Councilors must not have served in an elected office or party leadership position for the previous four years.[64] Although officially nonpartisan, political parties do in practice influence the selection of INE councilors.[65] Nevertheless, the INE is widely perceived to be impartial and professional.

The impartiality of EMBs is a big factor in explaining the quality and integrity of electoral processes. One study of Latin American presidential elections from 1980 to 2003 found that electoral processes were significantly more likely to be found acceptable by observers where the EMB was professional and nonpartisan.[66]

Also important is the functioning of the judiciary, since courts are often called on to resolve election-related disputes. A few Latin American countries have specialized electoral courts to hear challenges to election results or other aspects of the electoral process. One example is Mexico's Tribunal Electoral del Poder Judicial de la Federación, whose members are named by the Supreme Court, and which enjoys independence from political parties. Legal challenges involving the electoral process, which might involve the INE, are resolved by the tribunal—providing a neutral umpire that can overrule decisions taken by the INE. Brazil, Chile, the Dominican Republic, Ecuador, Honduras, and Peru also have specialized electoral courts. In other countries the EMB typically rules on election-related challenges, at least initially. If the EMB is the sole body to resolve election disputes, concerns arise about potential conflicts of interest, as many election complaints involve the conduct of election officials themselves. Indeed, some international election observers even recommend that countries separate the roles of administration and adjudication in different institutions.[67] In most countries, however, legal cases on at least some electoral issues can be appealed to the supreme or constitutional courts. To the extent that the courts are impartial (which is not always the case), parties to an election dispute can expect a fair ruling.

NOTES

1. One study counted almost 250 electoral reforms in the region from 1978 to 2015, not including minor administrative reforms. See Flavia Freidenberg and Tomáš Došek, "Las Reformas Electorales en América Latina (1978–2015)," in *Reformas*

Políticas en América Latina, Tendencias y Casos, ed. Kevin Casas-Zamora, Marian Vidaurri, Betilde Muñoz-Pogossian, and Raquel Chanto (Organization of American States, 2016).

2. Bolívar Lamounier and Octavio Amorim Neto, "Brazil," in *Elections in the Americas: A Data Handbook, vol. 2 South America,* ed. Dieter Nohlen (New York: Oxford University Press, 2005), 167–68.

3. Paul W. Drake, *Between Tyranny and Anarchy: A History of Democracy in Latin America, 1800–2006* (Stanford: Stanford University Press, 2009), 108.

4. Ibid., 42–44; Dieter Nohlen (ed.), *Elections in the Americas: A Data Handbook, vol. 2 South America* (New York: Oxford University Press, 2005).

5. Bolivia's 1967 Constitution, Art. 41, amended in 1994.

6. Fernando Tuesta Soldevilla, "Peru," in *Elections in the Americas: A Data Handbook, vol. 2 South America,* ed. Dieter Nohlen (New York: Oxford University Press, 2005), 450.

7. Nohlen, *Elections in the Americas,* 12.

8. European Union Election Observation Mission, El Salvador 2019 Final Report, 10.

9. Colombia's Constitution, Art. 219; Guatemala's Electoral and Political Parties Law, Art. 15; Honduras' Constitution, Art. 37; Paraguay's Electoral Code, Art. 91; Dominican Republic's Constitution, Art. 208.

10. José Molina and Bernard Thibaut, "Venezuela," in *Elections in the Americas: A Data Handbook, vol. 2 South America,* ed. Dieter Nohlen (New York: Oxford University Press, 2005), 552.

11. "100,632 Uniformados Pueden Votar en las Próximas Elecciones de Ecuador," *El Comercio,* January 8, 2017, https://www.elcomercio.com/actualidad/politica/uniformados-policias-militares-votacion-elecciones.html.

12. El Salvador's Electoral Code, Art. 7; Uruguay's Constitution, Art. 80.

13. Ley del Regimen Electoral, Art. 45.

14. Chile's Constitution, Art. 14; Ecuador's Constitution, Art. 63; Venezuela's Ley Orgánica de Procesos Electorales, Art. 29, 41; Uruguay's Constitution, Art. 78.

15. European Union Election Observation Mission, El Salvador 2019 Final Report, 33.

16. Ibid.

17. OAS, Informe Final de la Misión de Observación Electoral de la Organización de los Estados Americanos, Elecciones Generales del 24 de Noviembre de 2013 de la República de Honduras, 19; European Union Election Observation Mission, Honduras Final Report, General Elections 2013, 15.

18. "Voto en EE.UU. Será Cinco Veces Más Caro," *El Heraldo,* September 16, 2013, http://www.elheraldo.hn/csp/mediapool/sites/ElHeraldo/Pais/story.csp?cid=583176&sid=299&fid=214.

19. This section draws primarily on Kevin Pallister, *Election Administration and the Politics of Voter Access* (New York: Routledge, 2017), 42–51.

20. European Union, Election Expert Mission, Bolivia 2019, Final Report, 13.

21. Lawson, Chappell, Gabriel S. Lenz, Andy Baker, and Michael Myers, "Looking Like a Winner: Candidate Appearance and Electoral Success in New Democracies," *World Politics* 62, no. 4 (2010): 567, note 31, doi: 10.1017/S00438871 10000195.

22. Cynthia McClintock, *Electoral Rules and Democracy in Latin America* (New York: Oxford University Press, 2018), 108–9.

23. Ibid., 88.

24. Jorge Lazarte R., "Bolivia," in *Elections in the Americas: A Data Handbook*, *vol. 2 South America*, ed. Dieter Nohlen (New York: Oxford University Press, 2005), 128; Lamounier and Neto, "Brazil," 169.

25. Before 1990 the legislature chose from the top three candidates. Afterward it was from the top two candidates. McClintock, *Electoral Rules*, 14.

26. By one count, 61 percent of presidential elections held under majority runoff rules did in fact have a runoff round. Salvador Romero Ballivián, *Elecciones en América Latina* (Tribunal Supremo Electoral and Instituto Internacional para la Democracia la Asistencia Electoral, 2020), 100.

27. Adrián Lucardi, Juan Pablo Micozzi, and Agustín Vallejo, "Does the Early Bird Always Get the Worm? First Round Advantages and Second Round Victories in Latin America," *Electoral Studies* 81 (2023), https://doi.org/10.1016/j.electstud.2022.102570.

28. Gabriel L. Negretto, "Choosing How to Choose Presidents: Parties, Military Rulers, and Presidential Elections in Latin America," *Journal of Politics* 68, no. 2 (2006): 423, https://doi.org/10.1111/j.1468-2508.2006.00417.x.

29. McClintock's study of presidential elections in Latin America finds that in countries with plurality elections, the winning president's party won half or more of the seats in the legislature in 50 percent of cases; for runoff countries, this was so only in 36 percent of cases. McClintock, *Electoral Rules*, 37.

30. McClintock, *Electoral Rules*.

31. Ibid., 75, 95.

32. Ibid., 197.

33. Ibid., 165.

34. In the 1990s, Peru and Venezuela shifted from bicameral to unicameral legislatures.

35. Nohlen, *Elections in the Americas*, 22–23.

36. The most common calculation methods are the D'Hondt and the Hare Least Remainders systems.

37. Nohlen, *Elections in the Americas*, 34.

38. Gabriel L. Negretto and Giancarlo Visconti, "Electoral Reform under Limited Party Competition: The Adoption of Proportional Representation in Latin America," *Latin American Politics and Society* 60, no. 1 (2018): 30, https://www.jstor.org/stable/44684430.

39. This is quite a departure from the previous voting system in Honduras: legislative candidate names were not even included on the ballot until 2005. Ecuador also used panachage between 1998 and 2000. See McClintock, *Electoral Rules*, 88; Romero Ballivián, *Elecciones*, 104.

40. Rosario Aguilar, Saul Cunow, Scott Desposato, and Leonardo Sangali Barone, "Ballot Structure, Candidate Race, and Vote Choice in Brazil," *Latin American Research Review* 50, no. 3 (2015): 177, note 5, doi:10.1353/lar.2015.0044.

41. Compilations of candidate ads can be found online. See, for example, "Comédia Eleitoral Gratuita," August 1, 2014, https://www.youtube.com/watch?v=zwDAyYVoHsE.

42. Ryan Lloyd and Carlos Oliveira, "How Brazil's Electoral System Led the Country into Political Crisis," *Washington Post Monkey Cage*, May 25, 2016, https://www.washingtonpost.com/news/monkey-cage/wp/2016/05/25/how-brazils-electoral-system-led-the-country-into-political-crisis/?utm_term=.92a122b4f5a3.

43. Maurice Duverger, *Political Parties: Their Organization and Activity in the Modern State* (New York: Wiley, 1954).

44. Scott Morgenstern and Javier Vázquez-D'Elía, "Electoral Laws, Parties, and Party Systems in Latin America," *Annual Review of Political Science* 10 (2007), https://doi.org/10.1146/annurev.polisci.10.081205.094050.

45. Richard Snyder and David Samuels, "Devaluing the Vote in Latin America," *Journal of Democracy* 12, no. 1 (2001): 146, http://doi.org/10.1353/jod.2001.0016.

46. Ernesto Calvo, "Down to the Wire: Argentina's 2015 Campaign," in *Campaigns and Voters in Developing Democracies: Argentina in Comparative Perspective*, ed. Noam Lupu, Virginia Oliveros, and Luis Schiumerini (Ann Arbor: University of Michigan, 2019), 57.

47. Snyder and Samuels, "Devaluing the Vote."

48. Data from Nohlen, *Elections in the Americas*, 23, updated by author.

49. Monica Barczak, "Representation by Consultation? The Rise of Direct Democracy in Latin America," *Latin American Politics and Society* 43, no. 3 (2001), doi:10.1111/j.1548-2456.2001.tb00178.x.

50. Juve J. Cortés, "Self-Governance in Latin America: To What Extent Can Citizens Make Policy via Direct Democracy?" *Latin American Policy* 9, no. 1 (2018): 12, https://doi.org/10.1111/lamp.12139.

51. Costa Rica's Constitution, Art. 168

52. Cortés, "Self-Governance in Latin America," 17.

53. Ibid.

54. Ibid., 6–7; Anita Breuer, "The Use of Government-Initiated Referendums in Latin America: Towards a Theory of Referendum Causes," *Revista de Ciencia Política* 29, no. 1 (2009): 25, http://dx.doi.org/10.4067/S0718-090X2009000100002.

55. Simeon Nichter, *Votes for Survival: Relational Clientelism in Latin America* (New York: Cambridge University Press, 2018), 56.

56. For a detailed overview of the Venezuelan recall election, see the Carter Center, *Observing the Venezuela Presidential Recall Referendum, Comprehensive Report* (Atlanta, GA: 2005), https://www.cartercenter.org/documents/2020.pdf.

57. David Altman, "Direct Democracy in Latin America," in *Referendums around the World: The Continued Growth of Direct Democracy*, ed. Matt Qvortrup (New York: Palgrave Macmillan, 2014), 165.

58. Calculated from data at ElectionGuide: https://www.electionguide.org/.

59. European Union Election Observation Mission, Republic of Paraguay, Final Report, General Elections, 22 April 2018, 11.

60. Bolivia's Ley del Órgano Electoral Plurinacional, Art. 14.

61. Omar Sánchez-Sibony, "Competitive Authoritarianism in Morales's Bolivia: Skewing Arenas of Competition," *Latin American Politics and Society* 63, no. 1 (2021): 123, doi:10.1017/lap.2020.35.

62. Carter Center, Study Mission to the October 7, 2012, Presidential Election in Venezuela, 24.

63. ACE Electoral Knowledge Network, "Electoral Management," https://aceproject.org/ace-en/topics/em/annex/electoral-management-case-studies/costa-rica-a-powerful-constitutional-body.

64. Ley General de Instituciones y Procedimientos Electorales, Art. 38.

65. Federico Estévez, Eric Magar, and Guillermo Rosas, "Partisanship in Non-Partisan Electoral Agencies and Democratic Compliance: Evidence from Mexico's Federal Electoral Institute," *Electoral Studies* 27, no. 2 (2008), https://doi.org/10.1016/j.electstud.2007.11.013.

66. Jonathan Hartlyn, Jennifer McCoy, and Thomas M. Mustillo, "Electoral Governance Matters: Explaining the Quality of Elections in Latin America," *Comparative Political Studies* 41, no. 4 (2008), https://doi.org/10.1177/0010414007301701.

67. See, for instance, European Union Election Observation Mission, El Salvador 2018, "Supreme Electoral Tribunal Organises Complex Elections, Implementing Electoral Reforms Introduced by Constitutional Chamber—Preliminary Statement," https://eeas.europa.eu/election-observation-missions/eom-el-salvador-2018/40894/node/40894_en.

Chapter 4

Candidates

Every year, thousands of Latin Americans run for public office. Some run for president or congress, while others run for provincial and municipal offices. Even before launching a campaign, prospective candidates face myriad regulations that determine whether they can run. These include the requirements candidates must meet to be elected to office, whether candidates can run as independents or must be nominated by a political party, and whether incumbent officeholders can run for reelection. The path to being a candidate is also shaped by the recruitment and nomination practices of political parties.

This chapter examines running for office in Latin America. It begins with a look at the social characteristics of national-level candidates. It then explores the institutional factors that influence candidacies, including the legal requirements that candidates must meet for national office, the practices that parties use to nominate candidates, legal rules that promote candidacies of women, and the region's tumultuous experience with term limits.

These themes speak to enduring questions in politics: How important is it for candidates and officeholders to "look like" their constituents in order to adequately represent their interests? How can electoral rules ensure equitable representation of women and other marginalized groups? What are the consequences of different methods of nominating candidates? What restrictions on running for office are legitimate? Do term limits help ensure the survival of democracy or undermine its spirit by depriving voters of choice? Ultimately, the study of who runs for office, and under what institutional rules, helps us understand two concerns that have been central to Latin American politics since the third wave of democratization: representation and accountability.

WHO RUNS FOR OFFICE?

Candidates for national office in Latin America are often political-party insiders who have years of experience in politics, but outsider candidates and amateur politicians are not uncommon. In Argentina almost all members of Congress have prior experience in government or political-party positions, such as provincial legislator, municipal councilor, and appointed positions in the provincial and national executive branches.[1] The same is true of candidates for governor in Argentina's provinces, with candidates often previously serving in the national Senate or Chamber of Deputies.[2] In Colombia, all nineteen presidential candidates from 1974 to 2002 had served in Congress at some point in their career.[3] In Chile, most presidents between 1932 and 2007 had served in Congress and/or held a cabinet position prior to being elected president; half were lawyers, and their average age was sixty.[4] Gabriel Boric, elected president of Chile in December 2021, only half fit this pattern. He had been elected to Congress twice, but prior to that he had risen to prominence as a leader of a student protest movement. He had studied law but did not finish his degree. Elected president at age thirty-five (the minimum age to be president in Chile), he succeeded seventy-two-year-old Sebastián Piñera to become Chile's youngest president in its history. With tattoos and a beard, and openly discussing his obsessive-compulsive disorder, Boric "represented a break from the traditional image of presidential candidates."[5]

In addition to prior political experience, lawmakers tend to be well-off, with white-collar professional backgrounds (such as lawyer or business owner) being common. Some legislators have backgrounds in middle-class professions such as teachers and social workers. Politicians with a working-class background make up only a small share of legislators.[6] For example, of fifty-seven candidates elected as deputies in Costa Rica's Legislative Assembly in 2018, all had professional middle- or upper-class backgrounds. Fifteen were lawyers, while other common professions were in business, administration, engineering, and journalism. Six deputies were evangelical pastors. The average age of elected candidates was forty-six.[7] The elite backgrounds and educational qualifications are evident in Mexico as well, where by the mid-1990s most national-level politicians were highly educated and came from upper-middle-class backgrounds.[8]

Nevertheless, some legislative and presidential candidates have backgrounds in less elite fields, including labor unions, peasant organizations, and the military. Among the most notable have been successful presidential candidates Luiz Inácio Lula da Silva (first elected president of Brazil in 2002), a labor union leader prior to his political career; Evo Morales, a leader of the coca-growers movement before being elected president of Bolivia in 2005;

and former army officers Hugo Chávez (Venezuela), Otto Pérez Molina (Guatemala), and Jair Bolsonaro (Brazil), who all went on to successful presidential runs.

While many candidates rise through the ranks of political parties, not all do. In some countries with weak political parties, amateur politicians are much more common. Rather than rising through the ranks of stable parties, outsider candidates enter politics from other professions. This is the case in Peru, where parties are not institutionalized and the reelection rate for legislators is low. Without being able to rely on a useful party label, many politicians have a prior career in business, media, or other areas where they can make a name for themselves. Sports figures often use their fame to launch political campaigns, as when former members of the national women's volleyball team were elected to Congress.[9]

Some candidates run as independents rather than with a party label. A slight majority of Latin American countries allow independent candidates to run for national office. Getting on the ballot as an independent often requires submitting a large number of signatures, and so the vast majority of candidates are put forward by political parties.

Yet even where candidates cannot run as independents, many "outsider" politicians manage to run for office under the label of a political party—either a preexisting party or a party that they create as a vehicle for their own candidacy. In some cases, a person with no prior political experience runs as a candidate for a well-established party. This was the case with Mauricio Funes, who won the presidency in El Salvador in 2009 with the FMLN (Farabundo Martí National Liberation Front) party. In other cases, someone with no prior experience may form their own party. Such outsider presidential candidates who had never run for office before include Fernando Collor de Mello (president of Brazil, 1990–1992), Alberto Fujimori (president of Peru, 1990–2000), Rafael Correa (president of Ecuador, 2007–2017), and Fernando Lugo (president of Paraguay, 2008–2012).[10]

In presidential elections, outsider candidates generally receive more votes when the political-party system is weakly institutionalized and established parties have failed to address pressing problems.[11] Lacking the support of a well-organized party in the legislature, presidents who are elected as outsiders often confront executive-legislative gridlock and can be tempted to try to circumvent or undermine the legislative branch—as Fujimori did in Peru when he closed Congress and effectively established an authoritarian regime.

In legislative elections outsiders and amateur politicians likewise sometimes run even where independent candidacies are not allowed. This is the case in Brazil, where party leaders exercise little control over legislative candidate nominations and candidates effectively self-select themselves to run under a particular party label.[12]

Outsider candidates are often characterized as populists. In addition to a personalistic style, populists claim to represent "the people" against a corrupt and immoral "elite." Both "the people" and "the elite" are vague formulations that allow populist politicians flexibility in portraying their supporters and adversaries. In populist discourse the concept of "the people" "is imagined as a homogeneous body sharing interests and an identity that are embodied in a leader whose mission is to save the nation" from rapacious elites.[13] As Jan-Werner Müller puts it, "When running for office, populists portray their political competitors as part of the immoral, corrupt elite; when ruling, they refuse to recognize any opposition as legitimate."[14] For left-wing populists, the "elite" might signify wealthy business interests and foreign powers (especially the United States), while for right-wing populists the "elite" are more often progressive intellectual and cultural leaders.

Latin America has long been known for its charismatic populist politicians, most notably Juan Perón in Argentina and Hugo Chávez in Venezuela—outsiders who came to power and reshaped their countries' political systems. In a region with severe socioeconomic inequalities and discontent with political parties, even some insiders with long careers in party politics adopt a populist style. This is the case with Brazil's Jair Bolsonaro (president, 2019–2022) and Mexico's Andrés Manuel López Obrador (president, 2018–2024), for example.

TEXT BOX 4.1: NAYIB BUKELE: FROM PARTY POLITICIAN TO OUTSIDER TO THE "WORLD'S COOLEST DICTATOR"

After taking office as president in 2019, 38-year-old Nayib Bukele began eroding democratic norms and institutions that had been in place in El Salvador since the end of the country's civil war in 1992. A prolific tweeter who wears jeans and leather jackets, Bukele acts the part of a political outsider, routinely attacking the country's two traditional political parties and the political class as corrupt and ineffective.

Bukele comes from a family of Palestinian migrants to El Salvador. His father was a successful businessman, and when Bukele left school without finishing his law degree, he worked for the family business. His father had close ties to leaders of the leftist FMLN party, and when Bukele first ran for mayor of a small municipality in 2012, he ran under the FMLN banner. As mayor, he started using a slogan that tapped into widespread disgust with corruption: "El dinero alcanza cuando nadie está robando" (there is enough money when no one steals).[a]

In 2015 Bukele was elected mayor of the capital city, San Salvador. But he was later expelled from the FMLN for regularly criticizing the party in public. He went on to run for president in 2019 under the label of a conservative party with which he had no previous ties, while also forming his own party, Nuevas Ideas (New Ideas). Bukele won the 2019 election with 53 percent of the vote, outpolling the second-place candidate by more than twenty points. In the 2021 legislative elections, Bukele's New Ideas party won two-thirds of the seats in the legislative assembly.

With his charisma and ability to exploit Salvadorans' discontent with the status quo, the ostensible outsider Bukele remained popular in his first term in office, and his popularity allowed him and his new political party to stack the courts and attorney general's office with loyalists and to nullify the constitutional prohibition on presidential reelection. When critics labeled him a dictator, Bukele changed his Twitter profile to describe himself as "the coolest dictator in the world."

[a] Gabriel Labrador, "Bukele, el Autoritario Cool," *El Faro*, Sept. 29, 2021, https://elfaro.net/es/202109/el_salvador/25753/Bukele-el-autoritario-cool.htm.

LEGAL REQUIREMENTS FOR OFFICE

While candidates for office in Latin America range from experienced party insiders to amateur outsiders, they must meet certain minimum legal requirements pertaining to age, citizenship, and other criteria. Table 4.1 contains select legal requirements for each country.

The minimum age requirements for presidential candidates range from twenty-five (El Salvador and Nicaragua) to forty (Guatemala). Eight countries set the minimum age at thirty-five, while seven set it at thirty. The minimum age for legislators is eighteen in Bolivia, Ecuador, and Guatemala, while other countries require legislators to be at least twenty-one or twenty-five years old. Most countries with bicameral legislatures set a higher minimum age for senators than for members of the lower house.

Citizenship is a requirement for running for national office throughout the region. A large majority of countries require presidential candidates to be citizens by birth, but countries vary in requirements for legislative candidates. Mexico requires that candidates for both chambers of the legislature be natural-born citizens, while Uruguay allows naturalized citizens to be candidates for both chambers.[15] Colombia requires Senate candidates to be natural-born citizens, but candidates for the Chamber of Representatives can be naturalized citizens. Some countries that allow naturalized citizens to run for the legislature require a residency period, as in Costa Rica, where naturalized citizens must have resided in the country for ten years after obtaining citizenship.[16]

Table 4.1   Select Requirements for Office

	Presidency	Legislature (Lower Chamber)	Legislature (Upper Chamber)
Argentina	30; citizen (natural born); minimum income	25; citizen (4y); district residency (2y)	30; citizen (6y); district residency (2y); minimum income
Bolivia	30; citizen; residency (5y)	18; citizen; district residency (2y)	18; citizen; district residency (2y)
Brazil	35; citizen; literacy	21; citizen; district residency; literacy	35; citizen; district residency; literacy
Chile	35; citizen	21; voting rights; district residency (2y)	35; voting rights
Colombia	30; citizen (natural born)	25; citizen	30; citizen (natural born)
Costa Rica	30; citizen (natural born)	21; citizen	-
Dominican Republic	30; citizen (natural born)	25; citizen; district residency (5y)	25; citizen; district residency (5y)
Ecuador	35; citizen (natural born)	18; citizen; district residency (2y)	-
El Salvador	25; citizen (natural born)	25; citizen (natural born)	-
Guatemala	40; citizen (natural born)	18; citizen (natural born)	-
Honduras	30; citizen (natural born)	21; citizen (natural born); district residency (5y)	-
Mexico	35; citizen (natural born); residency (20y total, 1y preceding election)	21; citizen (natural born); district residency (6 months)	25; citizen (natural born); district residency (6 months)
Nicaragua	25; citizen; residency (4y)	21; citizen; district residency (2y)	-
Panama	35; citizen (natural born)	21; citizen; district residency (1y)	-
Paraguay	35; citizen (natural born)	25; citizen (natural born)	35; citizen (natural born)
Peru	35; citizen (natural born); voting rights	25; citizen (natural born); voting rights	-
Uruguay	35; citizen (natural born)	25; citizen	30; citizen
Venezuela	30; citizen (natural born)	21; citizen; district residency (4y)	-

Source: ACE Electoral Knowledge Network, Comparative Data: Parties and Candidates, https://aceproject
.org/epic-en/CDTable?view=country&question=PC003, with updates by the author from each country's
constitution and electoral laws.
Note: cells display minimum age for office followed by other criteria.

Aside from age and citizenship, there exists a variety of restrictions on candidacies for the legislature or presidency. Most constitutions specify that candidates must be in full enjoyment of their legal rights, and in some cases in possession of voting rights. This effectively bars individuals currently serving criminal sentences from running for office. In a few cases, conviction for certain crimes carries a permanent ban on election, such as terrorism and drug trafficking in Peru.[17] The most extensive ban on candidates for criminal convictions is Brazil's "Clean Record Law," which in the interest of fighting corruption prohibits individuals convicted of a wide range of financial and administrative crimes from running for office.[18]

Most countries also prohibit current ministers in executive branch agencies and active-duty military officers from running for national office. Some countries also prohibit people with contracts with the state from running for the legislature or presidency (e.g., Ecuador, El Salvador) and require that people who have managed government funds provide an official document showing that there are no legal claims against their management of those funds (e.g., El Salvador, Guatemala). Some countries—Costa Rica, Guatemala, Honduras, Mexico, Nicaragua, and Venezuela—prohibit religious officials from running for the presidency. Nicaragua and Paraguay apply this prohibition to legislative elections as well.

Most Latin American countries also prohibit family members of the sitting president from running for the presidency, out of a concern that presidents might circumvent term limits through the election of a spouse or other relative.[19] In Guatemala, first lady Sandra Torres attempted to run for president in 2011 after divorcing her husband, President Álvaro Colom. But the courts blocked her candidacy, ruling that her divorce was a ploy to circumvent the constitutional prohibition.[20] In Argentina, where a president can be succeeded by a family member, President Néstor Kirchner (2003–2007) decided not to run for reelection in 2007, and his wife, Cristina Fernández de Kirchner, was elected.

Some Latin American countries (including Ecuador, Guatemala, and Nicaragua) also prohibit anyone who has previously led a military coup or an unconstitutional government from running for president. In Guatemala this rule affected Efraín Ríos Montt, who had led a coup in 1982 and presided over a brutal military dictatorship until the following year. When Ríos Montt tried to run for president in 1990 and again in 1995, the courts blocked his candidacy. (He was elected to Congress, however.) Finally in 2003 Ríos Montt ran (unsuccessfully) for president after a dubious court ruling allowing him to run. Guatemala's ban on presidential candidacies of coup leaders even extends to family members. As a result, Zury Ríos, congresswoman and daughter of Efraín Ríos Montt, was blocked from running for president in 2019.[21]

Several countries have taken steps to promote the election of indigenous and Afrodescendant candidates. Bolivia, the Latin American country with the largest proportion of indigenous citizens, created seven reserved seats in its Chamber of Deputies for indigenous minority groups. Colombia and Venezuela created smaller numbers of reserved seats for indigenous communities in their legislatures, and Colombia also created two seats for black communities. Peru requires that political parties running candidates in local elections in the heavily indigenous Amazon region include indigenous candidates on their lists. Despite such rules, indigenous peoples remain underrepresented in Latin American legislatures, as do Afrodescendants in some countries.[22]

NOMINATING CANDIDATES

Historically, candidates for office in Latin America have been chosen by political-party elites, or individual politicians have formed their own parties as vehicles for their election campaigns. Election laws did not require parties to hold primary elections to select their candidates for general elections, and most parties eschewed primaries. Of more than eight hundred candidates that ran in democratic presidential elections from 1978 to 2004, only forty-seven were selected via primaries.[23] Instead, party executive committees or small nominating conventions chose the candidates.

This has been changing in recent years, however, as more parties have adopted primary elections—in which all voters or all voters affiliated with the party can participate—and more countries have added requirements for primary elections in their electoral laws. Elections in 2019 in Bolivia and El Salvador were the first in those countries in which parties were required to hold primary elections.[24] Other countries that have legally mandated the use of primaries include Honduras, Panama, Paraguay, Peru, and Uruguay.[25]

Even when primaries are legally mandated, candidates may be unopposed within their parties and party leaders may still exercise great influence over who gets nominated. In Argentina, for instance, where open primaries are used, provincial party bosses choose legislative candidates while presidential candidates are often agreed upon by the leadership of party factions.[26] When primaries are not mandated, some political parties use them anyway. This has been the case in Mexico, where only some of the largest parties have used primaries to select their presidential nominees. Prior to the 2000 election, only one of the three big parties, the Institutional Revolutionary Party (PRI), held a primary. Before the 2012 election, only the National Action Party (PAN) held a primary. To nominate candidates for Congress, parties have used a mix of primaries, conventions, and selection by party leadership.[27]

Even as primary elections have become more common, the nomination of presidential and legislative candidates is marked by variation across Latin America. A mix of primaries, party nominating conventions, and party governing committees select candidates. Not only is there variation across countries but often across political parties within the same country. Primaries may be open (allowing all registered voters to participate) or closed (allowing only registered party affiliates to vote). In some countries, parties themselves are responsible for organizing and paying for primaries, as in Mexico and El Salvador.[28] In some cases, the party's presidential candidate has influence over the selection of legislative candidates. For example, in Ecuador the legislative candidates for President Rafael Correa's party, Alianza PAIS, were selected directly by Correa and his closest advisers.[29] In general, parties exercise only rudimentary vetting of legislative candidates, and there is marked variation across parties in their requirements for candidates in terms of length of party membership and fit with the party's ideology.[30]

Primaries are generally seen as more democratic and transparent than candidate selection by party elites or party conventions. One study has found that candidates selected via primary get a boost in the general election because of the legitimacy effect they get from being selected in a more democratic process.[31] Primaries may also help achieve consensus on candidates within parties that contain rival factions, and within coalitions of parties that must decide on a single candidate to nominate in a race. Rather than fight over which faction's or party's preferred candidate is nominated, the decision can be left to primary voters. Indeed, where primaries have not been legally required, the parties most likely to voluntarily use them are those with intraparty divisions that might be reconciled through primary elections.[32]

This doesn't mean that primaries always unify a factionalized party. In Mexico, the PRI party used primary elections to select its gubernatorial candidates but replaced primaries with party conventions in 2003, in part because primaries "allowed losing primary candidates to obtain recognition, declare the elections to be fraudulent, and then leave the party and become a candidate from one of the other parties."[33] More generally, primary election campaigns can generate intraparty conflicts as candidates compete against (and criticize) one another. Some evidence from other parties in Mexico suggests that legislative candidates nominated via primary elections do not gain a competitive advantage in general elections compared to other candidates.[34]

The effects of primaries on internal party divisions, as well as issues such as who votes in primaries and how primaries affect the types of candidates nominated, are still not well understood. While a number of case studies rigorously analyze features of primary elections in select countries,[35] primaries remain an understudied area in Latin American politics.

ELECTING WOMEN

One of the most notable features of candidate recruitment in Latin America in recent decades has been the increase in women running for office. The election of women matters in a number of ways, with scholars distinguishing three main forms of representation in understanding the significance of electing women (or members of other identifiable social groups).[36] First, electing women provides descriptive representation: elected institutions like congress bear greater resemblance to the population they are meant to represent if they include a significant number of women. Second, electing women may affect substantive representation or the extent to which representatives advance the interests and policy preferences of their constituents. Finally, women in office may manifest symbolic representation, whereby members of a particular group feel represented by officeholders who "stand for" them.

Latin America is in the global forefront of electing women to public office. Seven countries in the region had elected a woman president by the end of 2021: Violeta Chamorro (Nicaragua 1990), Mireya Moscoso (Panama 1999), Michelle Bachelet (Chile 2006, 2014), Cristina Fernández de Kirchner (Argentina 2007, 2011), Laura Chinchilla (Costa Rica 2010), Dilma Rousseff (Brazil 2010, 2014), and Xiomara Castro (Honduras 2021).[37] Other countries have had competitive women presidential candidates, such as Keiko Fujimori in Peru, who lost both the 2016 and 2021 elections by less than one percentage point.

Across Latin America women made up an average of 34 percent of the members of the lower chamber of national legislatures in early 2023, putting the region well above the global rate of 26.6 percent. Latin American countries ranged from a high of 55.7 percent in authoritarian Cuba to a low of 17.5 percent in Brazil. (For comparison, women made up 28.7 percent of the House of Representatives in the United States.)[38] For the region's national senates, the average was nearly 31 percent.

While women have seen increasing descriptive representation at the national level, women remain underrepresented in local elected office, making up only 15 percent of mayors and 27 percent of city councilmembers in 2020.[39] Few women are elected as governors in the federal countries where those positions are elected, such as Argentina, Brazil, and Mexico.[40] In Bolivia, despite constituting nearly half of the national legislature, women accounted for only 8 percent of mayors, four out of twenty cabinet ministers, and no governors in 2019.[41]

Explanations for the differences across countries and over time in the election of women tend to focus on socioeconomic development, cultural views of gender roles, and political institutions. It is the latter that best explains the election of women in Latin America. Numerous studies find that women tend to be elected at higher rates in proportional representation electoral systems (which are used at least to some degree in all Latin American countries) compared to single-member district systems. As Leslie Schwindt-Bayer puts it, proportional representation systems that elect more than one representative from each district

> influence the election of women by making it easier for parties to nominate women without eliminating men from the ballot. This occurs because parties can win multiple seats in any district and because seats get allocated in proportion to the votes that parties receive. Consequently, political parties may be more likely to "risk" the nomination of nontraditional candidates (i.e., women) for the nth seat in multimember districts with proportional representation rather than for the only seat in single-member district plurality systems.[42]

Yet an even more important institutional factor than proportional representation has been gender quotas. Quotas require that political parties include a minimum number of women on their candidate lists for legislative elections. Gender quotas are typically set between 20 and 50 percent, and the strongest quotas also include placement mandates requiring parties to alternate men and women on their candidate lists or to include at least one woman in every three spots on the list. Over 130 countries have some form of electoral gender quota in their laws or political-party statutes, or they have established reserved seats in their legislature for women.[43]

Latin America has been the world leader in adopting gender quotas for national legislative elections. Argentina was the first country in the world to adopt a gender quota for legislative elections in 1991. By 2021 all Latin American countries except for Guatemala had some type of gender quota for legislative elections. The biggest force for the adoption of gender quotas in many Latin American countries was the mobilization of women activists and politicians, especially in early quota adopters like Argentina and Mexico. International norms and the strategic motives of political parties seeking popular support were also influential.[44]

In most cases gender quotas have become stricter over time as countries have raised the minimum percentage of candidates that must be women, added a placement mandate, or included additional requirements.[45] In Costa Rica, for instance, political parties first adopted voluntary (non-binding) quotas in 1994, followed several years later by the adoption of a legally binding quota for all parties but with no placement mandate, then a binding quota with a placement mandate.[46] More recently Ecuador strengthened its placement mandate in a 2020 reform, requiring that half of party lists be headed by women beginning in 2025,[47] while Honduras increased its threshold from 40 to 50 percent and added a placement mandate in its 2021 election law. Table 4.2 shows data on gender quotas and women in legislatures in each country.

Quotas have proven remarkably effective at increasing the number of women elected to legislative office. In Argentina, for instance, "the first election of the current democratic period in 1983 resulted in only 4 percent of those in the Chamber of Deputies being female. By 2001, women comprised 31 percent of the lower house of Congress."[48] Many other countries have also seen significant increases in the number of women elected after instituting gender quotas.

Yet the effectiveness of gender quotas depends on their design and the effective enforcement of the rules. Quotas are most effective when the minimum percentage of women candidates is not set too low, when a placement mandate is included, and when the rules are enforced by electoral authorities. Over time, most countries have increased the minimum threshold to 40 or 50 percent, and party lists that do not comply with the quota rules are not placed on the ballot. Placement mandates are particularly important, because in a

Table 4.2   Electing Women to Legislatures, 2023

World Rank	Country	Women in Lower Chamber (%)	Gender Quota (%)	Placement Mandate
2	Cuba	55.7	n/a	n/a
3	Nicaragua	51.7	50	Yes
4	Mexico	50.0	50	Yes
8	Costa Rica	47.4	50	Yes
11	Bolivia	46.2	50	Yes
17	Argentina	44.8	50	Yes
31	Peru	38.8	50	Yes
32	Ecuador	38.7	50	Yes
43	Chile	35.5	40	No
70	Colombia	28.9	30–50[a]	No
80	Dominican Republic	27.9	33	Yes
83	El Salvador	27.4	30	No
84	Honduras	27.3	50	Yes
90	Uruguay	26.3	33	Yes
102	Panama	22.5	50	No
104	Venezuela	22.2	50	Yes
119	Guatemala	19.4	none	n/a
123	Paraguay	18.8	20	No
131	Brazil	17.5	30	No

Source: InterParliamentary Union, Monthly Ranking of Women in National Parliaments, https://data.ipu.org /women-ranking?month=4&year=2023 (data as of April 1, 2023; Venezuela's data is from prior years); International IDEA, Gender Quota Database, https://www.idea.int/data-tools/data/gender-quotas, with updates by the author.
[a] In Colombia, the quota is 50 percent for districts that elect five or more representatives, and 30 percent for districts that elect fewer than five representatives. See Colombia's electoral code, Art. 80.

given district only the top few candidates on a party list might have a chance of winning election. If parties comply with a quota by placing women candidates only at the bottom of the party list, few women will be elected.

In the past some parties exploited loopholes in quota laws to minimize their impact. Parties in Bolivia could comply with the quota by naming women only as alternate candidates, who take office only if the primary candidate resigns or is removed from office.[49] In Costa Rica, parties would follow the placement mandate by alternating male and female candidates on their lists (known as vertical parity), but the first position on each district list would usually go to a male candidate (thus lacking horizontal parity). (Both vertical and horizontal parity are now required.)[50] And Brazil's quota law continues to be lax and weakly enforced. Even in Mexico, with a strict quota law, parties in the state of Oaxaca in the 2018 elections "attempted to fill the quota with fake transgender candidates—men who dressed as women but had never done so until their nomination."[51]

However, over time most gender quotas in the region have become stricter, and more women have been elected as a result. Strong quota rules have been found to have their biggest effect in closed-list proportional representation systems, where candidates are elected in the order that the party lists them on the ballot.[52] Under open-list proportional representation, where voters choose individual candidates from party lists, the placement mandates of gender quotas are less relevant since the order of candidates on the party list does not directly determine which candidates get elected from each party.

While gender quotas achieve women's descriptive representation, their effects on substantive and symbolic representation are less clear cut. In terms of substantive representation, it is important not to overgeneralize the political interests and preferences of women as a monolithic group. Nevertheless, surveys tend to show that women give greater priority to issues such as poverty and healthcare than do men,[53] and women share interests on issues such as gender discrimination in employment and violence against women. Research on several Latin American legislatures finds that women legislators more often sponsor bills related to women's issues (such as women's rights and family issues), speak on behalf of women's issues in legislative debates, and actively perform constituent service on behalf of women constituents.[54] Although women rarely hold leadership positions or chair powerful committees in Latin American legislatures,[55] the election of women—facilitated by gender quotas—produces a degree of substantive representation of women.

Gender quotas, and the election of women more generally, seem to have less impact in terms of symbolic representation. Gender quotas are theorized to strengthen a norm that women should be involved in politics, with elected women serving as symbolic role models to other women. However, survey research finds no relationship between quotas and women's attitudes (such as political interest) or political behavior (e.g., contacting elected officials or participating in campaigns).[56]

TEXT BOX 4.2: MICHELLE BACHELET: BREAKING THE GLASS CEILING IN CHILE

In 2006 Michelle Bachelet became the first woman elected to the presidency in Chile. As the candidate for the center-left Concertación coalition, which had won every presidential election since the country's return to democracy in 1989, Bachelet was able to benefit from the Concertación's positive performance in office while also presenting herself as something new, thus promising both continuity (in terms of policy) and change (in terms of style).[a]

A doctor by training, Bachelet was involved in left-wing politics from a young age. Bachelet's father, a military officer, served in the leftist government of Salvador Allende in the early 1970s and died in military custody after being tortured following the coup that brought Augusto Pinochet to power. In 1975 Bachelet and her mother were arrested by the military regime's security forces and tortured in detention. After being released, Bachelet went into exile, making her way to Germany before returning to Chile in 1979.

After Chile's return to democracy, Bachelet worked in the Socialist Party, one of the parties in the Concertación coalition. When Socialist Ricardo Lagos became president in 2000, he named Bachelet minister of health and subsequently minister of defense (making Bachelet the first woman in Latin America to serve as defense minister).

Bachelet's cabinet experience and education certainly qualified her for the presidency. But in many ways she was an unlikely candidate in a conservative Catholic country: a divorced mother of three children from two different fathers, and a self-described agnostic. In her first presidential run, Bachelet evoked her identity as a middle-class single mother. During a presidential debate, Bachelet said, "I know that as a woman, people are going to be looking at me through a magnifying glass to see if I am doing it well or not, and I have a tremendous responsibility, not just with the people who vote for me, with those who believe in me, but also with the women of this country, to demonstrate also that women can do it."[b]

Gender played a large role in Bachelet's campaign, which sought to cultivate a sense of shared identity with women voters and promised to implement reforms such as early childhood education and universal access to kindergarten.[c] Her campaign ads skillfully blended Bachelet's stereotypically feminine traits (such as empathy) with her experience, skills, and strength, stereotypically associated with male candidates.[d] Bachelet also benefited from her charisma and down-to-earth personality that distinguished her from the traditionally elitist style of many Chilean politicians.[e]

Bachelet won the 2006 race by a seven-point margin. After sitting out the one required presidential term, she was again elected to the presidency in 2013 in a lopsided contest, outpolling her rival in the runoff round by 24 points. Bachelet ended her second term with low approval ratings, with her administration dogged by corruption scandals and slow economic growth, although she oversaw significant reforms to education, marriage equality, and the tax code.[f] After leaving the presidency, Bachelet went on to become the United Nations High Commissioner for Human Rights.

[a] Susan Franceschet and Gwynn Thomas, "Renegotiating Political Leadership: Michelle Bachelet's Rise to the Chilean Presidency," in *Cracking the Highest Glass Ceiling: A Global Comparison of Women's Campaigns for Executive Office*, ed. Rainbow Murray (Santa Barbara, CA: Praeger, 2010), 182; Marcela Rios Tobar, "Seizing a Window of Opportunity: The Election of President Bachelet in Chile," *Politics & Gender* 4, no. 3 (2008): 515, doi:10.1017/S1743923X0800041X.

[b] Catherine Reyes-Housholder, "Women Mobilizing Women: Candidates' Strategies for Winning the Presidency," *Journal of Politics in Latin America* 10, no. 1 (2018): 83, https://doi.org/10.1177/1866802X1801000103.

[c] Reyes-Housholder, "Women Mobilizing Women."

[d] Franceschet and Thomas, "Renegotiating Political Leadership"; Alberto Pedro López-Hermida Russo, "Political Advertising in Chile: State of Play in a Period of Changes," in *Routledge Handbook of Political Advertising*, ed. Christina Holtz-Bacha and Marion R. Just (New York: Routledge, 2017), 105.

[e] Franceschet and Thomas, "Renegotiating Political Leadership," 185.

[f] Beryl Seiler and Ben Raderstorf, "Michelle Bachelet's Underappreciated Legacy," *Americas Quarterly*, March 9, 2018, https://www.americasquarterly.org/article/michelle-bachelets-underappreciated-legacy-in-chile/.

TERM LIMITS

While Latin America has been at the vanguard of adopting gender quotas, the region has also been a laboratory for experimenting with term limits. Latin America has a tradition of leaders continuing in power for extended periods, known as continuismo. Examples are many—including Manuel Estrada Cabrera in Guatemala (1898–1920), Rafael Trujillo in the Dominican Republic (1930–1961), and Alfredo Stroessner in Paraguay (1954–1989). In Mexico, Porfirio Díaz was in power for a nearly uninterrupted period from 1877 to 1910, and a rallying cry of the revolution that overthrew him was "effective suffrage, no reelection."

While many personalist leaders held power for extended periods, Latin America saw a tremendous number of constitutional amendments adopting, altering, and abolishing term limits throughout the nineteenth and twentieth centuries.[57] In response to the threat of leaders perpetuating themselves in power, countries throughout the region adopted prohibitions on immediate presidential reelection in the 1800s. But in the early to mid-twentieth century, presidents often changed their country's constitution to eliminate term limits and stay in office. Augusto Leguía in Peru in the 1920s, Getúlio Vargas in Brazil in the 1930s, Juan Perón in Argentina in the 1940s, and Victor Paz Estenssoro in Bolivia in the 1960s all secured constitutional changes to allow for reelection. But in all these cases, "disillusionment with the performance of these presidencies and the upheaval with which they ended fueled a reaction against continuismo and the reestablishment of constitutional prohibitions on reelection."[58]

During the transitions to democracy in the late twentieth century, most countries limited presidents to one or two terms. Where two terms were allowed, in most cases an incumbent president could only run for election after sitting out at least one interim term—a rule that was the most common term limit historically in Latin America. Only the Dominican Republic allowed immediate reelection at the start of the recent democratization period.[59]

But over time sitting presidents have chipped away at term limits, and since the 1990s many countries have loosened or eliminated restrictions on reelection. Argentina, Brazil, Ecuador, Peru, and Venezuela all amended their constitutions to allow immediate reelection. Colombia did likewise in 2005, although a subsequent reform reinstated the prohibition on reelection.[60] Typically these constitutional amendments allowed then-popular presidents like Alberto Fujimori in Peru, Carlos Menem in Argentina, and Fernando Henrique Cardoso in Brazil to run for a second term.

Other countries have followed suit in more recent years. In Bolivia, El Salvador, Honduras, Nicaragua, and Venezuela, term limits have been eliminated as part of a process of democratic backsliding, with presidents concentrating power in their own hands and undermining democratic institutions.[61] In Venezuela, President Hugo Chávez organized a constituent assembly that produced a new constitution allowing one immediate reelection and extending presidential terms to six years. He later pushed through a referendum vote in 2009 that eliminated term limits altogether. In Nicaragua (2009), Honduras (2015), and Bolivia (2017), high courts amenable to the interests of incumbent presidents struck down constitutional prohibitions on reelection on the dubious grounds that they violated a person's human right to run for office. In El Salvador, the Supreme Court's Constitutional Chamber ruled in 2021 that presidents must be allowed to run for a second term. In all four cases the judges who issued these rulings had ties to the ruling party.[62] In Bolivia's case, the court ruling came after Bolivian voters had rejected the elimination of term limits in a 2016 referendum.

Table 4.3 shows the term limits in place in each Latin American country at the beginning of 2023. Only four countries maintain a total prohibition on reelection. Five countries only allow reelection after one or more interim terms. Only three Latin American countries follow the U.S. model of allowing two and only two terms, which may be consecutive.

Not all attempts to loosen term limits are successful. Panamanian president Ernesto Pérez Balladares failed to loosen term limits in a 1998 referendum. Argentine president Carlos Menem failed to get the constitution changed to allow a third term, as did President Álvaro Uribe in Colombia. In Paraguay, President Horacio Cartes's effort to run for reelection was voted down by the lower house of the Congress in 2017 after protesters had set fire to the legislature.[63] In the Dominican Republic, President Danilo Medina tried unsuccessfully to get the courts to annul the constitutional term limits in 2019.[64] But despite these instances of presidential reelection ambitions being frustrated, the regional trend has been toward allowing reelection, and in the less democratic states, toward indefinite reelection.[65] As of 2023, Latin America was evenly divided between countries prohibiting immediate reelection (some of which allow a second term after an interim term) and countries that allow two or more consecutive terms.

Term limit rules have real consequences for election outcomes. In countries where immediate reelection is allowed, incumbents usually win. One analysis found that from the mid-1980s to 2014, only two of the nineteen incumbent presidents who had run for reelection had lost.[66] Since then, Mauricio Macri's 2019 defeat in Argentina and Jair Bolsonaro's loss in 2022 in Brazil have been two rare cases of incumbent defeat. When former presidents can only run for reelection after an interim term, the picture is different. Ex-presidents running for non-consecutive election win less than half the time.[67] Examples of successful reelection bids by ex-presidents include Michelle Bachelet (2006–2010, 2014–2018) and Sebastián Piñera (2010–2014, 2018–2022) in Chile and Julio María Sanguinetti (1985–1990, 1995–2000) and Tabaré Vásquez (2005–2010, 2015–2020) in Uruguay.

Unlike for presidents, term limits for legislators and mayors are rare. Members of Costa Rica's Congress cannot seek immediate reelection after

Table 4.3   Presidential Term Limits

No Reelection	Reelection only after 1+ interim terms	Two consecutive terms, no reelection	Two consecutive terms, reelection after interim term	No term limits
Colombia	Chile	Dominican Republic	Argentina	Bolivia
Guatemala	Costa Rica	Ecuador	Brazil	Honduras
Mexico	Panama	El Salvador		Nicaragua
Paraguay	Peru			Venezuela
	Uruguay			

Note: Based on the author's review of each country's constitution and court rulings.

serving their four-year terms, and as a result most legislators are newcomers.[68] A 2019 reform in Peru also instituted a ban on immediate reelection to Congress.[69] Members of Mexico's Congress could not run for reelection until 2014. Legislators in the lower house can now serve up to four 3-year terms and senators can serve two 6-year terms. Ecuador eliminated its term limits for legislators by constitutional reform in 1998.[70] Even without term limits, legislatures tend to see high rates of legislator turnover between terms. This is partly because many legislators choose not to run for indefinite reelection, viewing the legislature (with its limited powers) as a steppingstone to more powerful executive offices at the local or national level.[71]

Policymakers and political analysts have long debated the merits of term limits.[72] Those in favor of strict term limits argue that they help prevent the consolidation of power in the hands of an aspiring autocrat. If reelection is possible, presidents may abuse their powers of office to stay in power—a risk illustrated by presidents such as Alberto Fujimori in Peru (1990–2000) and Hugo Chávez in Venezuela (1999–2013), both of whom exploited state resources and harassed the opposition to help win reelection. In this view, limiting presidents to one or two terms can prevent an elected executive from becoming a dictator. Indeed, given the striking success that incumbents have when running for reelection, term limits may be a necessary condition for alternation in power. As a historical study of term limits in Latin America notes,

> [n]o country that allowed for consecutive reelection ever experienced a relatively long and stable democratic period before 1985. . . . Where presidents were able to stand for reelection, they always won, and a disgruntled opposition had to turn to other strategies such as coups, revolutions, or assassinations to provide alternation. In a region where elections have as long a history as the countries' independence, the first Latin American incumbent president to ever lose an election was President Joaquín Balaguer in 1978 in the Dominican Republic.[73]

Thus, term limits may not only prevent continuismo but also incentivize a president's rivals to try to win power via elections rather than attempting unconstitutional methods like coups. Where the president is limited to one or two terms, opponents know they will have a chance to compete for power without the incumbent manipulating the playing field to stay in office. This argument about the perils that reelection poses for democracy is supported by statistical evidence that reforms loosening term limits and the possibility of immediate presidential reelection are associated with lower democracy scores in Latin America.[74]

In addition to ensuring the rotation of individuals in the presidency, term limits also encourage the alternation of political parties in power. As Gideon

Maltz shows with data from around the world, "the political opposition fares better against successor candidates than against incumbents. Presidential term limits thus reduce incumbency advantages and substantially improve the chances of political-party alternation in power."[75] This alternation can incentivize parties to institutionalize safeguards against the abuse of power by incumbents, since they can expect to find themselves out of power after future elections.

While allowing indefinite reelection can lead to presidential continuismo, allowing presidents to run for reelection after sitting out one interim term has its critics as well. On the one hand, the possibility of standing for election again in the future can encourage a sitting president to leave office rather than cling to power.[76] On the other hand, such a system can lead an outgoing incumbent to undermine their own party's presidential candidate in order to retain leadership of the party in the hopes of later winning reelection. If the incumbent party's successor candidate loses the next election, "the outgoing president may retain prominence as leader of the opposition, along with an aura as the champion capable of winning a national election."[77]

While the history of continuismo in Latin America offers strong grounds for adhering to strict term limits, opponents of term limits offer compelling arguments of their own. First, prohibition on reelection can deprive the country of a particularly capable leader and restrict the right of voters to choose to retain a popular president. For instance, constitutional changes allowing for immediate reelection have permitted voters to reelect presidents that successfully tackled economic crises, such as Fernando Henrique Cardoso in Brazil (reelected in 1998) and Carlos Menem in Argentina (reelected in 1995).

Second, allowing for immediate reelection allows presidents sufficient time to gain experience and implement policy reforms. By making presidents lame ducks early in their first term, strict term limits can limit policy effectiveness and force politicians to have short time horizons when making policy. Carrying out significant policy agendas, such as Colombian president Juan Manuel Santos's (2010–2018) negotiation of a peace accord with the FARC guerrilla group, can require more than one term in office.[78]

The third and perhaps most compelling line of argument against strict term limits relates to the responsiveness of presidents to constituents and the ability of voters to hold politicians accountable. When reelection is prohibited, citizens have no way of punishing officials for performing poorly or rewarding them for performing well (by reelecting them to office). Term limits can thus diminish responsiveness to voters and make politicians more dependent on political-party elites for their future career prospects. This has been documented in Mexico, where strict term limits for presidents and legislators made politicians "indebted to party leaders (who nominate them for future posts) rather than voters."[79]

For these reasons, some analysts argue that excessive presidential powers, and not permissive reelection rules, are the problem facing many Latin American countries.[80] But as presidents in several Latin American countries continue to chip away at term limits as part of broader efforts to concentrate power in their hands, the debate over term limits is likely to continue.

NOTES

1. Mark P. Jones, "The Recruitment and Selection of Legislative Candidates in Argentina," in *Pathways to Power: Political Recruitment and Candidate Selection in Latin America*, ed. Peter Siavelis and Scott Morgenstern (University Park, PA: Penn State University Press, 2008), 59, 63.

2. Miguel de Luca, "Political Recruitment and Candidate Selection in Argentina: Presidents and Governors, 1983 to 2006," in *Pathways to Power: Political Recruitment and Candidate Selection in Latin America*, ed. Peter Siavelis and Scott Morgenstern (University Park, PA: Penn State University Press, 2008), 204–5.

3. Steven L. Taylor, Felipe Botero, and Brian F. Crisp, "Precandidates, Candidates, and Presidents: Paths to the Colombian Presidency," in *Pathways to Power: Political Recruitment and Candidate Selection in Latin America*, ed. Peter Siavelis and Scott Morgenstern (University Park, PA: Penn State University Press, 2008), 275.

4. David Altman, "Political Recruitment and Candidate Selection in Chile, 1990 to 2006: The Executive Branch," in *Pathways to Power: Political Recruitment and Candidate Selection in Latin America*, ed. Peter Siavelis and Scott Morgenstern (University Park, PA: Penn State University Press, 2008), 256.

5. "Gabriel Boric: From Student Protest Leader to Chile's President," BBC News, December 20, 2021, https://www.bbc.co.uk/news/world-latin-america-59694056.

6. Nicholas Carnes and Noam Lupu, "Rethinking the Comparative Perspective on Class and Representation: Evidence from Latin America," *American Journal of Political Science* 59, no. 1 (2015), https://doi.org/10.1111/ajps.12112; Tiffany D. Barnes and Gregory W. Saxton, "Working-Class Legislators and Perceptions of Representation in Latin America," *Political Research Quarterly* 72, no. 4 (2019), https://doi.org/10.1177/1065912919829583.

7. Author's calculations from data at "Yo Voto Elecciones 2018," https://www.crhoy.com/site/dist/especiales/elecciones-cr-2018/candidatos-diputados.html.

8. Roderic Ai Camp, "Political Recruitment, Governance, and Leadership in Mexico: How Democracy Has Made a Difference," in *Pathways to Power: Political Recruitment and Candidate Selection in Latin America*, ed. Peter Siavelis and Scott Morgenstern (University Park, PA: Penn State University Press, 2008), 298.

9. Steven Levitsky, "Peru: The Institutionalization of Politics without Parties," in *Party Systems in Latin America: Institutionalization, Decay, and Collapse*, ed. Scott Mainwaring (New York: Cambridge University Press, 2018), 351.

10. Miguel Carreras, "The Rise of Outsiders in Latin America, 1980–2010: An Institutionalist Perspective," *Comparative Political Studies* 45, no. 12 (2012), https://

doi.org/10.1177/0010414012445753; Scott Mainwaring, "Party System Institution-alization, Predictability, and Democracy," in *Party Systems in Latin America: Insti-tutionalization, Decay, and Collapse,* ed. Scott Mainwaring (New York: Cambridge University Press, 2018), 75–76.

11. Mainwaring, "Party System Institutionalization"; Carreras, "Rise of Outsid-ers." Carreras also finds that nonconcurrent elections, the absence of an incumbent running for reelection, and compulsory voting are associated with higher vote shares for outsider candidates.

12. David Samuels, "Political Ambition, Candidate Recruitment, and Legislative Politics in Brazil," in *Pathways to Power: Political Recruitment and Candidate Selec-tion in Latin America,* ed. Peter Siavelis and Scott Morgenstern (University Park, PA: Penn State University Press, 2008).

13. Carlos De La Torre, "Technocratic Populism in Ecuador," *Journal of Democ-racy* 24, no. 3 (2013): 34, doi:10.1353/jod.2013.0047.

14. Jan-Werner Müller, *What Is Populism?* (Philadelphia: University of Pennsyl-vania Press, 2016), 3.

15. Naturalized citizens must wait until five years after obtaining citizenship to run for the Chamber of Representatives and seven years before running for the Senate.

16. Panama and Venezuela require a longer residency period, fifteen years.

17. Peru's Ley Orgánica de Elecciones, Art. 113.

18. Kevin Casas and Tomás Quesada, "Legislative Candidate Vetting Mechanisms in Latin American Political Parties," National Democratic Institute and National Endowment for Democracy, 2019, 17–18.

19. The only countries with no kinship bans for president are Argentina, Colom-bia, Chile, Mexico, Dominican Republic, and Uruguay. See Mario D. Serrafero, "El Control de la Sucesión: Reelección y Limitaciones de Elección Presidencial por Par-entesco en América Latina," *Revista de Estudos e Pesquisas sobre as Américas* 9, no. 1 (2015), https://periodicos.unb.br/index.php/repam/article/view/16051.

20. Torres was allowed to run for president in 2015 and subsequent elections, as her ex-husband did not serve as president leading up to those contests.

21. Because of inconsistent court rulings, Zury Ríos had been allowed to run for president in 2015 and was again allowed to run in 2023. She lost both elections.

22. Mala Htun, *Inclusion without Representation in Latin America: Gender Quo-tas and Ethnic Reservations* (New York: Cambridge University Press, 2016).

23. John M. Carey and John Polga-Hecimovich, "Primary Elections and Candidate Strength in Latin America," *Journal of Politics* 68, no. 3 (2006), https://doi.org/10.1111/j.1468-2508.2006.00443.x.

24. European Union, Election Expert Mission, Bolivia 2019, Final Report; Euro-pean Union Election Observation Mission, El Salvador 2019 Final Report, 1.

25. Ozge Kemahlioglu, Rebecca Weitz-Shapiro, and Shigeo Hirano, "Why Prima-ries in Latin American Presidential Elections?" *Journal of Politics* 71, no. 1 (2009): 340 note 5, https://doi.org/10.1017/S0022381608090221; European Union Election Observation Mission, Honduras Final Report, General Elections 2017, 18; Peru's Ley de Organizaciones Políticas, Art. 19–24.

26. Susan Franceschet and Jennifer M. Piscopo, "Gender and Political Backgrounds in Argentina," in *The Impact of Gender Quotas*, ed. Susan Franceschet, Mona Lena Krook and Jennifer M. Piscopo (New York: Oxford University Press, 2012), 43–56; "Argentina's PASO Primaries: What You Need to Know," *Buenos Aires Times*, August 8, 2019, https://www.batimes.com.ar/news/argentina/argentinas-paso-primaries-what-you-need-to-know.phtml.

27. Kathleen Bruhn, "Electing Extremists? Party Primaries and Legislative Candidates in Mexico," *Comparative Politics* 45, no. 4 (2013): 401-2, https://www.jstor.org/stable/43664073.

28. Ibid., 409; European Union Election Observation Mission, El Salvador 2019 Final Report, 12.

29. Catherine M. Conaghan, "Diminished by Design: Ecuador's Alianza PAIS," in *Diminished Parties: Democratic Representation in Contemporary Latin America*, ed. Juan Pablo Luna, Rafael Piñeiro Rodríguez, Fernando Rosenblatt, and Gabriel Vommaro (New York: Cambridge University Press, 2022), 210–11.

30. Casas and Quesada, "Legislative Candidate Vetting."

31. Carey and Polga-Hecimovich, "Primary Elections."

32. Kemahlioglu, Weitz-Shapiro, and Hirano, "Why Primaries."

33. Camp, "Political Recruitment," 297.

34. Kathleen Bruhn, "Too Much Democracy? Primaries and Candidate Success in the 2006 Mexican National Elections," *Latin American Politics and Society* 52, no. 4 (2010), https://doi.org/10.1111/j.1548-2456.2010.00097.x.

35. Examples include Carlos Cantillana Pena, Gonzalo Contreras Aguirre, and Mauricio Morales Quiroga, "Elecciones Primarias y Personalización de la Política: El Caso de las Elecciones Locales en Chile 2012," *Revista de Ciencia Politica* 35, no. 2 (2015), http://dx.doi.org/10.4067/S0718-090X2015000200002; Bruhn, "Electing Extremists?"; and Sergio J. Ascencio, "Party Influence in Presidential Primaries: Evidence from Mexico," *Party Politics* 27, no. 6 (2021), https://doi.org/10.1177/1354068820946424.

36. These forms of representation come from Hanna Pitkin's classic work, *The Concept of Representation* (University of California Press, 1967).

37. Several other women have served as president but were unelected, taking office after the death or resignation of the president. Prominent examples include Isabel Perón in Argentina in 1974, who as vice president took office when her husband Juan Perón died, and Jeanine Áñez in Bolivia, who became interim president in late 2019 when President Evo Morales resigned.

38. All data come from the Inter-Parliamentary Union: https://data.ipu.org/women-ranking?month=4&year=2023.

39. Betilde Muñoz-Pogossian and Flavia Freidenberg, "What It's Really Like to Be a Female Candidate in Latin America," *Americas Quarterly*, October 22, 2020, https://americasquarterly.org/article/what-its-really-like-to-be-a-female-candidate-in-latin-america/. This represents a significant increase from ten years earlier, when women made up only about 5 percent of mayors. See Magda Hinojosa, *Selecting Women, Electing Women: Political Representation and Candidate Selection in Latin America* (Philadelphia: Temple University Press, 2012), 5.

40. Htun, *Inclusion without Representation*, 28.

41. European Union, Election Expert Mission, Bolivia 2019, Final Report, 22.

42. Leslie A. Schwindt-Bayer, *Political Power and Women's Representation in Latin America* (New York: Oxford University Press, 2010), 9.

43. Amanda Clayton, "How Do Electoral Gender Quotas Affect Policy?" *Annual Review of Political Science* 24 (2021), https://doi.org/10.1146/annurev-polisci-041719-102019.

44. Susan Franceschet, Mona Lena Krook, and Jennifer M. Piscopo, "Conceptualizing the Impact of Gender Quotas," in *The Impact of Gender Quotas*, ed. Susan Franceschet, Mona Lena Krook, and Jennifer M. Piscopo (New York: Oxford University Press, 2012), 5–6; Pär Zetterberg, "Do Gender Quotas Foster Women's Political Engagement? Lessons from Latin America," *Political Research Quarterly* 62, no. 4 (2009): 718, https://doi.org/10.1177/1065912908322411; Htun, *Inclusion without Representation*, chapter 3.

45. For a summary of reforms to quotas through 2015, see Htun, *Inclusion without Representation*, 39, table 2.6.

46. Mark P. Jones, "Quota Legislation and the Election of Women: Learning from the Costa Rican Experience," *Journal of Politics*, 66, no. 4 (2004): 1207, https://doi.org/10.1111/j.0022-3816.2004.00296.x.

47. Ricardo Ortiz Ortiz, "Reforma Electoral 2020 y Sistemas Electorales Nacionales y Locales: Igualdad, Proporcionalidad y Paridad," *Democracias* 8 (2020), http://institutodemocracia.gob.ec/wp-content/uploads/2020/08/reforma_electoral.pdf.

48. Schwindt-Bayer, *Political Power*, 3. It is worth noting that women elected through quotas were no less qualified than men elected to Congress. One study found that women legislators held university degrees at a higher rate than male legislators and had similar levels of prior legislative experience. See Susan Franceschet and Jennifer M. Piscopo, "Gender and Political Backgrounds in Argentina," in *The Impact of Gender Quotas*, ed. Susan Franceschet, Mona Lena Krook, and Jennifer M. Piscopo (New York: Oxford University Press, 2012).

49. Mark P. Jones, "Gender Quotas, Electoral Laws, and the Election of Women: Evidence from the Latin American Vanguard." *Comparative Political Studies* 42, no. 1 (2009): 63, https://doi.org/10.1177/0010414008324993.

50. Jennifer M. Piscopo, "When Do Quotas in Politics Work? Latin America Offers Lessons," *Americas Quarterly*, October 22, 2020, https://americasquarterly.org/article/when-do-quotas-in-politics-work-latin-america-offers-lessons/.

51. Ibid.

52. Jones, "Gender Quotas"; Schwindt-Bayer, *Political Power*, ch. 2.

53. Clayton, "Electoral Gender Quotas."

54. Ibid.; Schwindt-Bayer, *Political Power*.

55. Schwindt-Bayer, *Political Power*, 186.

56. Zetterberg, "Gender Quotas."

57. Leiv Marsteintredet, "Presidential Term Limits in Latin America: c.1820–1985," in *The Politics of Presidential Term Limits*, ed. Alexander Baturo and Robert Elgie (New York: Oxford University Press, 2019).

58. John Carey, "The Reelection Debate in Latin America," *Latin American Politics and Society* 45, no. 1 (2003): 124, doi:10.1111/j.1548-2456.2003.tb00234.x.

59. Marsteintredet, "Presidential Term Limits," 106, 114; José Antonio Cheibub and Alejandro Medina, "The Politics of Presidential Term Limits in Latin America: From Re-democratization to Today," in *The Politics of Presidential Term Limits*, ed. Alexander Baturo and Robert Elgie (New York: Oxford University Press, 2019).

60. In Colombia, President Juan Manuel Santos's popularity was declining, and he agreed to prohibit reelection to block his rival, former president Álvaro Uribe, from possibly returning to the presidency. Javier Corrales, *Fixing Democracy: Why Constitutional Change Often Fails to Enhance Democracy in Latin America* (New York: Oxford University Press, 2018), 201.

61. Ecuador also removed term limits in a 2015 reform, but then reinstated them through a 2018 referendum.

62. On Honduras, see Elisabeth Malkin, "Distaste for Honduran Leaders Who Linger Fuels Distrust in Elections," *New York Times*, November 25, 2017, https://www.nytimes.com/2017/11/25/world/americas/honduras-election-juan-hernandez.html. On El Salvador, see "El Salvador Court Rules Presidents Can Serve Two Consecutive Terms," BBC News, September 4, 2021, https://www.bbc.com/news/world-latin-america-58451370.

63. "Paraguay MPs Reject Amendment Allowing President Re-Election," BBC News, April 27, 2017. https://www.bbc.com/news/world-latin-america-39728675.

64. This was just a few years after his party had amended the constitution to allow for immediate reelection for one term. See Leiv Marsteintredet, "How the Dominican Republic Successfully Resisted Presidential Term Extension," ConstitutionNet, July 25, 2019. https://constitutionnet.org/news/how-dominican-republic-successfully-resisted-presidential-term-extension.

65. Studies find that the strongest predictors of whether presidents succeed in loosening term limits are the president's approval rating, partisan majority in the legislature, and a history of weak institutional checks on the executive. See Corrales, *Fixing Democracy*; and Gabriel L. Negretto, "Tinkering with Executive Term Limits: Partisan Imbalances and Institutional Legacies in Latin America," *Democratization* 29, no. 1 (2022), https://doi.org/10.1080/13510347.2021.1980539.

66. Javier Corrales and Michael Penfold, "Manipulating Term Limits in Latin America," *Journal of Democracy* 25, no. 4 (2014): 162, http://doi.org/10.1353/jod.2014.0066. The two incumbents who lost their reelection bids were Hipólito Mejía in the Dominican Republic in 2004 and Daniel Ortega in Nicaragua in 1990.

67. Corrales and Penfold, "Manipulating Term Limits," 163. Ex-presidents do frequently run and obtain a significant share of the vote, however. See Javier Corrales, "Latin America's Neocaudillismo: Ex-presidents and Newcomers Running for President . . . and Winning," *Latin American Politics and Society* 50, no. 3 (2008), doi:10.1111/j.1548-2456.2008.00020.x.

68. Bruce M. Wilson, "Enforcing Rights and Exercising an Accountability Function: Costa Rica's Constitutional Chamber of the Supreme Court," in *Courts in Latin America*, ed. Gretchen Helmke and Julio Rios-Figueroa (New York: Cambridge University Press, 2011), 62.

69. Constitución Política del Perú, article 90-A.

70. Cynthia McClintock, *Electoral Rules and Democracy in Latin America* (New York: Oxford University Press, 2018), 166–67.

71. See various contributions in Peter Siavelis and Scott Morgenstern (eds.), *Pathways to Power: Political Recruitment and Candidate Selection in Latin America* (University Park, PA: Penn State University Press, 2008).

72. A summary of some of these arguments can be found in Carey, "The Reelection Debate"; and Karel Kouba and Jan Pumr, "The Democratic Cost of Consecutive Re-election and Presidential Term-Limit Evasion in Latin America," *Government and Opposition* 58, no. 3 (2023), doi:10.1017/gov.2021.51.

73. Marsteintredet, "Presidential Term Limits," 116.

74. Kouba and Pumr, "The Democratic Cost."

75. Gideon Maltz, "The Case for Presidential Term Limits," *Journal of Democracy* 18, no. 1 (2007): 131, doi:10.1353/jod.2007.0010.

76. Marsteintredet, "Presidential Term Limits," 108.

77. Carey, "The Reelection Debate," 128.

78. "Debating Term Limits and Presidential Reelection in Latin America," *The Dialogue*, April 20, 2017, https://www.thedialogue.org/blogs/2017/04/debating-term-limits-and-presidential-reelection-in-latin-america/.

79. Shannon O'Neil, "Mexico: Democratic Advances and Limitations," in *Constructing Democratic Governance in Latin America*, 4th edition, ed. Jorge I. Domínguez and Michael Shifter (Baltimore: Johns Hopkins University Press, 2013), 262.

80. Patricia Navia, "Limit the Power of Presidents, Not Their Term in Office," *Americas Quarterly*, April 14, 2009, https://americasquarterly.org/fulltextarticle/limit-the-power-of-presidents-not-their-term-in-office/.

Chapter 5

Political Parties

Political parties are critically important actors in democratic elections. They play important roles in recruiting and nominating candidates, providing campaign resources to candidates, coordinating campaign messaging, and providing labels or brands representing different ideas about government policy that help voters decide who to vote for.

How well parties perform these functions varies depending on the specific party and the country's broader political-party system. Some Latin American countries have fairly stable party systems, with several parties winning most legislative seats and enjoying the loyalty of a sizable share of the electorate. More often, however, party systems are unstable, highly fragmented (with many parties contesting each election), and lacking strong roots in society. In fact, political parties are one of the least trusted institutions throughout the region.[1] The animosity felt toward political parties was captured by a chant from demonstrators in Chile in 2011: "el pueblo unido, avanza sin partidos" (the people united advance without parties).[2] It is a sentiment widely shared throughout the region.

This chapter provides an overview of the types of political parties found in Latin America and the main features of political-party systems in the region. It concludes with case studies that illustrate the fragility of many Latin American party systems. The study of Latin American political parties sheds light on several fundamental questions about how democracies, and democratic elections, work: What role do parties play in representing and mobilizing voters and structuring electoral competition? What does democracy look like under different political party systems? If political parties are necessary for democracy to function, why do so many democracies struggle to develop institutionalized party systems?

TYPES OF PARTIES

There are several ways that political parties can forge links to the electorate and generate partisan identities. One is by promoting certain types of public policies or a coherent ideology. With this type of linkage, known as programmatic, parties offer voters distinct policy programs from which to choose. In other words, where party systems are highly programmatic, "teams of politicians compete for votes by offering citizens alternative packages of policies that they commit to enact if elected to political office."[3]

When a party offers voters a consistent programmatic package, it can develop a party brand—a clear sense of what the party stands for and what types of citizens the party represents. A distinct party brand can help parties attract supporters, while frequently changing policy positions or forming coalitions with ideologically different parties can dilute a party's brand and cause it to lose supporters.[4]

In contrast to programmatic appeals, parties can also connect to the electorate through clientelistic exchange (providing private goods such as government jobs or smaller handouts to supporters) and through charismatic or symbolic appeals. Many Latin American parties primarily appeal to voters through clientelism and/or the charisma of their candidates. In the latter case, some political parties are highly personalistic—they are little more than the legal vehicle for powerful personalities to compete for office and have no organizational existence apart from the party's leader. This is the case with most political parties in Guatemala and Peru, for instance. In reality, parties often employ different types of appeals to different constituencies, combining programmatic appeals with clientelism and charismatic or symbolic appeals.[5]

Latin America offers a wide range of programmatic parties. In the nineteenth century, the primary parties in most countries were conservatives and liberals. Conservatives were centered on the traditional rural elites and liberals on emerging elites in commercial agriculture who advocated free-market policies and greater separation of church and state. The differences between the two camps were partly programmatic and partly clientelist but were not anchored in social class distinctions: both were elitist parties. In some countries, such as Honduras and Colombia, the divide between liberals and conservatives continued through the twentieth century, although the original issues dividing the parties became less relevant over time.

As new social sectors emerged with economic development, new types of political parties began to form in the twentieth century that advocated expanded political rights and social services. Elite and middle-class-oriented reformist parties included the Radical Civic Union in Argentina, the Chilean Radical Party, the Colorado Party in Uruguay, and moderate Christian Democratic parties in several countries. More left-wing and populist reform parties formed as the century progressed, such as APRA in Peru, Democratic Action in Venezuela, and in the latter part of the century the Workers' Party in Brazil and the Frente Amplio (Broad Front) in Uruguay. Other leftist parties emerged from armed revolutionary movements, including the FSLN in Nicaragua, the FMLN in El Salvador, and the small URNG party in Guatemala. In most cases, leftist parties were more ideologically moderate by the end of the twentieth century than they had been in decades past.

In some countries, conservatives and business interests have formed well-organized parties. The National Action Party (PAN) in Mexico, the Independent Democratic Union (UDI) and National Renewal (RN) in Chile, ARENA in El Salvador, and Republican Proposal (PRO) in Argentina have been among the most electorally successful.

The most distinctive type of party to emerge since the 1990s has been the ethnic party. These are parties based on indigenous ethnic identity, whose members and leadership are predominantly indigenous peoples. Latin America is home to several hundred distinct indigenous peoples, with the largest including millions of members. Indigenous people tend to have lower socioeconomic outcomes compared to other Latin Americans and have historically suffered political and social marginalization. Indigenous political parties formed in several countries to represent the interests of indigenous communities, including the recognition of indigenous customary law and languages, land reform, and regional autonomy. In addition to such programmatic goals, indigenous parties also employ clientelism and symbolic appeals (e.g., using indigenous cultural symbols, such as language and dress, and appealing to shared identities and values), as do most parties.[6]

Bolivia's Movement toward Socialism (MAS), led by Evo Morales, has been the most well-known indigenous party in the region. Formed from social movements of rural coca growers in 1995, it forged links to other grassroots social movements and quickly rose to become the country's dominant political party, with Morales winning the presidency in 2005. The party has held the presidency and a majority in the legislature almost continuously ever since.

The indigenous Packakutik party in Ecuador has been another successful ethnic party. Pachakutik first participated in elections in 1996, electing eight members of Congress and two mayors.[7] It went on to support a presidential candidate that became deeply unpopular after winning the presidency. Yet Pachakutik rebounded, and in 2021 the party's presidential candidate won 19 percent of the vote in the first round, just missing the runoff round, while the party also won 27 of 137 seats in the National Assembly, making it the second-largest party in the legislature.

Indigenous parties face the challenge of uniting diverse indigenous communities of varying sizes that speak different languages and are often beset by regional, ideological, and personal rivalries. The most successful cases have had the support of an organized social movement, have avoided exclusionary ethnic appeals that might alienate non-indigenous voters, and have adopted a populist style that mobilizes lower and middle classes against elites and espouses anti-free-market economic policies. Parties that have done this have successfully forged coalitions between a mostly rural indigenous base and left-leaning urban mestizos.[8]

PARTY SYSTEMS

Individual political parties vary greatly in terms of their ideology, organization, stability over time, and so on. The same is true of national party systems, which vary in the number of competitive parties, how stable the set of parties is from one election to the next, and the manner in which parties appeal to the electorate. While voters in some countries face a stable and manageable set of party options each election, in other countries voters can face a bewildering array of parties that fluctuate wildly between election cycles.

Even in cases where voters typically choose between two party blocs, the party system beneath the surface can be fluid and complex. In Argentina, for instance, competition in national elections is dominated by the Peronist and the anti-Peronist coalitions. Yet the parties themselves are fluid and divided into factions, and national parties coexist with provincial parties that compete only in elections in their home provinces. Politicians routinely break away from their parties and sometimes return to the fold, and parties form alliances at both the national and provincial levels. The national parties sometimes form different coalitions in different provinces, meaning that two parties can be allies in one province but competitors in others.[9] Thus in Argentina as in most countries in the region, the party system can present voters with complex and volatile offerings.

The Number of Parties

When it comes to political parties, one thing is for sure: Latin American voters have a lot of options from which to choose. Two-party systems have not been uncommon. Costa Rica had a two-party system from the mid- to late twentieth century, with the two largest parties together winning the overwhelming majority of votes.[10] Colombia, Venezuela, Uruguay, and Paraguay also had two-party systems in the latter half of the twentieth century.[11] But many countries have more than two parties that win local races and legislative seats and are viable contenders for the presidency. And even former two-party systems like in Costa Rica have become more fragmented in recent decades, with more parties winning seats in the legislature.[12]

Brazil is a notorious case of such party fragmentation. In the 2018 general election, thirty-five parties competed for seats in the Chamber of Deputies (and thirty of them won at least one seat), while thirteen parties ran presidential candidates. And Brazil isn't alone: Guatemala and Peru routinely see a dozen or more parties compete in each general election, as does Ecuador, where the 2021 election saw nineteen parties run for legislative seats and sixteen parties field presidential candidates.

There are no widely agreed upon explanations for why the number of political parties varies across Latin American countries. But a number of factors may contribute to party system fragmentation, including the ethnic and ideological diversity of voters, proportional representation electoral rules that allow for smaller parties to remain viable by winning some legislative seats, and majority runoff rules for presidential races that encourage a proliferation of parties to field presidential candidates.[13] As for the consequences of fragmented party systems, more voters might be able to find a party that they feel represents them, but sifting through all the parties on the ballot also poses significant cognitive demands on even the most attentive voters.[14]

TEXT BOX 5.1: PARTY REGISTRATION RULES AND PARTY SYSTEM FRAGMENTATION

In response to the fragmentation and volatility of many party systems, some Latin American countries have adopted legal rules aimed at strengthening political parties. In particular, some measures have sought to make forming new parties more difficult and thereby limit party system fragmentation. Such measures include strict requirements to register new parties.

In all countries, registering a new political party requires demonstrating some level of party organization. Usually this requires submitting to election authorities a minimum number of signatures of party members. The number might be an absolute number or a percentage of the number of registered voters or the number of votes cast in the previous election.[a] Some signature requirements are daunting—Peru requires 3 percent of the total number of votes in the previous election, Bolivia 1.5 percent of registered voters—while others are easily met, as in Guatemala (0.3 percent of registered voters) and Uruguay (a miniscule 0.05 percent of registered voters). Stricter signature requirements generally lower the number of parties, although Peru bucks that trend.[b] Most countries also impose a spatial registration requirement, which "mandates that new party applicants must

collect signatures or organize local party branches in a specified geograph-
ical manner that exceeds more than one constituency."[c]

   Despite occasionally burdensome party registration rules, many party
systems remain highly fragmented. And in contrast to adopting stricter
rules, some countries allow organizations other than parties to run candidates, most notably in Bolivia, where citizen groups and indigenous
peoples can run candidates outside of political parties. Likewise in Guatemala, citizen groups known as civic committees can run candidates in
municipal elections (while parties maintain a monopoly on candidacies at
the national level).

[a] Yen-Pin Su, "Party Registration Rules and Party Systems in Latin America," *Party Politics* 21, no. 2 (2015), https://doi.org/10.1177/1354068812472585.
[b] Ibid.; European Union, Election Expert Mission, Bolivia 2019, Final Report, 8.
[c] Su, "Party Registration Rules," 296.

Institutionalization

Another feature of party systems is their degree of institutionalization, or the
degree to which parties are stable over time, maintain consistent ideological
positions, and develop clear social bases among voters.[15] When institutionalization is low, political parties come and go, and they may shift their policy
positions drastically over time or fail to offer clear policy positions at all.
When this is the case, voters lack clear informational cues that help them
make voting decisions and struggle to hold politicians accountable for their
behavior in office.[16]

   Institutionalization varies significantly across countries in the region. Party
systems have remained somewhat stable (though with important evolution
over time) in Uruguay, Chile, and Mexico, while party systems have been
extremely volatile and poorly institutionalized in Ecuador, Peru, Venezuela,
and Guatemala.

   One of the more institutionalized systems has been Mexico, with its stable
three-party system: the economically and socially conservative PAN party
formed in 1939, the leftist PRD party formed in 1989, and the broadly centrist
PRI party that ruled the country for seventy years before losing the presidency
in 2000. The three parties dominated national elections after 2000, collectively winning over 94 percent of the vote in the 2006 and 2012 presidential
races.[17] Yet like many Latin American countries, the party system has seen
destabilizing trends. The PRD's leader and two-time presidential candidate,
Andrés Manuel López Obrador (widely known as AMLO), left the party to
form his own. AMLO won the presidency in 2018, and his Morena party (in

alliance with several smaller parties) won control of the legislature. Morena's meteoric rise led the PAN, PRD, and PAN to join together in a coalition to try to defeat AMLO's party in the 2021 midterm elections, illustrating how Morena's success had reshuffled party competition.

Average rates of electoral volatility, meaning the shift in vote shares between parties from one election to the next, are quite high across Latin America.[18] This is seen particularly where new parties regularly form to compete in one or two elections and then disappear. Since many Latin American countries made transitions to democracy starting in the late 1970s, hundreds of political parties have formed, but only a relative handful have built durable party organizations that remain electorally competitive over time.[19] In some cases new parties can briefly rise to prominence, even winning the presidency, and then quickly fade from the scene. In presidential elections from 1990 to 2015, the average vote share received by new parties was 40 percent in Guatemala and over 20 percent in Colombia, Ecuador, Peru, and Venezuela.[20] The Guatemalan case is notable: all presidents elected since its transition to democracy in the 1980s have come from different political parties. In such cases voters can face a bewildering whirlwind of new party names and logos from one election to the next.

Related to the consistency of the parties competing from one election to the next is parties' organizational development, which can facilitate voter mobilization and effective campaigning at the local level. Party organizational development varies widely across parties and party systems. Some parties, such as the Workers' Party (PT) in Brazil, enjoy significant organizational development: branch offices and committee structures throughout the country's territory, large numbers of staff workers and volunteers, databases of party members, and other types of party infrastructure. But in many cases parties are poorly developed organizationally, based primarily on a small number of elites rather than a mass base of members and activists at the grassroots level. In fact, many parties in the region are little more than a name and lack any real organizational existence.

Also indicative of the fragile organizational development and stability of some parties is the prevalence of party switching among legislators. In several countries, including Brazil, Colombia, Guatemala, and Peru, party switching is common. After getting elected on one party's list, many legislators subsequently change parties in search of better opportunities for reelection or access to patronage resources. In Brazil, about one-third of deputies switch parties during their term.[21] In Guatemala, party switching has reached nearly 50 percent, leading to a reform in 2016 that tried to outlaw the practice.[22] As a consequence of party switching, voters have little certainty that parties will retain the legislative seats that they win or that individual candidates are loyal to a particular party brand.

Party Identification

Political-party systems are more stable and institutionalized when parties are strongly rooted in society, and one indicator of such rootedness is party identification: when people identify with a political party. Such identification is often thought of not only as a cumulative assessment of a party's performance in office over time, but as a psychological attachment that forms part of a person's social identity.

Across Latin America party identification tends to be low, with a majority of survey respondents reporting that they do not identify with a party. Figure 5.1 shows the percentage of people who identified with a party in Latin American countries in 2018. Partisanship ranges from a high of 48 percent in Uruguay to just 10 percent in Guatemala, and in two-thirds of countries the level of party identification is below 30 percent—showing a high level of detachment of ordinary citizens from political parties.[23] Aside from affirmative party identification, many Latin Americans—even those who don't identify with a party—exhibit negative partisanship, or an aversion to a particular political party that they would never support.[24]

Programmatic Structuration

Party systems also vary by the degree to which parties represent coherent policy programs that are distinguishable from the programs of other parties

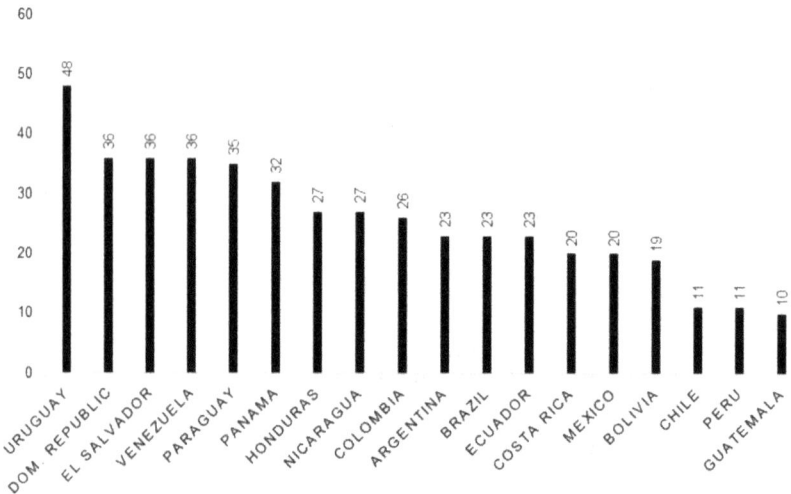

Figure 5.1 Party Identification in Latin America, 2018. *Source*: Data from The AmericasBarometer by the LAPOP Lab, http://www.vanderbilt.edu/lapop. *Note*: Data for Venezuela is from 2016, as no data is available for subsequent years. Percentages are rounded.

(what is called programmatic structuration). Some scholars have argued that the few programmatic party systems in Latin America in the late 1990s resulted from mass mobilization around social welfare policies in the early to mid-twentieth century. Where heavy government regulation of the economy and the introduction of welfare programs occurred, political parties competed over alternative visions of the role of the state in the economy—and this programmatic competition tended to persist in subsequent decades. In countries that didn't experience similar political mobilization over social welfare policies, sustained programmatic competition did not develop.[25]

Similar contestation over economic policies played a role in solidifying or undermining programmatic competition beginning in the late twentieth century. In the 1980s and 1990s countries across Latin America adopted market-friendly economic policies, reducing government regulation of the economy. Where conservative parties implemented market reforms and a left-wing party opposed the reforms, party competition tended to align along clear programmatic lines: pro-market conservative parties versus pro-regulation left-wing parties. In contrast, where a left-wing party implemented free-market reforms (often due to economic necessity), the party system tended to destabilize: the programmatic commitments of leftist parties were muddled by their adoption of policies that were inconsistent with their traditional platforms, and voters opposed to market reforms turned to new political movements and populist outsiders.[26]

From the late 1990s to the mid-2000s left-wing parties won power in many countries throughout the region. In what was called the Left Turn or the Pink Tide, left-wing populists won the presidency in Venezuela, Bolivia, and Ecuador, while institutionalized leftist parties won in Argentina, Brazil, Chile, Uruguay, and El Salvador. In some of these cases, consensus over economic policies broke down, and ideological polarization grew.[27] In many countries, however, competition between parties remained centered on clientelism and on promises to deliver on valence issues (such as jobs and security) rather than distinct policy-centered platforms.

TEXT BOX 5.2: EXTREME DEINSTITUTIONALIZATION: PARTY SYSTEM COLLAPSE

Many Latin American countries have weakly institutionalized party systems. In some cases, party system deinstitutionalization reached such an extreme that the party system collapsed. In these cases—Venezuela, Bolivia, and Peru in the 1990s and early 2000s—corruption scandals and the failure of major parties to represent the ideological positions of many voters undermined party identification. As left-wing parties implemented free-market reforms, the programmatic positions of parties became blurred. And as all parties failed to deal effectively with economic crisis, voters withdrew support from traditional parties and flocked to new outsiders.[a]

In Venezuela, party system collapse paved the way for the election of outsider Hugo Chávez and the gradual erosion of democracy. Venezuela had a two-party system dominated by center-left and center-right parties (AD and COPEI). Faced with economic crisis in the 1980s and 1990s, the two parties converged on neoliberal economic policies, thus blurring the programmatic differences between them. Neither party successfully resolved the economic crisis while in power, and economic decline meant fewer resources to use for clientelism, leading to declining popular support.

After Chávez was elected president in 1998, he implemented far-reaching economic and political reforms and concentrated power in his own hands. Since then, party competition has centered on an axis of Chavismo versus anti-Chavismo. The socialist party created by Chávez (PSUV) has had a sizeable share of members and party identifiers, but exists parallel to Chavista grassroots organizations and has ultimately been under the authoritarian rule of Chávez and his successor, Nicolás Maduro. The opposition to Chavismo has been splintered into several parties with limited territorial organization, divided by ideology and personalities. No single opposition party enjoys much party identification, and attempts to unite the opposition under a single coalition have had limited success. Thus, even several decades after party system collapse, Venezuela's party system remains inchoate and marked by a dominant party under authoritarian rule.[b]

[a] Jason Seawright, *Party System Collapse: The Roots of Crisis in Peru and Venezuela* (Stanford, CA: Stanford University Press, 2012); Jana Morgan, *Bankrupt Representation and Party System Collapse* (University Park, PA: Pennsylvania State University Press, 2011).
[b] Jana Morgan, "Deterioration and Polarization of Party Politics in Venezuela," in *Party Systems in Latin America: Institutionalization, Decay, and Collapse*, ed. Scott Mainwaring (New York: Cambridge University Press, 2018).

PARTY PROBLEMS: CASE STUDIES IN UNDER-INSTITUTIONALIZED PARTY SYSTEMS

Brazil: Extreme Multipartism

Brazil's party system is extremely fragmented, with twenty-four parties represented in the lower house of Congress in 2022 and with no party ever coming close to winning a majority in the legislature. Following the 2018 general election, for example, the party winning the most seats in the Chamber of Deputies took just 11 percent of the seats. Yet despite high fragmentation, electoral volatility has been relatively low since the 1990s, with some stability in which parties are the main contenders for the presidency until recent years (the PT and PSDB). Parties also often form coalitions for presidential and gubernatorial elections, lending a degree of coherence to competition in the highly fragmented system.[28]

Programmatically, the Brazilian system offers voters a wide array of options on the left, center, and right, along with many parties that rely on clientelistic practices as much as on ideological appeals. Many parties have maintained their ideological positions over time, although the system overall has shifted right, as left-of-center parties adopted centrist economic programs.[29]

Most Brazilian parties fail to cultivate partisan loyalty or build substantial party infrastructure. As one study puts it, "most Brazilian parties play little or no active role in legislative campaigns—parties do not provide candidates with volunteers, campaign finance, or consulting services—candidates must generate these resources on their own. Party labels are generally not used by most voters as information cues; most citizens cast votes based on candidates' reputations, not based on their partisanship."[30] One exception has been the Workers' Party (PT), a programmatic, organized, and disciplined party formed in 1980 with ties to labor unions and urban social movements. A left-wing party at its origin, the party moderated ideologically over time as the broader economic environment shifted in the 1990s. The party leader, Luiz Inácio Lula da Silva (widely known simply as Lula), finished second in presidential races in 1989, 1994, and 1998 before winning the presidency in 2002 and again in 2006 (and after being out of office for several terms, again in 2022). During Lula's administration and that of his PT successor, Dilma Rousseff, far more Brazilians identified with the PT than with any other party. The PT also generated a great deal of negative partisanship, with many Brazilians feeling antipathy toward the party.[31]

The PT suffered from several corruption scandals and a recession during Rousseff's second term and lost the presidency to far-right candidate Jair Bolsonaro in 2018. Yet it remained the most formidable party organization in the country.[32]

Colombia: From Duopoly to Fragmentation

For much of its history since independence, Colombia has been a two-party system. The liberal and conservative parties dominated electoral politics from the mid-nineteenth century until 2002. The parties originally were divided over trade policy, the role of the church, civil and political rights, and federalism versus centralism. Fierce conflict between the parties generated strong partisan identification. Partisan conflict degenerated into civil war from 1948 to 1953. After a brief period of dictatorship, the two parties subsequently agreed to alternate the presidency and equally divide other state offices during a period known as the National Front (1958–1974). During this period they colluded to exclude other parties and became clientelist machines with few programmatic differences. The parties also became factionalized during the National Front, as competition for office occurred within each party rather than between the parties.[33]

The two-party system cracked with the election of Liberal dissident Álvaro Uribe as president in 2002. Uribe, a right-leaning former governor and senator, ran as an independent and promised to clean up corruption and crack down hard on violent left-wing guerrilla groups. As he appeared headed for victory, other independent candidates and the Conservative Party threw their support to Uribe.[34] Politicians that supported Uribe went on to form a new party, the Partido de la U. After Uribe served two terms as president, his successor, Juan Manuel Santos, won the presidency in 2010 under the banner of the Partido de la U. Following a schism between Santos and Uribe, Uribe formed a personalistic party, Centro Democrático, which was the largest opposition to Santos during his two-term presidency. Several small parties with ties to right-wing paramilitaries also aligned with Uribe while several leftist parties have also formed since 2002.[35]

Following Uribe's election, Colombia saw increased electoral volatility and the weakening of party organizations and ties to society.[36] The party system was fragmented, with the leading party in the Chamber of Representatives following the 2022 elections winning just 32 of 172 seats. Recent presidential elections have seen shifting coalitions between parties, although generally with distinguishable placements on the ideological left-right axis. Party switching was rampant, with Senate candidates routinely running with different parties from one election to the next.[37] Individual candidates were much more important than party organizations. Illustrating this fact was a survey of Colombian mayors that found that two-thirds of mayors reported not receiving any campaign support from their political parties.[38]

Peru: Elections without Parties

Peru has perhaps the most volatile and un-institutionalized party system in Latin America. Peru's party system collapsed in the 1990s. Profound economic crisis and a violent insurgency from the far-left Shining Path group in the 1980s had discredited the existing parties, and voters elected outsider Alberto Fujimori president in 1990. Fujimori subsequently closed down Congress and ruled as a semi-autocratic strongman for the rest of the decade before being forced from office in 2000.

The major parties were eviscerated: the four largest parties that had collectively won 97 percent of the vote in 1985 were reduced to only 6 percent in 1995.[39] Countless new parties sprouted into existence, but they were almost all personalistic vehicles for prominent political figures and lacked programs and organizational development. Fujimori himself created a string of parties that were in fact just vehicles to support his own candidacy: Change 90 (Cambio 90) for the 1990 election, followed by New Majority (Nueva Mayoría) for constituent assembly elections in 1992, then Let's Go Neighbor (Vamos Vecino) in 1998, then Peru 2000 National Independent Front, which "was so lacking in grassroots capacity that Fujimori had to resort to a massive forgery operation to generate the signatures necessary to register the new party."[40]

After Fujimori's fall from power, parties continued to be highly personalist, described as "electoral labels created by, and exclusively for, a single presidential aspirant."[41] This is evident by the fate of parties associated with winning presidential candidates. After Alejandro Toledo's presidency (2001–2006), his Peru Posible party was reduced from forty-five congressional seats following the 2001 elections to two seats in 2006. The APRA party that won the 2006 election declined from thirty-six seats in 2006 to four seats in 2011, while President Ollanta Humala's party declined from forty-seven seats in 2011 to not even running candidates in 2016.[42]

As short-lived personalistic vehicles, parties had almost no organizational development in the form of branch offices, staff members, volunteers, and other organizational infrastructure. The party system also became denationalized: many regional parties emerged and largely displaced national parties in local elections.[43] Party switching in Congress became common, as did local and legislative candidates buying their spots on party candidate lists—reportedly paying between $20,000 and $120,000 for spots on the congressional candidate lists.[44] Rather than rising through the ranks of an established party, candidates were increasingly amateur politicians with little experience and no commitment to a party's program.

After Fujimori's fall, electoral reforms sought to construct a stable party system. With the goal of reducing the number of parties, smaller congressional districts were created and a 5 percent threshold was established for parties to win congressional seats. More rigorous rules for party registration were adopted, and independent candidacies were banned. Nevertheless, Peru's party system remained highly fragmented, volatile, and personalistic.[45]

El Salvador: From Institutionalized Party System to Outsider Takeover

In 1994 El Salvador held what were hailed as the "elections of the century." They marked the country's transition from bloody civil war in the 1980s to democratic electoral competition. The elections pitted the former left-wing guerrilla insurgents, the FMLN, against the right-wing incumbent party,

ARENA. Over the following years the country settled into a multiparty system with the FMLN and ARENA as the leading contenders and several small parties remaining viable competitors.

ARENA, or the Nationalist Republican Alliance, is an example of an authoritarian successor party—a party that inherited from a prior authoritarian regime resources such as territorial organization and clientelistic networks that help it transition successfully to democratic electoral competition. The party was founded by Major Roberto D'Aubuisson, a protégé of an infamous death squad leader and once described by a U.S. ambassador as a "pathological killer." During El Salvador's civil war, D'Aubuisson read off names of suspected left-wing subversives on television; the suspects would often later be found murdered. Violent anticommunism was at the heart of ARENA's ideology. At ARENA campaign rallies, D'Aubuisson would cut open watermelons with a machete to illustrate that they were green on the outside but red on the inside, just like Christian Democratic Party (whose party color was green). ARENA's party anthem contains the line "El Salvador will be the tomb where the Reds meet their end."[46]

Despite the macabre imagery, ARENA gradually shifted to a more moderate pro-business conservative identity while still retaining ties to its counterinsurgency past. By the late 1980s ARENA had largely displaced other right-wing parties that had operated under the military regime. ARENA was a well-organized party with a territorial organization, a broad support base, and ample resources—in part inherited from paramilitary structures during the civil war years.[47] With these resources, ARENA held the presidency for four consecutive terms beginning in 1989.

The FMLN had been the umbrella organization for Marxist guerrillas during the civil war. Following the 1992 peace accords that ended the war, the FMLN transformed from armed insurgency to a political party. In the transitional 1994 elections the FMLN allied with other small left-wing parties and placed second in the presidential contest. The party improved its performance at the local level in subsequent elections, and it first won the presidency in 2009 when it put forward television news broadcaster Mauricio Funes (himself not a party member) as its candidate. The party retained the presidency in 2014 with former guerrilla commander Salvador Sánchez Cerén. Although born of a Marxist insurgency, the FMLN pursued moderate policies once in power.

From 1994 to 2019 El Salvador's politics was dominated by ARENA and the FMLN. In the 2003 legislative elections, the two parties combined won nearly 70 percent of the seats. That increased to around 80 percent over the next several elections. (Several smaller parties split the remaining seats.) Party identification was high by Latin American standards. Voters' ideology was consistently associated with vote choice, with those on the left supporting the FMLN and those on the right supporting ARENA. The FMLN tended to perform strongly in San Salvador and other urban areas, while ARENA was strongest in rural areas.[48]

Yet beneath the surface, all was not well with the parties. Party elites dominated the candidate nomination process, and the parties continued to put forward former guerrilla leaders (the FMLN) or individuals with elite connections (ARENA) as candidates. Both parties were beset by corruption scandals, with several recent presidents being implicated in massive embezzlement cases. Despite the polarized origins of the two parties, their programmatic differences seemed to shrink over time. Perhaps most importantly, neither party effectively addressed the most pressing policy issue when in power: street gangs. Salvadoran gangs are large organizations that pervade the country's social life and control significant parts of the country's territory, and neither party found a formula for addressing the problem.

As a result, Salvadoran voters abandoned the two parties. Party identification plummeted, and in 2018 "a remarkable 82.3 percent of Salvadorans said that there were no meaningful differences between ARENA and the FMLN," viewing both parties as part of an out-of-touch and corrupt political class.[49] In 2019 Salvadorans elected outsider Nayib Bukele as president, and in the 2021 legislative elections ARENA and FMLN captured just 20 percent of assembly seats, as Bukele's New Ideas party captured a majority. In their frustration with the corrupt and ineffectual established parties, Salvadorans handed power to a leader with autocratic inclinations who set about dismantling the country's hard-won checks and balances. Ineffective and unresponsive parties appeared to be the death knell of democracy.

NOTES

1. Survey data from Latin American countries from 2021 show that 41 percent of respondents say they have no trust at all in parties, while only 6 percent say they have a lot of confidence in parties. See the AmericasBarometer by the LAPOP Lab, https://www.vanderbilt.edu/lapop.

2. Fernando Rosenblatt, *Party Vibrancy and Democracy in Latin America* (New York: Oxford University Press, 2018), 3.

3. Herbert Kitschelt, Kirk A. Hawkins, Juan Pablo Luna, Guillermo Rosas, and Elizabeth J. Zechmeister, *Latin American Party Systems* (New York: Cambridge University Press, 2010), 16.

4. Noam Lupu, *Party Brands in Crisis: Partisanship, Brand Dilution, and the Breakdown of Political Parties in Latin America* (New York: Cambridge University Press, 2016).

5. Juan Pablo Luna, *Segmented Representation: Political Party Strategies in Unequal Democracies* (New York: Oxford University Press, 2014).

6. Karleen Jones West, *Candidate Matters: A Study of Ethnic Parties, Campaigns, and Elections in Latin America* (New York: Oxford University Press, 2020).

7. Marc Becker, *Pachakutik: Indigenous Movements and Electoral Politics in Ecuador* (Lanham, MD: Rowman & Littlefield Publishers, 2011), 51.

8. Raúl L. Madrid, *The Rise of Ethnic Politics in Latin America* (New York: Cambridge University Press, 2012). On the formation of indigenous parties, see Donna Lee Van Cott, *From Movements to Parties in Latin America: The Evolution of Ethnic Politics* (New York: Cambridge University Press, 2005).

9. Carlos Gervasoni, "Argentina's Declining Party System: Fragmentation, Denationalization, Factionalization, Personalization, and Increasing Fluidity," in *Party Systems in Latin America: Institutionalization, Decay, and Collapse*, ed. Scott Mainwaring (New York: Cambridge University Press, 2018), 275.

10. Cynthia H. Chalker, "Elections and Democracy in Costa Rica," in *Elections and Democracy in Central America Revisited*, ed. Mitchell A. Seligson and John A. Booth (Chapel Hill: University of North Carolina Press, 1995).

11. Smaller parties also competed in elections, in addition to the two largest parties. Particularly in Colombia and Uruguay, the main parties were highly factionalized, with party factions competing against each other in elections. Thus what looked like two-party systems on the surface sometimes resembled multiparty systems in practice.

12. On Costa Rica, see Forrest D. Colburn and Arturo Cruz S., "The Fading of Costa Rica's Old Parties," *Journal of Democracy* 29, no. 4 (2018), doi:10.1353/jod.2018.0061.

13. For a review of the literature on the effects of institutions on the number of political parties, see Scott Morgenstern and Javier Vázquez-D'elía, "Electoral Laws, Parties, and Party Systems in Latin America," *Annual Review of Political Science* 10, no. 1 (2007), https://doi.org/10.1146/annurev.polisci.10.081205.094050.

14. Ryan E. Carlin, Matthew M. Singer, and Elizabeth J. Zechmeister, "Introduction to the Latin American Voter," in *The Latin American Voter: Pursuing Representation and Accountability in Challenging Contexts*, ed. Ryan E. Carlin, Matthew M. Singer, and Elizabeth J. Zechmeister (Ann Arbor: University of Michigan Press, 2015), 10.

15. Scott Mainwaring (ed.), *Party Systems in Latin America: Institutionalization, Decay, and Collapse* (New York: Cambridge University Press, 2018).

16. Scott Mainwaring, "Party System Institutionalization, Predictability, and Democracy," in *Party Systems in Latin America: Institutionalization, Decay, and Collapse*, ed. Scott Mainwaring (New York: Cambridge University Press, 2018), 98.

17. Kenneth F. Greene and Mariano Sánchez-Talanquer, "Authoritarian Legacies and Party System Stability in Mexico," in *Party Systems in Latin America: Institutionalization, Decay, and Collapse*, ed. Scott Mainwaring (New York: Cambridge University Press, 2018), 205.

18. For different views on the causes of volatility, see Mollie J. Cohen, Facundo E. Salles Kobilanski, and Elizabeth Zechmeister, "Electoral Volatility in Latin America," *Journal of Politics* 80, no. 3 (2018), https://doi.org/10.1086/697464; and Scott Mainwaring and Yen-Pin Su, "Electoral Volatility in Latin America, 1932–2018,"

Studies in Comparative International Development 56, no. 3 (2021), https://doi.org /10.1007/s12116-021-09340-x.

19. One study finds that of the parties formed from 1978 to 2005 that won at least 1 percent of the national vote, only eleven had won at least 10 percent of the vote in five consecutive legislative elections and survived the departure of their founding leader, while 244 parties had failed to meet this benchmark. Steven Levitsky, James Loxton, and Brandon Van Dyck, "Introduction: Challenges of Party-Building in Latin America," in *Challenges of Party-Building in Latin America*, ed. Steven Levitsky, James Loxton, Brandon van Dyck, and Jorge Dominguez (New York: Cambridge University Press, 2017).

20. Scott Mainwaring, "Party System Institutionalization in Contemporary Latin America," in *Party Systems in Latin America: Institutionalization, Decay, and Collapse*, ed. Scott Mainwaring (New York: Cambridge University Press, 2018), 37.

21. Scott W. Desposato, "Parties for Rent? Ambition, Ideology, and Party Switching in Brazil's Chamber of Deputies," *American Journal of Political Science* 50, no. 1 (2006): 63, https://doi.org/10.1111/j.1540-5907.2006.00170.x; Scott Mainwaring, Timothy J. Power, and Fernando Bizzarro, "The Uneven Institutionalization of a Party System: Brazil," in *Party Systems in Latin America: Institutionalization, Decay, and Collapse*, ed. Scott Mainwaring (New York: Cambridge University Press, 2018), 185.

22. In just the first three months of the new Congress in 2016, 44 percent of congressional deputies switched parties, many of them joining the new president's party. Jessica Gramajo, "El 44% de los Diputados Son Tránsfugas," *Prensa Libre*, April 13, 2016, http://www.prensalibre.com/guatemala/politica/el-44-de-los-diputados -son-transfugas.

23. While party identification is low, there are no regionwide trends over time— either increasing or declining party identification. Jason Seawright, "Roots in Society: Attachment between Citizens and Party Systems in Latin America," in *Party Systems in Latin America: Institutionalization, Decay, and Collapse*, ed. Scott Mainwaring (New York: Cambridge University Press, 2018). At the country level, higher party identification is correlated with higher party polarization and lower numbers of political parties—such that more people identify with a party when there are fewer parties and those parties represent clear alternatives. Noam Lupu, "Partisanship in Latin America," in *The Latin American Voter: Pursuing Representation and Accountability in Challenging Contexts*, ed. Ryan E. Carlin, Matthew M. Singer, and Elizabeth J. Zechmeister (Ann Arbor: University of Michigan Press, 2015).

24. Agustina Haime and Francisco Cantú, "Negative Partisanship in Latin America," *Latin American Politics and Society* 64, no. 1 (2022), doi:10.1017/lap.2021.54.

25. Kitschelt et al., *Latin American Party Systems*.

26. Kenneth Roberts, *Changing Course in Latin America: Party Systems in the Neoliberal Era* (New York: Cambridge University Press, 2014).

27. Matthew Singer, "Elite Polarization and the Electoral Impact of Left-Right Placements: Evidence from Latin America," *Latin American Research Review* 51, no. 2 (2016), doi:10.1353/lar.2016.0022.

28. Mainwaring, Power, and Bizzarro, "Uneven Institutionalization," 170–71, 178.

29. Ibid., 180.

30. Desposato, "Parties for Rent," 71.

31. David J. Samuels and Cesar Zucco, *Partisans, Antipartisans, and Nonpartisans: Voting Behavior in Brazil* (New York: Cambridge University Press, 2018).

32. For a review of the large scholarly literature on the PT, see Oswaldo E. do, Amaral and Timothy J. Power, "The PT at 35: Revisiting Scholarly Interpretations of the Brazilian Workers' Party," *Journal of Latin American Studies* 48, no. 1 (2016), doi:10.1017/S0022216X15001200.

33. Juan Albarracín, Laura Gamboa, and Scott Mainwaring, "Deinstitutionalization without Collapse: Colombia's Party System," in *Party Systems in Latin America: Institutionalization, Decay, and Collapse*, ed. Scott Mainwaring (New York: Cambridge University Press, 2018); Laura Wills-Otero, Bibiana Ortega, and Viviana Sarmiento, "The Colombian Liberal Party and Conservative Party: From Political Parties to Diminished Subtypes," in *Diminished Parties: Democratic Representation in Contemporary Latin America*, ed. Juan Pablo Luna, Rafael Piñeiro Rodríguez, Fernando Rosenblatt, and Gabriel Vommaro (New York: Cambridge University Press, 2022), 152–55; Eduardo Dargent and Paula Muñoz, "Democracy against Parties? Party System De-Institutionalization in Colombia," *Journal of Politics in Latin America* 3, no. 2 (2011): 50, https://doi.org/10.1177/1866802X1100300202.

34. Dargent and Muñoz, "Democracy against Parties," 55.

35. Albarracín, Gamboa, and Mainwaring, "Deinstitutionalization without Collapse," 230–31.

36. Dargent and Muñoz, "Democracy against Parties."

37. Albarracín, Gamboa, and Mainwaring, "Deinstitutionalization without Collapse," 237.

38. Claudia N. Avellaneda and María C. Escobar-Lemmon, "All by Myself: Personal Qualifications versus Party Affiliation in Colombian Mayoral Elections," *Latin American Politics and Society* 54, no. 2 (2012): 118, https://doi.org/10.1111/j.1548-2456.2012.00155.x.

39. Steven Levitsky and Mauricio Zavaleta, "Why No Party-Building in Peru?" in *Challenges of Party-Building in Latin America*, ed. Steven Levitsky, James Loxton, Brandon van Dyck, and Jorge Dominguez (New York: Cambridge University Press, 2017), 413.

40. Taylor C. Boas, *Presidential Campaigns in Latin America: Electoral Strategies and Success Contagion* (New York: Cambridge University Press, 2016), 141.

41. Steven Levitsky, "Peru: The Institutionalization of Politics without Parties," in *Party Systems in Latin America: Institutionalization, Decay, and Collapse*, ed. Scott Mainwaring (New York: Cambridge University Press, 2018), 328.

42. Ibid., 331.

43. Ibid.

44. Levitsky and Zavaleta, "Why No Party-Building," 418.

45. Ibid., 414.

46. James Loxton, "Authoritarian Successor Parties and the New Right in Latin America," in *Challenges of Party-Building in Latin America*, ed. Steven Levitsky, James Loxton, Brandon van Dyck, and Jorge Dominguez (New York: Cambridge University Press, 2017), 266 note 51, 271.

47. Elisabeth J. Wood, "Civil War and the Transformation of Elite Representation in El Salvador," in *Conservative Parties, the Right, and Democracy in Latin America*, ed. Kevin J. Middlebrook (Baltimore: The Johns Hopkins University Press, 2000), 247.

48. Dinorah Azpuru, "The Salience of Ideology: Fifteen Years of Presidential Elections in El Salvador," *Latin American Politics and Society* 52, no. 2 (2010), doi:10.1111/j.1548-2456.2010.00083.x.

49. Manuel Meléndez-Sánchez, "Latin America Erupts: Millennial Authoritarianism in El Salvador," *Journal of Democracy* 32, no. 3 (2021): 29, http://doi.org/10.1353/jod.2021.0031.

Chapter 6

Campaigning

When legislative elections approach in Brazil, voters are barraged by some of the most unusual campaign advertisements in the world. Most famous are the ads from a candidate dressed as a clown campaigning under his stage name Tiririca. In one of his viral YouTube videos, he asks, "What does a federal deputy do? Truly, I don't know. But vote for me and I will find out for you." Tiririca won more votes than any other congressional candidate in 2010.[1] Other candidates change their names to grab attention—candidates named Barack Obama, Donald Trump, and Osama bin Laden have all run for Congress. Other candidates dress up as Batman, Robin, Wonder Woman, and other superheroes.

Underlying these unorthodox campaign ads is Brazil's open-list proportional representation system, in which voters choose an individual candidate for Congress out of dozens or hundreds of options. With voters awash in campaign advertisements for so many candidates, each candidate tries to stand out from the crowd—leading to campaigning styles that would be unthinkable in many other countries.[2]

While Brazil's congressional electioneering is unique, campaigning in other Latin American countries is no less colorful. Stump speeches, boisterous rallies, caravans of vehicles blaring loud music, public spaces plastered with posters, campaign staff handing out fliers, slick television ads, a deluge of social media posts—all of these characterize modern election campaigns in Latin America. But there are also significant variations across countries and candidates in the mix of tactics used and the types of messages disseminated to voters.

Campaigns are critical periods of democratic engagement. They are a time of heightened political awareness and citizen participation, when citizens are called on to reflect on the best options for representing their interests and governing the country. The quality of candidates and their campaigning styles can produce voter enthusiasm and hope or apathy and cynicism. The campaign's tone, including how frequently candidates attack each other, can affect citizen attitudes about politics. And the specificity of campaign messaging "helps determine whether elected officials can be held accountable for their promises, versus claiming a right to govern at will based on a vague mandate of 'change.'"[3]

Campaigns are the moments when politicians most directly engage with citizens. This chapter addresses fundamental questions about modern election campaigns: How do candidates and parties appeal to voters? What tactics do they use to reach voters, and what messages do they employ to persuade or mobilize them? In short, how do they try to win votes? The chapter provides an overview of campaign practices in Latin America, ranging from the typical electioneering tools used by campaigns to the messages that campaigns utilize to mobilize and persuade voters. The chapter shows that since Latin America's transitions to democracy in the 1980s, election campaigns have evolved into modernized media-centered affairs while still retaining elements of more traditional electioneering. We start, however, with a look at how campaign activity is regulated by law throughout the region.

LEGAL REGULATIONS OF ELECTION CAMPAIGNING

While the example of Brazil's legislative campaigns might suggest a free-for-all style of electioneering, Latin American countries tend to place tight legal restrictions on campaigning activities, at least on paper. The length of time allowed for campaigning is typically short. In Brazil, the campaigning period begins just forty-five days before election day. In Chile, it is sixty days, while in Mexico it is sixty days for legislative elections and ninety days for presidential elections. Bolivia kicks off campaigning ninety days before election day but allows media advertising starting just thirty days prior to voting. Argentina allows campaign media advertising starting only thirty-five days before election day.[4]

In addition to short campaign periods, most countries in the region also prohibit campaigning in the few days before election day. For example, campaigning is not allowed in the two days prior to election day in Argentina and for three days in Bolivia, Chile, and Mexico. To further encourage a time of reflection for voters and avoid last-minute manipulation of public expectations, the publication of public opinion polls is prohibited in the days leading up to voting in some countries—as in Mexico (for three days) and Bolivia (for one week).[5]

Campaigns' access to television airtime is also highly regulated in many countries. Most countries provide free or subsidized airtime to political parties, and some prohibit the direct purchase of airtime to run campaign ads. In Brazil, free radio and TV airtime have been available to candidates and parties since the 1960s. Campaigns cannot directly purchase advertising in electronic media. The free airtime comes in two types: thirty-second spots and longer programs that air at specified times during the day and evening. The electoral authority allocates airtime to the political parties based on a formula, with some time being distributed evenly to all parties and some being allocated based on the size of each party in the legislature. Television stations are required to broadcast the campaign ads allocated by the electoral authority. The content of broadcast ads is regulated to some degree as well: during the free broadcasts, parties are prohibited from degrading other candidates or parties. Ads that run afoul of this rule can be removed from the air by the election authorities.[6]

In Argentina, campaign advertising was largely unregulated before 2009, when Congress passed a law that prohibited the purchase of television airtime by campaigns. Instead, free airtime is made available to all parties, half of which is divided equally across all parties and half of which is divided according to parties' vote share in the previous election. Television stations are required to provide 10 percent of their airtime to parties during the campaign season, and specific time slots are allocated to parties by lottery.[7]

Chile also prohibits parties and candidates from buying television advertising, with free airtime provided in the month preceding an election; campaigns can purchase print and radio ads, however. Broadcast television stations are required to provide two 20-minute blocs daily that are divided among the parties.[8]

Mexico passed a reform in 2007 that placed more regulations on campaigning. The reform prohibited the direct purchase of campaign ad time, with the electoral authorities allocating airtime to the campaigns instead. Thirty percent of the allotted ad time is divided equally, with the remaining 70 percent divided based on each political party's vote share in the previous election. TV and radio stations are required to broadcast forty-eight minutes of electoral advertising per day between 6:00 a.m. and midnight. Campaign advertising is also expected to "abstain from any expressions denigrating institutions and political parties, or slandering individuals,"[9] although in practice this does not prevent attack ads.

Finally, in Colombia, campaign advertising is allowed starting sixty days before the first round of an election. Other means of promoting a presidential candidate are allowed to begin three months prior to the election. Limited free airtime is provided to candidates on television and radio, and candidates can purchase additional ads—though there are daily limits on how many spots a candidate can air. The content of campaign advertising is also regulated: attack ads are prohibited, as is the use of national symbols like the Colombian flag.[10]

As these cases illustrate, Latin American countries impose quite rigid restrictions on campaigns' access to the television airwaves, and often provide free airtime to political parties in an effort to limit the influence of private campaign finance. Some countries also try to limit negative advertising, although these rules are not always vigorously enforced.

CAMPAIGNING TACTICS

Campaign tactics in Latin America have evolved significantly over the past half century, as technological change has opened new ways of reaching voters. In the mid- to late-twentieth century, candidates often met with small groups of community leaders to seek their votes, held boisterous rallies, and walked the streets and markets to meet voters. Observers of Latin American elections commonly noted a carnival atmosphere surrounding campaigning.[11]

By end of the twentieth century these campaigning methods were often combined with focus groups, opinion polls, television advertising, and domestic and foreign campaign consultants. In recent years social media has become an indispensable part of campaigns. Large rallies are still held often, and now provide images to use in TV spots and social media posts. Observers of campaigns have distinguished between a "classic" style of electioneering focused on meetings and rallies and a "modern" style centered on reaching audiences through mass media, especially television.[12]

Ground Game: Canvassing and Rallies

Before the campaign rally starts, the party faithful mill about the plaza, chatting or sitting patiently, waiting for the spectacle to begin. Many attendees wear shirts and wave flags bearing the party logo. Recorded ads are playing through the sound system on the stage. Street vendors hawk snacks, sunglasses, and vuvuzelas to the crowd and to passersby. When the rally begins, members of the campaign on stage begin to fire up the crowd with generic messages and slogans. A party atmosphere begins to develop, with party activists waving flags, blowing their vuvuzelas, and taking pictures with their phones. One person on stage does some singing while music plays through the speakers; a band playing live music follows. Then come the stump speeches from some of the party's congressional candidates, and finally the presidential candidate arrives to deliver her stump speech.

This is a typical experience at a campaign rally,[13] and even in the digital age such rallies remain a staple of many campaigns in Latin America. The campaign or party organization typically buses people to the rally from surrounding areas. While attendees include genuine supporters of the candidate or party, turnout is also boosted by giving attendees a free meal, hats, t-shirts, or other merchandise. The entertainment provided by the rally also draws some spectators as live music, raffles, and games provide an afternoon or evening of family fun. In some cases the rally involves the main candidate working her way through the crowd to shake hands and take selfies; always the rally includes stump speeches from the candidates.

Candidates and political parties hold rallies for a number of reasons. Rallies can fire up the enthusiasm of supporters, helping to ensure that they turn out to vote. Mobilizing attendance at the rally can even serve as practice for the party to mobilize voters to polling stations on election day. By visiting cities, towns, and villages throughout the country, the candidate attempts to show people that she listens to and sympathizes with their concerns. As one study puts it, "the appearances generate attractive photo opportunities that the campaigns put to good use—endless pictures of the candidates pressing the flesh, eating local delicacies, and interacting with everyday people in a way that signals their empathy and understanding of their day-to-day problems."[14] Big turnout at rallies can also indicate that a candidate is competitive, helping to attract media and voter attention. Large rally turnout can also deter potential defectors from the political party by showing the party's ability to turn out voters—showing individual party politicians that they are better off staying with the party rather than leaving it and trying to defeat it at the polls.[15]

Perhaps less intuitively, campaign rallies can provide top party leaders with information about lower-level party officials, who can act as brokers who distribute goods and favors to voters in exchange for their political support. Rallies also provide party officials with information about individual voters. This has been shown in a study of campaign rallies in Argentina, where party brokers closely monitor attendance at rallies and sometimes punish voters who fail to attend, and where party leaders monitor the performance of party brokers. As Szwarcberg puts it, rallies

> provide party brokers with an opportunity to display their ability to turn out voters and get promoted within the party. In addition rallies enable brokers to gather information about voters' responses to material inducements by monitoring their attendance (or failure to participate) at rallies. Voters find in rallies an opportunity to display their gratitude towards party brokers for distributing material benefits and solving their everyday problems. Rallies can also force voters' participation due to their fear of losing the flow of goods if they fail to turn out.[16]

Figure 6.1   Campaign Posters, Guatemala City, 2011 and 2019. *Source*: Author.

The so-called ground campaign consists of more than just mass rallies. Campaigns often plaster posters all over public spaces, from telephone poles to billboards (see figure 6.1). Conflicts sometimes break out between parties accusing each other of tearing down or painting over the other side's campaign materials. Campaign volunteers can often be found on busy street corners handing out small fliers with the names and photos of the candidates, sometimes accompanied by slogans or information about their issue stances. Candidates also canvas neighborhoods house to house and stroll busy markets to meet and greet potential voters. Caravans of cars with mounted loudspeakers blasting loud music occasionally roam the streets to publicize the party. While some campaigns now rely almost exclusively on social media, the ground game continues to be a staple of most Latin American elections.

Television

While the face-to-face and low-tech tactics of rallies and canvassing characterize the so-called classic style of campaigning, television is the hallmark of "modern" campaigning. Television also remains the dominant communication medium in the region, watched by 97 percent of people in Brazil and the main source of information about politics for three-quarters of people in Mexico[17]—although social media is rapidly gaining ground on television.

By the early 1990s television had become a dominant medium for election campaigns throughout Latin America. Candidates give frequent interviews with television outlets, hold televised press conferences, and in some countries even pay television stations to provide favorable news coverage. But the centerpiece of electioneering on television is the spot, or short advertisement that is often slickly produced and mixes jingles, emotion-inducing music, and imagery.

Spots take many different forms. Some are "talking head" format, in which the candidate speaks directly into the camera. In one such spot, Mexican presidential candidate Andrés Manuel López Obrador addresses viewers and promises to cut government waste by selling the country's presidential airplane.[18] Other spots combine a candidate making promises with music and video footage, often showing the candidate meeting with ordinary folks. For instance, Otto Pérez Molina's 2011 presidential campaign in Guatemala featured a spot with the candidate addressing an audience promising harsh measures against criminals, spliced with footage depicting crime. Some spots appeal to voters' fears or anger. But much more common are montages combining uplifting music, footage of happy people going about their day, and a candidate appealing to shared aspirations. Applicable throughout the region is a description of campaign spots in Colombia as "characterized by the presentation of images of iconic places and positive representations of Colombia (people, folklore, nature, etc.)" and "attempt[ing] to link candidates with ideas like prosperity, peace, equality, progress and happiness."[19]

During campaign season television spots are ubiquitous. In Mexico's 2012 presidential election, the campaign of winning candidate Enrique Peña Nieto produced eighty-one distinct spots broadcast over twenty-nine thousand times across ten major television stations.[20] The general election that year saw millions of spots broadcast, saturating the airwaves to the point that sometimes "the same ad by the same party or coalition was broadcast twice in a single bloc of commercials."[21] While that is an extreme case, it is not uncommon for campaign spots to fill the airwaves. For instance, in Colombia's 2014 election, the campaign of incumbent president Juan Manuel Santos produced 109 distinct television spots.[22]

With voters bombarded by television advertisements, any individual spot is unlikely to sway voters. However, sometimes a particularly effective or ineffective spot can have an impact. Colombia's 2014 presidential race provides an example. Óscar Iván Zuluaga was running against incumbent Juan Manuel Santos, and Zuluaga's campaign ran a spot that became known as "mad lady with oranges." The spot featured an actor depicting a Colombian storekeeper complaining about government inaction in improving education. As she speaks, she grows angrier and throws an orange. The over-the-top tone of the ad is thought to have backfired on Zuluaga by illustrating his lack of moderation.[23]

While campaigns use television advertising as part of their electioneering strategies, they are also affected by how the news media, particularly television, covers election races. In this there is substantial variation across countries. In some cases television coverage focuses overwhelmingly on the horse race, emphasizing which candidates are winning.[24] Some countries historically have had extremely biased media coverage, with concentrated ownership of major media outlets and news coverage used to sway election outcomes. In Mexico, the media conglomerate Televisa "once displayed images of Benito Mussolini and Fidel Castro next to videos of the ruling party's right- and left-wing opponents giving campaign speeches" in order to paint them as extremists.[25] But in Mexico, Brazil, and Chile in the 2000s, media coverage of presidential campaigns was relatively unbiased. In Venezuela and Bolivia, in contrast, coverage was polarized: commercial media was generally fiercely opposed to the leftist candidates Hugo Chávez and Evo Morales (only 1 percent of television coverage of Morales was positive in his 2005 campaign, for example), while state media gave each candidate overwhelmingly positive coverage when they were in office.[26] Media ownership continues to be highly concentrated in the region, giving rise to concerns about a level playing field for all candidates.

Internet and Social Media

By the 2000s many Latin American presidential campaigns were using the internet. In Chile's 2005 presidential election, candidate websites included videos of their television spots, downloadable campaign jingles, photos and information on the candidate, and each candidate's governing plan.[27] In Mexico's 2006 election, Felipe Calderón's website included the candidate's speeches, photos of campaign events, chat rooms, games, and a page to make donations.[28] Colombian presidential candidates all had a campaign website in that country's 2006 election.[29]

By the 2010s social media became a prominent part of campaigning and largely displaced the relevance of websites. By the 2010 elections in Brazil, for instance, almost all candidates for Senate and governor used some form of social media, although often in limited ways—such as simply tweeting out the number that voters needed to enter to vote for the candidate on the country's electronic voting devices.[30] In 2012 Mexico's presidential candidates were active on social media, with frontrunner Enrique Peña Nieto enjoying ten million followers on YouTube and three million likes on Facebook.[31] More recent studies have found candidate use of social media to be widespread. In Guatemala's 2019 presidential election, for instance, all twenty-two candidates used Facebook for campaigning, and most also used Twitter and Instagram; only seven candidates had a functioning campaign website.[32] Likewise in Argentina's 2019 presidential race, the candidates maintained an active social media presence, with winning candidate Alberto Fernández tweeting on average 3.5 times per day and his opponent Mauricio Macri tweeting 4.5 times per day.[33]

The digital component of campaigns can be quite sophisticated. In Brazil presidential candidates "tap into teams of content producers who work around the clock to keep their respective candidates' online presence 'fresh' for the voting public."[34] Campaigns use social media to disseminate photos and videos quickly and relatively cheaply and interact with voters in novel ways—such as through Facebook Live broadcasts where candidates can respond to user questions in real time. Candidates' social media presence often complements and multiplies the impact of ground campaigning, as when photos and videos of campaign rallies (whether captured with a smartphone, a professional camera crew, or a drone flying overhead) are posted to social media accounts to reach voters that did not attend the rally.

Nowhere has the role of social media been more prominent than in El Salvador's 2019 presidential election, which was won by thirty-seven-year-old Nayib Bukele. Bukele's victory was the first time a candidate from outside the country's two major parties won the presidency since the country's transition to democracy in the 1990s. His stunning victory was the result of a campaign that relied almost entirely on Facebook and Twitter. Bukele avoided interviews with the press and traditional campaign rallies, and declined to participate in debates. Instead he relied almost entirely on social media to connect directly with voters, including through Facebook Live videos. Combined with an informal style—he frequently appeared in jeans and a leather jacket—and his campaign promises to fight corruption in a country where three recent presidents have been charged with stealing hundreds of millions of dollars, Bukele's social media savvy propelled him to the presidency.

Some other politicians have followed Bukele's lead. In Colombia's 2022 presidential election, seventy-seven-year-old Rodolfo Hernández made it to the runoff round with a campaign centered almost entirely on social media. Hernández was known as "the king of Tik Tok" for his viral videos on the platform. Hernández lost by just three points in the runoff.

Campaigns also use social media for more nefarious purposes, such as creating fake accounts to artificially boost a candidate's perceived popularity, promote a particular narrative, or to attack opponents. These tactics are discussed in chapter 2.

Professionalization, Modernization, Americanization

Since Latin America's transitions to democracy in the late twentieth century, election campaigns have become more professionalized or "modern." Whereas campaigns traditionally relied on party activists to mobilize supporters, and candidates made direct contact with voters through rallies and canvassing, modern campaigning is more media intensive and relies on professional campaign staff. National-level campaigns use public opinion polling, focus groups, and voter data to craft their messages. They also often employ professional campaign consultants, whether national or international.

A paradigmatic example of campaign professionalization and modernization is Vicente Fox's successful presidential campaign in Mexico in 2000. Fox created his own campaign organization, "Friends of Fox," separate from his political party. The campaign developed a daily tracking poll, used focus groups, and hired a private polling firm that conducted seven nationwide surveys during the campaign. This data was used to develop campaign messages for distinct segments of the electorate. The campaign also produced almost sixty television spots.[35] Many other campaigns have similarly employed polling and focus groups to craft their campaign messages. In the successful presidential campaign of Fernando Henrique Cardoso in Brazil in 1994, for example, "[s]urvey-based strategic recommendations determined nearly every move; one journalist went so far as to describe the campaign as a 'survey dictatorship.'"[36]

Some observers have noted an "Americanization" of campaigns. In this view candidates adopt campaigning techniques from the United States and adapt them to local circumstances. The American model includes "a fixation on the candidate's image, strategic product development, target group marketing, news management, spin control, permanent campaigning, and negative advertising."[37] This style of campaigning spreads in part through the work of U.S. political consultants who advise Latin American campaigns. High-profile American consultants like James Carville and Dick Morris have advised a number of campaigns in the region, including in Argentina, Bolivia, Colombia, and Mexico.[38] In Bolivia, the role of American consultants in the winning 2002 presidential campaign of Gonzalo Sánchez de Lozada was depicted in the documentary film *Our Brand Is Crisis*, which was later popularized in a Hollywood dramatization of the same name.

However, it is easy to overstate the extent of Americanization of campaigns and the influence of U.S. consultants. Many Latin American countries have their own well-developed networks of campaign professionals. In Brazil, for instance, political consulting is highly professionalized: consultants routinely publish how-to books on campaigning and are organized in an association that conducts training seminars and conferences. When hiring international consultants, Latin American campaigns often look to other Latin American countries. For example, in Peru, Ollanta Humala's successful 2011 presidential campaign hired consultants from Brazil's Workers' Party, who designed a campaign that was less confrontational and more policy-focused than Humala's previous presidential run.[39]

More importantly, campaign style in Latin America has not converged on a U.S. model of electioneering. Not only are more traditional campaign tactics still widely used, but campaigning style varies from country to country and candidate to candidate. A major study of Latin American presidential campaigning by Taylor Boas argues that campaigning style—as measured by the level of policy focus, the types of linkages candidates develop with voters (either personal or mediated through organizations like parties), and the extent to which candidates prime societal divisions to appeal to segments of voters—can be explained in part by his theory of success contagion.[40] According to this theory, candidates emulate the campaign style used by the first winning presidential candidate that goes on to have a successful term in office. Where presidents routinely leave office unpopular or disgraced, candidates "are wary of adopting strategies that voters associate with discredited politicians" and presidential campaigns don't converge on a single style.[41]

Nevertheless, while campaigns haven't all Americanized or become homogeneous, they have become more modern in their reliance on television and social media. In at least one case, a campaign has gone even further to incorporate "neuropolitics" into its strategy. Enrique Peña Nieto's 2012 presidential campaign in Mexico "employed tools to measure voters' brain waves, skin arousal, heart rates and facial expressions," while his political party used "facial coding to help pick its best candidates," the *New York Times* reported.[42] It is not at all clear whether such techniques are effective, but they indicate how advanced some techniques used in Latin American campaigns have become. Developments in artificial intelligence promise to push election campaigns even further into uncharted territory.

TEXT BOX 6.1: MODERNIZATION AND TRADITION IN CHILE'S PRESIDENTIAL CAMPAIGNS

For most of the time since Chile's return to democracy in 1989, the country's politics has centered on two political coalitions, one on the center-left (under the names Concertación and Nueva Mayoria) and one on the right (including two prominent conservative parties, the UDI and the RN). Chile's campaigning style has included a mix of tactics, an avoidance of negative advertising, an emphasis on showing candidates' empathy with ordinary citizens, and little focus on specific policy proposals.

In the 1999 presidential election both coalitions combined modern and traditional campaign methods. Both campaigns utilized television advertisements. But the ground game—holding rallies and fielding campaign activists "to cover every wall, lamppost and public space with posters, or just to paint them with the candidates' names"—was still central to both campaigns.[a] The candidate for the right-wing coalition, Joaquín Lavín, focused on touring the country's provinces. His campaign staff prepared for each campaign stop so that Lavín's arrival was met with great fanfare, with crowds and bands playing music. To gain ample media coverage, the campaign recorded each visit and provided the footage to the media, while also providing free transportation and meals to television reporters and camera crews to accompany the candidate on his campaign trips. The campaign also paid young people who attended campaign events "and stood at street junctions in city centres waving [the coalition's] blue flags and leafleting drivers and pedestrians."[b]

The Concertación campaign also fielded an impressive ground game. The campaign "stressed door-to-door canvassing, motorcades and neighbourhood meetings that combined carnival-style bands, performances by local artists, games for children, chess competitions and free services provided by supporters, from legal, medical and social work advice, to hairdressing and fortune-telling. In other words, Concertación unleashed its infantry."[c]

While utilizing these more traditional campaign tactics, both campaigns also made extensive use of opinion polls, focus groups, and professional campaign advisers (both foreign and domestic).[d] The Concertación campaign initially attacked Lavín for his ties to the country's previous military regime. But when forced to a runoff election, the coalition's candidate, Ricardo Lagos, brought in a new team of campaign strategists and shifted to a less divisive strategy, adopting the slogan "A much better Chile" (Chile mucho mejor).[e]

In Chile's 2005 presidential election Michelle Bachelet, the candidate of the Concertación, emulated many tactics of previous campaigns. Her campaign established citizen networks like Women with Bachelet that distributed campaign pamphlets and organized festive campaign events. Bachelet also used listening tours as previous candidates had done, meeting with groups of people for "citizen dialogues" around the country. Bachelet's campaign ads discussed policy issues in general rather than specific terms and also included "segments designed to emphasize Bachelet's leadership qualifications—images of her reviewing troops as defense minister or fluently speaking English, French, and German at a press conference."[f]

In more recent elections social media has become an integral part of campaigns, with candidates using Facebook, YouTube, and TikTok to reach voters. In 2021, one presidential candidate lived in the United States and campaigned entirely on social media without ever visiting Chile.[g] Yet for the most part, social media has been added to a repertoire of campaign tactics that still includes traditional ground campaigning and television ads.[h] Chile's party coalitions have also evolved over time, and the 2021 election was more polarized than previous contests, with the runoff pitting left-wing Gabriel Boric against right-wing Antonio Kast. Yet while politics has grown more polarized, Chile's campaigning style still bears the mark of moderation and conciliation that originated with the country's transition to democracy after the Pinochet dictatorship.

[a] Espíndola, "Electoral Campaigning," 122.
[b] Ibid.
[c] Ibid.
[d] Ibid., 122–23.
[e] Boas, *Presidential Campaigns*, 64–65.
[f] Ibid., 79.
[g] The candidate, Francisco Parisi, came in third place with almost 13 percent of the vote. Maritza Tapia, "¿Cómo Influyen las Redes Sociales en las Campañas Políticas?" Universidad de Chile, Nov. 24, 2021, https://uchile .cl/noticias/182049/elecciones-cuanto-influyen-las-redes-sociales-en-las-campanas.
[h] Juan Pablo Luna et al., "Much Ado About Facebook? Evidence from 80 Congressional Campaigns in Chile," *Journal of Information Technology & Politics* 19, no. 2 (2021), https://doi.org/10.1080/19331681.2021.1936334.

CAMPAIGN MESSAGING: WHAT CAMPAIGNS SAY TO VOTERS

Beyond the diverse media that campaigns use, the centerpiece of election campaigning is messaging: what the campaigns say to voters about issues and values and the candidate or party image that the campaign seeks to create. Campaign teams are strategic in choosing what issues to prioritize, what positions to take on issues (or how to avoid taking positions), and what sort of candidate image to promote. Vicente Fox's 2000 campaign in Mexico is emblematic of the strategizing involved, as the campaign used polling "to determine who could be persuaded, how other candidates' messages resonated with the public, how to press the campaign's central theme, and how to court undecided but important electoral groups."[43]

Campaign messaging strategies can take a few general forms. In his groundbreaking study of presidential campaigns, Taylor Boas distinguishes between personalist, neopopulist, and technocratic approaches. In personalistic campaigns, candidates "tend to portray themselves as likable individuals" who empathize with the problems of everyday people.[44] In contrast, technocratic campaigns focus on policy issues and offer fairly detailed policy proposals, while neopopulists portray themselves as charismatic figures fighting for the common man against established interests (such as the wealthy, the elites, or foreign powers). As Boas puts it, "If a neopopulist promises that 'I will fight for you,' and a technocrat says 'I will solve your problems,' a personalistic politician claims to 'feel your pain.'"[45]

Naturally, most campaigns employ at least some elements of these different approaches. The sections below look at several dimensions of campaign messaging: how much campaigns focus on the individual candidate or the political party, the use of slogans, how campaigns address policy issues and craft candidate images, and the use of negative messaging to attack opposing candidates.

Candidate or Party Focus

One element of messaging is how much a campaign focuses on the individual candidate or the political party under whose label the candidate runs. At the presidential level, campaigns tend to be candidate-centered—although the visibility of the political party label varies from case to case. The general trend is for candidates to deemphasize party affiliations in their campaign messaging. For example, in Costa Rica's 2010 election, the television spots for candidate Laura Chinchilla never mentioned her party at all.[46] In Chile's 2005 presidential election, the website of Michelle Bachelet contained no symbols or links to the websites of her party or coalition.[47] Where party identification is strong, however, candidates are more likely to make use of their party's symbols and logos.

There is greater variation at the legislative level, where the utility of party labels for campaign messaging is affected by the electoral system in place (proportional representation or single-member district; open-list or closed-list) and the party system. In Mexico, non-presidential elections tend to be focused on the image of the political party, and the political party leadership rather than the candidate tends to centralize the campaign's organization and messaging.[48] Some major parties in Costa Rica require candidates to use standardized logos and colors in their campaign materials.[49] At the other extreme, congressional elections in Brazil tend to be highly personalistic, as thousands of candidates compete for name recognition in a context of open-list proportional representation and weak party identification. In Ecuador, Karleen Jones West documents differences across candidates in how much they run a personalist or party-centered campaign, depending on the attributes of the individual candidate and the district in which they campaign.[50] As distrust of political parties grows over time, however, the general trend is for candidates to increasingly run personalist campaigns rather than putting their party affiliation front and center.

Slogans

Because most citizens pay relatively little attention to politics, campaigns often focus on a small number of issues or themes that are presented to voters in simple terms. This is seen in campaign slogans, short expressions that are repeatedly used by candidates and serve as a motto for the campaign. Slogans express highly simplified ideas such as change or unity that aim to appeal to everyone. In Mexico, Ernesto Zedillo's 1994 slogan was "well-being for everyone" (bienestar para todos); in Argentina, Mauricio Macri's 2019 campaign used the famous expression "yes we can" (sí se puede), while in 2003 Carlos Menem's slogan referred to better economic conditions when he had been president in the 1990s—"With Menem We Lived Better."[51] In Guatemala's 2019 presidential election, slogans included "for you and your family," "a country for everyone," and the Trumpian "make Guatemala great."

Some slogans are bereft of content, but others serve to emphasize the main policy focus of the campaign. In Colombia's 2010 presidential campaign, Juan Manuel Santos used slogans that emphasized unity ("United with Juan Manuel") and economic well-being ("Jobs and More Income: Juan Manuel") while also "highlight[ing] his first name, in an effort to bring his candidacy closer to the average citizen and to distance the candidate from a last name that in Colombia is synonymous with wealth and power."[52] Running for reelection four years later, Santos emphasized ongoing peace negotiations with the FARC rebel group, using slogans such as "Vote to Win Peace" and "In Peace We Will Do More." His opponent's use of the slogan "Siding with Colombians" implied that Santos was on the side of the rebels in negotiating a peace deal.[53] More often, however, slogans offer a generic message to voters that seeks to tap into shared values and aspirations, such as "Government for all" (Daniel Ortega, Nicaragua, 1996) and "Love for Peru" (Ollanta Humala, Peru, 2006), or to signal the candidate's competence, such as Enrique Peña Nieto's slogan "I deliver" (Yo sí cumplo) in Mexico's 2012 election.[54]

Image

As the use of campaign slogans suggests, candidate rhetoric is commonly full of clichés, platitudes, and proposals that lack specifics. A common lament is that campaigns in the region lack meaningful discussion of policy issues, opting instead to focus on candidate image. Indeed, campaigns often employ image consultants who go so far as to advise candidates on what to wear in public appearances. In Ecuador's 2006 election, for instance, Rafael Correa employed a former Miss Ecuador to choose his wardrobe.[55] In Colombia's 2010 presidential election, Juan Manuel Santos employed American advisers who coached the candidate on verbal and nonverbal gestures to prepare for televised candidate debates.[56] In Argentina, the communications team for Mauricio Macri's party "provided guidelines on how candidates and activists should dress at campaign events and the profiles they should adopt in the photographs taken at those events, which they should then share on social media."[57]

Without a doubt, candidates are highly attentive to their public image. Candidates may try to appear empathetic, honest, down to earth, competent, and strong. Some avoid clarifying where they stand on issues in favor of focusing entirely on image. In Mexico's pivotal 2000 election, Vicente Fox's campaign focused largely on the candidate's image as an honest man of the people rather than offering specific policy proposals. The entire message of the campaign revolved around the idea of change, with the slogan "'the change that is right for you' (el cambio que a ti te conviene)."[58] Twelve years later the presidential campaign of Enrique Peña Nieto similarly emphasized the candidate's image and was almost entirely devoid of policy issues.[59]

In Chile, presidential candidates likewise generally avoid focusing on policy differences and instead "aim primarily to demonstrate their empathy with the electorate by arguing that they understand the problems of various social groups and will implement largely unspecified solutions once in office."[60] Michelle Bachelet's successful 2005 campaign illustrates this pattern, with her slogan "I'm with you" (estoy contigo) that "emphasized closeness to and identification with the people and an intimate understanding of their problems."[61]

Sometimes candidates seek to modify their image from one election to the next, and they shift their campaign tone accordingly. In Mexico, for example, Andrés Manuel López Obrador (AMLO) changed his campaign tone in 2012 after losing the 2006 election. After presenting a combative persona in 2006, his 2012 campaign put forward an image of a family man who promised to build a "republic of love." In line with this new image, AMLO avoided the confrontational style and personal insults that had characterized his previous campaign.[62]

Cultivating an image of a sympathetic figure who understands the problems of ordinary people can be difficult for long-time politicians. One tactic sometimes used for this purpose is the listening tour, when a candidate travels around the country meeting with people from different walks of life to hear about their concerns. In the United States, Hillary Clinton famously undertook a listening tour in 2015 prior to her presidential run the following year. But the tactic had been practiced in Latin America for many years. In Brazil's 1994 election, Luiz Inácio Lula da Silva focused his campaign messaging on empathy and carried out a series of "citizenship caravans" where he visited 653 small towns to talk to ordinary people.[63] In Peru, Lourdes Flores's unsuccessful 2006 presidential campaign similarly conducted listening tours throughout the country to hear the concerns of ordinary citizens.[64]

To appear to be in touch with everyday people, candidates include images of themselves meeting with ordinary citizens in their campaign ads and social media feeds. Argentine presidential candidate Mauricio Macri effectively used video of himself meeting with ordinary citizens in their homes to portray himself as an ordinary Argentinian (despite his status as a wealthy businessman). Some candidates pepper their social media with photos of their family and household pets to humanize themselves. Peru's Alberto Fujimori drove home his common-man image with his 1990 campaign slogan, "a president like you."

Issues

While all candidates must tend to their image, the degree to which they also offer voters a clear policy platform varies. Some studies of the content of campaign advertisements show a lack of policy focus from the candidates. Analysis of presidential campaign spots from leading political parties in Costa Rica and Nicaragua shows that the spots overwhelmingly focus on image rather than issues and lack concrete policy proposals.[65] Likewise, an analysis of a sample of spots from the campaigns of Cristina Kirchner (in Argentina, 2011), Hugo Chávez (in Venezuela, 2012), and Enrique Peña Nieto (in Mexico, 2012) found that only one-third of content related to policy issues.[66] Research on congressional campaigns in Mexico has also found very little policy content in candidates' social media posts.[67]

Not all campaigns lack policy content, however. Taylor Boas documents a heavy policy focus in presidential campaigns in Brazil. In the 2006 presidential election, both the incumbent Lula and his opponent devoted about 70 percent of their free television broadcast time to discussing policy. Lula's broadcasts offered detailed descriptions of his policy accomplishments in his first term; his opponent's program highlighted his own policy accomplishments as governor of São Paulo.[68] Lula's previously successful 2002 presidential campaign also included a heavy dose of policy diagnosis and proposals.[69] In contrasting the policy-oriented campaign messaging in Brazil with the empathy-centered approach common in Chile, Boas observes that "[i]f Chilean candidates argue that they can 'feel your pain,' Brazilian candidates specify how they have alleviated people's pain in the past and how they plan to do so in the future."[70]

Research has also shown a moderate to high degree of policy focus in some other countries. In Colombia's 2014 presidential election, 74 percent of Juan Manuel Santos's campaign spots mentioned the peace process, while his rival emphasized education, health care, and crime.[71] Among the leading candidates in Guatemala's 2019 presidential election, half of candidates' Facebook posts mentioned at least one policy issue and nearly 29 percent offered some form of policy proposal.[72] In Argentina's 2019 presidential campaign, slightly more than half of the leading candidates' tweets mentioned one or more policy issue, although far fewer offered policy proposals—and specific policy proposals were even rarer in the candidates' television spots.[73]

While candidates may talk about policy issues, they don't always offer voters a clear sense of where they stand on those issues. Ambiguity allows candidates to avoid taking clear stances that would alienate some voters. Thus, candidates commonly promise to create jobs, but avoid specific proposals to accomplish this goal—which would involve issues of taxation, government spending, trade policy, and other areas on which voters disagree.

As in many elections around the world, the economy is often the issue that receives the most attention from campaigns. Candidates promise to deliver jobs and prosperity, although usually offering few details about how they will do so. Candidates also often promise to deliver improvements in education, health care, social welfare programs, the environment, and so on. But while promising the world, once in office politicians find it difficult to follow through—leaving many voters feeling distrustful of politicians' promises.

Given the high levels of crime in the region, especially related to drug trafficking and street gangs, some candidates campaign on a tough-on-crime message. Public security is among the top concerns to voters in many Latin American countries. Some candidates in Brazil, Colombia, El Salvador, Guatemala, and Honduras, among other countries, have made security and fighting crime the centerpiece of their campaigns. Right-wing candidates often adopt an "iron fist" (mano dura) approach, promising more police, longer prison sentences, fewer legal protections for criminals, and involving the military in the fight against crime. In Colombia in 2002, Álvaro Uribe campaigned successfully on a slogan of "mano firme, corazón grande" (firm hand, big heart). In 2007 in Guatemala, former military officer Otto Pérez Molina campaigned for the presidency with an almost exclusive focus on a hardline approach to crime. Although he lost that race, softer campaign messaging won him the presidency four years later. In Honduras in 2013, Juan Orlando Hernández's presidential campaign emphasized a tough-on-crime message, calling for fusing the military and police to combat crime; in contrast, his opponent focused on community policing and rights abuses committed by the police.[74]

Right-wing candidates tend to benefit from campaigning on public security because the issue splits voters along non-economic lines and allows rightists to appeal to poor voters who otherwise might be drawn to the economic appeals of the left. However, one study argues that the use of public security as a campaign issue is constrained by human rights concerns and low trust in the security forces. As a result, candidates are more likely to campaign on security when the country faces organized criminal groups (such as drug cartels and large street gangs such as MS-13) and when there is no recent history of state repression (so human rights concerns do not undercut the impact of security-oriented campaign messaging). According to this argument, civilian candidates rather than former military officers and candidates with a balanced mix of campaign issues are more likely to win votes through appeals to public security.[75]

Going Negative

Because voting is a comparative act—selecting one option over others—campaign messaging often involves not just promoting one's own candidacy but also criticizing one's election opponents. Such criticism, or negative messaging, often takes the form of "attack" ads. Attacks can focus on a candidate's policy positions, their past performance in office, or their character and personal conduct. There are several reasons to attack one's opponent: the negative message might reduce the opponent's popularity among voters, people tend to remember negative messages more readily than positive messages, and attack ads are likely to receive more media attention than positive ads.[76]

Research on negative campaign messaging, mostly from the United States and Europe, suggests that incumbents use attack ads less than challengers and are the target of more attack ads. Incumbents have a track record in office that they can emphasize in their campaign, whereas challengers will likely attack the incumbent's performance in office.[77] Underdog candidates and those at a funding disadvantage are also more likely to attack than are campaign front-runners and more well-funded candidates.[78] Candidates can face a backlash for attacking their opponent, as voters might give the target of the attack sympathy and view the attacker as unduly aggressive. However, those trailing in the polls have little to lose from going negative. Campaigns might also try to avoid a backlash by outsourcing attack messaging to outside groups or anonymous social media sources. In this way the negative messages won't be perceived as coming directly from a candidate.

The limited research on negative campaigning in Latin America finds substantial differences across countries. In Chile, negative campaigning is mostly avoided, as it is believed to alienate voters that recall the country's violent polarization before and during the military regime of Augusto Pinochet.[79] Analyses of presidential campaign ads in Argentina and Colombia and candidate Facebook posts in Guatemala have also found attacks to be limited.[80] In contrast, attack messages have been common in Brazil.[81]

In Mexico, attack ads are common despite being prohibited by law. The 2006 presidential campaign included candidate Felipe Calderón running television ads that asserted that his opponent López Obrador was "a danger to Mexico" and "the candidate of lies." In 2012, one campaign ad targeting Enrique Peña Nieto of the Institutional Revolutionary Party (PRI) included the line, "they say that in the PRI of Peña, there is no longer room for corruption (ya no caben corruptos). Of course—because it's already full of them (porque ya está lleno)."[82] An analysis of the 2012 presidential race identified over twelve thousand broadcasts of negative campaign spots,[83] while analyses of congressional campaign ads have similarly found frequent use of negative ads.[84] Negative messaging took innovative forms in the country's 2009 midterm elections, when the National Action Party (PAN) ran ads in newspapers in the form of a letter soup game where readers could find hidden words that characterized the opposing PRI. The hidden words included robbery, narco, corruption, poverty, and crime.[85]

Several factors might help explain differences in the level of negative campaigning across countries. The more political parties and candidates that compete in an election, the less attacks there should be, because attacking one rival might not benefit the attacker but another opponent instead.[86] In countries with a runoff election round, attacks might be less common in the first round, because candidates eliminated in the first round may seek political alliances with one of the candidates still participating in the second round (such as trading support in the second round for a cabinet position or other benefit). Anticipating a later round of alliance making, candidates may refrain from alienating potential coalition partners with attacks.

The characteristics of candidates matter as well. Some evidence from Latin America supports the view that challengers are more likely to go negative than incumbents. In Argentina's 2019 presidential campaign, for instance, the challenger Alberto Fernández often included attacks in his tweets and campaign spots, while incumbent Mauricio Macri rarely did so.[87] Candidates' standing in the polls also has an effect. In Mexico's 2012 presidential race, leading candidate Enrique Peña Nieto refrained from negative messaging until opponent AMLO appeared to gain ground—at which point Peña Nieto's campaign began to air attacks against AMLO. Similarly, third-place candidate Josefina Vázquez Mota turned to attack ads as she failed to gain in the polls during the campaign.[88]

Latin American elections see their share of attack messaging. But the degree to which campaigns attack their opponents can vary greatly by country and by candidate, depending on the institutional and cultural context.

TEXT BOX 6.2: ARGENTINA'S 2019 PRESIDENTIAL CAMPAIGN

In Argentina's 2019 election, incumbent president Mauricio Macri, a center-right businessman and former mayor of Buenos Aires, faced off against the country's longstanding populist party (the Peronists). The Peronists ran former cabinet member Alberto Fernández as their presidential candidate, with former president Cristina Fernández de Kirchner (CFK) running as the vice presidential candidate. While many suspected that CFK would be the real power behind an Alberto Fernández presidency, his presence on the ticket offered a more moderate image from the confrontational style of CFK.

CFK's presence on the ballot created the unusual situation of a former two-term president running for vice president, and doing so while facing myriad corruption charges. CFK is a polarizing figure, but she remained popular among her large base despite her legal problems. During the campaign she kept a low profile to avoid mobilizing anti-Kirchner voters and to keep the campaign's focus on Macri's performance in office.

The dominant issue of the campaign was the economy. During the second half of Macri's term, Argentina's economy entered a severe recession. As the incumbent, Macri was vulnerable on the economy issue, and Fernández kept his campaign messaging focused there, regularly mentioning the economy in his campaign spots and tweets.

To shift voters' focus away from the flailing economy, Macri focused heavily on infrastructure and to a lesser extent on public security. The focus on infrastructure allowed Macri to present the accomplishments of his administration in building or repairing roads and train terminals. Many of his campaign spots took the form of montages in which people took cell phone footage of newly repaired or completed roads or train stations and praised the Macri administration for its work.

While most campaign spots and tweets mentioned policy issues, the campaigns did little to offer concrete policy proposals. Instead, campaign messaging was dominated by vague references to policy issues combined with generic appeals to serve the interests of the country. The campaign included a fair amount of attack messaging, the majority of which came from Fernández's campaign (nearly one-third of his campaign tweets included an attack on Macri).

The two campaigns disseminated their messages through multiple channels: television spots, rallies, door-to-door canvassing, and social media. After the primaries, Macri's campaign increased its door-to-door canvassing, which had been important in Macri's 2015 election. The renewed emphasis on a ground game included Macri undertaking a tour of 30 cities in 30 days and adopting the optimistic slogan and social media hashtag #SíSePuede. Macri's campaign included a massive rally in Buenos Aires in October, dubbed the "March of a Million," which was heavily advertised on social media beforehand and documented on social media as it occurred. The Peronists similarly held numerous large campaign rallies.[a]

Ultimately the state of the economy, along with the unification of the often fractious Peronist movement on a single ticket, proved decisive to the election's outcome. The Peronist ticket defeated Macri in October's general election, 48.1 to 40.4 percent. While becoming one of the few incumbent presidents in Latin America to lose a reelection bid, Macri made Argentina history by becoming the first non-Peronist president to finish his term in office since 1928.

[a] Kevin Pallister and Erin Fitzpatrick, "The Medium and the Message in Argentina's Presidential Campaigns," *International Journal of Press/Politics* (2023), https://doi.org/10.1177/19401612221149272.

NOTES

1. "No Joke as Brazil Clown Tops Votes for Congress," BBC News, October 10, 2010, https://www.bbc.com/news/world-latin-america-11465127.

2. Jason Gilmore and Philip N. Howard, "Does Social Media Make a Difference in Political Campaigns? Digital Dividends in Brazil's 2010 National Elections," Center for Communication and Civic Engagement, University of Washington, Working Paper 2013–2 (2013), 8.

3. Taylor C. Boas, *Presidential Campaigns in Latin America: Electoral Strategies and Success Contagion* (New York: Cambridge University Press, 2016), 176. Despite the importance of campaigns for citizen engagement and democratic accountability, campaigning in the region is somewhat understudied. There are few comparative analyses of campaign styles across countries. As a result, not a lot is known about how campaign style is affected by electoral rules such as term limits, majority runoff rules, compulsory voting, campaign finance regulations, and so on.

4. Chile's Ley Orgánica Constitucional sobre Votaciones Populares y Escrutinios, Art. 31; Mexico's Ley General de Instituciones y Procedimientos Electorales, Art. 251; Bolivia's Ley del Régimen Electoral, Art. 116; Argentina's Ley de Financiamiento de Los Partidos Políticos, Art. 33–34.

5. Argentina's Codigo Electoral Nacional, Art. 64-bis; Bolivia's Ley del Régimen Electoral, Art. 116, 130; Chile's Ley Orgánica Constitucional sobre Votaciones Populares y Escrutinios, Art. 31; Mexico's Ley General de Instituciones y Procedimientos Electorales, Art 251.

6. Aldé Alessandra Aldé and Felipe Borba, "Prime Time Electoral Propaganda: The Brazilian Model of Free Airtime," in *Routledge Handbook of Political*

Advertising, ed. Christina Holtz-Bacha and Marion R. Just (New York: Routledge, 2017), 89, 91; Maria Page and Julia Pomares, "The Move Toward State-Run Mass Media Electoral Campaigns in Latin America: An Evaluation of the First Implementation in the 2011 Argentine Presidential Elections," *Election Law Journal* 11, no. 4 (2012): 536, https://doi.org/10.1089/elj.2012.1145; Mauro Porto, "Framing Controversies: Television and the 2002 Presidential Election in Brazil," *Political Communication* 24, no. 1 (2007): 20, https://doi.org/10.1080/10584600601128705.

7. Martin D'Alessandro, "Political Advertising in Argentina," in *Routledge Handbook of Political Advertising*, ed. Christina Holtz-Bacha and Marion R. Just (New York: Routledge, 2017), 77.

8. Taylor Boas, "Chile: Promoting the Personal Connection—The Internet and Presidential Election Campaigns," in *Making a Difference: A Comparative View of the Role of the Internet in Election Politics*, ed. Diana Owen and David Taras (Lanham: Lexington Books, 2008); Alberto Pedro López-Hermida Russo, "Political Advertising in Chile: State of Play in a Period of Changes," in *Routledge Handbook of Political Advertising*, ed. Christina Holtz-Bacha and Marion R. Just (New York: Routledge, 2017), 103–4.

9. Julio Juárez-Gámiz and Marco Arellano-Toledo, "The Lousy Avalanche: Political Advertising in Mexico," in *Routledge Handbook of Political Advertising*, ed. Christina Holtz-Bacha and Marion R. Just (New York: Routledge, 2017), 180.

10. Miguel García-Sánchez and Jair Alberto Arciniegas, "Political Advertising in Colombia: Between the Narratives of War and Peace," in *Routledge Handbook of Political Advertising*, ed. Christina Holtz-Bacha and Marion R. Just (New York: Routledge, 2017), 322–23.

11. Alan Angell, Maria D'Alva Kinzo, and Diego Urbaneja, "Latin America," in *Electioneering: A Comparative Study of Continuity and Change*, ed. David Butler and Austin Ranney (Oxford: Clarendon Press, 1992), 43–44.

12. John Martz, "Electoral Campaigning and Latin American Democratization: The Grancolombian Experience," *Journal of Interamerican Studies and World Affairs* 32, no. 1 (1990): 23, doi:10.2307/166128.

13. The description above is based on the author's attendance at a campaign rally of the MLP party in Guatemala City's Plaza de la Constitución on June 8, 2019.

14. Carlos De la Torre and Catherine Conaghan, "The Hybrid Campaign: Tradition and Modernity in Ecuador's 2006 Presidential Election," *International Journal of Press/Politics* 14, no. 3 (2009): 345, https://doi.org/10.1177/1940161209334523.

15. Mariela Szwarcberg, "Political Parties and Rallies in Latin America," *Party Politics* 20, no. 3 (2014), https://doi.org/10.1177/1354068811436049; Joy Langston and Scott Morgenstern, "Campaigning in an Electoral Authoritarian Regime: The Case of Mexico," *Comparative Politics* 41, no. 2 (2009): 170, http://www.jstor.org/stable/40599208.

16. Szwarcberg, "Political Parties and Rallies," 456.

17. Aldé and Borba, "Prime Time Electoral Propaganda," 87; Juárez-Gámiz and Arellano-Toledo, "The Lousy Avalanche," 181.

18. Available at https://www.youtube.com/watch?v=-ZfezQcMTbE&list=PLzpapITwQtIX1v-jnmZCxoTS1rWhJoX6p&index=1.

19. García-Sánchez and Arciniegas, "Political Advertising in Colombia," 330.
20. Juárez-Gámiz and Arellano-Toledo, "The Lousy Avalanche," 183–84.
21. Ibid., 182.
22. García-Sánchez and Arciniegas, "Political Advertising in Colombia," 326.
23. Ibid., 335.
24. D'Alessandro, "Political Advertising," 78.
25. Taylor Boas, "Mass Media and Politics in Latin America," in *Constructing Democratic Governance in Latin America*, 4th edition, ed. Jorge I. Domínguez and Michael Shifter (Baltimore: Johns Hopkins University Press, 2013), 68.
26. Ibid., 66–70.
27. Boas, "Promoting the Personal Connection," 25.
28. Leticia Heras Gómez and Oniel Francisco Díaz Jiménez, "Las Redes Sociales en las Campañas de los Candidatos a Diputados Locales del PRI, el PAN y el PRD en las Elecciones de 2015 en el Estado de México," *Apuntes Electorales* 57 (2017): 78.
29. García-Sánchez and Arciniegas, "Political Advertising in Colombia," 324.
30. Gilmore and Howard, "Does Social Media."
31. Alberto Venzor Coronado, "Análisis de las Estrategias del *Marketing* Político y el Uso de Redes Sociales entre los Candidatos a la Presidencia de México en 2012," in *Campañas Electorales en México y Una Visión a Centroamérica*, ed. María Antonia Martínez and Rubén Aguilar Valenzuela (Ciudad de México: Miguel Angel Porrúa/Instituto Federal Electoral/Asociación Latinoamericana de Investigadores en Campañas Electorales/Fundación José Ortega y Gasset-Gregorio Marañón, 2013), 129.
32. Kevin Pallister, "Digital Caudillos: The Use of Social Media in Guatemalan Presidential Campaigns," *Journal of Politics in Latin America* 13, no. 2 (2021), https://doi.org/10.1177/1866802X211010319.
33. Kevin Pallister and Erin Fitzpatrick, "The Medium and the Message in Argentina's Presidential Campaigns," *International Journal of Press/Politics* (2023), https://doi.org/10.1177/19401612221149272.
34. Gilmore and Howard, "Does Social Media," 6.
35. Oniel Francisco Díaz Jiménez, "*Marketing* Político y Profesionalización de las Campañas Electorales del Partido Acción Nacional y el Partido de la Revolución Democrática," *Polis: Investigación y Análisis Sociopolítico y Psicosocial* 11, no. 1 (2015): 131–32, https://www.scielo.org.mx/scielo.php?script=sci_arttext&pid=S1870-23332015000100119; Brandon Rottinghaus and Irina Alberro, "Rivaling the PRI: The Image Management of Vicente Fox and the Use of Public Opinion Polling in the 2000 Mexican Election," *Latin American Politics and Society* 47, no. 2 (2005), doi:10.1111/j.1548-2456.2005.tb00312.x.
36. Boas, *Presidential Campaigns*, 97.
37. Fritz Plasser, "American Campaign Techniques Worldwide," *Harvard International Journal of Press/Politics* 5, no. 4 (2000): 35, https://doi.org/10.1177/1081180X00005004003.
38. Roberto Espíndola, "Electoral Campaigning in Latin Americas' New Democracies: The Southern Cone," in *Mass Media and Political Communication in New Democracies*, ed. Katrin Voltmer (New York: Routledge, 2006), 123; Díaz Jiménez,

"*Marketing* Político," 133; García-Sánchez and Arciniegas, "Political Advertising in Colombia," 320.

39. Boas, *Presidential Campaigns*, 107, 171–72. Some regional campaign consultants can be found on the website of the Latin American Association of Political Consultants (*Asociación Latinoamericana de Consultores Políticos*): http://alacoplatam.org/.

40. Boas, *Presidential Campaigns*; Taylor C. Boas, "Varieties of Electioneering: Success Contagion and Presidential Campaigns in Latin America," *World Politics* 62, no. 4 (2010), doi:10.1017/S0043887110000213.

41. Boas, "Varieties of Electioneering," 637.

42. Kevin Randall, "Neuropolitics, Where Campaigns Try to Read Your Mind," *New York Times*, November 3, 2015, https://www.nytimes.com/2015/11/04/world/americas/neuropolitics-where-campaigns-try-to-read-your-mind.html.

43. Rottinghaus and Alberro, "Rivaling the PRI," 146.

44. Boas, *Presidential Campaigns*, 10.

45. Ibid.

46. Óscar Jímenez Alvarado and Mariano Salas Narango, "Los Partidos Oficialistas en Centramérica y sus Campañas Electorales en Televisión: Análisis de los *Spots* del PLN (Costa Rica) y el FSLN (Nicaragua)," in *Campañas Electorales en México y Una Visión a Centroamérica*, ed. María Antonia Martínez and Rubén Aguilar Valenzuela (Ciudad de México: Miguel Angel Porrúa/Instituto Federal Electoral/Asociación Latinoamericana de Investigadores en Campañas Electorales/Fundación José Ortega y Gasset-Gregorio Marañón, 2013), 165–66.

47. Boas, "Promoting the Personal Connection," 25–26.

48. Aquiles Chihu Amparán, "El Framing Audiovisual del Discurso de Reparación de Imagen: Elecciones Federales, México 2009," in *Campañas Electorales en México y Una Visión a Centroamérica*, ed. María Antonia Martínez and Rubén Aguilar Valenzuela (Ciudad de México: Miguel Angel Porrúa/Instituto Federal Electoral/Asociación Latinoamericana de Investigadores en Campañas Electorales/Fundación José Ortega y Gasset-Gregorio Marañón, 2013).

49. Ronald Alfaro-Redondo and Steffan Gómez-Campos, "PLN and PAC: Two Costa Rican Parties with Constituencies Evolving in Opposite Directions," in *Diminished Parties: Democratic Representation in Contemporary Latin America*, ed. Juan Pablo Luna, Rafael Piñeiro Rodríguez, Fernando Rosenblatt, and Gabriel Vommaro (New York: Cambridge University Press, 2022), 115.

50. Karleen Jones West, *Candidate Matters: A Study of Ethnic Parties, Campaigns, and Elections in Latin America* (New York: Oxford University Press 2020).

51. On Zedillo, see Fabián Echegaray, *Economic Crises and Electoral Responses in Latin America* (Lanham, MD: University Press of America, 2005), 11; On Menem, see Francois Gélineau and Matthew M. Singer, "The Economy and Incumbent Support in Latin America," in *The Latin American Voter: Pursuing Representation and Accountability in Challenging Contexts*, ed. Ryan E. Carlin, Matthew M. Singer, and Elizabeth J. Zechmeister (Ann Arbor: University of Michigan Press 2015).

52. García-Sánchez and Arciniegas, "Political Advertising in Colombia," 331.

53. Ibid., 333.

54. On Peña Nieto, see Kathleen Bruhn, "Chronicle of a Victory Foretold: Candidates, Parties, and Campaign Strategies in the 2012 Mexican Presidential Election," in *Mexico's Evolving Democracy: A Comparative Study of the 2012 Elections*, ed. Jorge I. Domínguez, Kenneth F. Greene, Chappell H. Lawson, and Alejandro Moreno (Baltimore: Johns Hopkins University Press, 2015), 36.

55. De la Torre and Conaghan, "The Hybrid Campaign," 346.

56. Néstor J. Restrepo Echavarría, "La Profesionalización de las Campañas Electorales: Las Elecciones Presidenciales de Colombia 2010," *Revista Española de Ciencia Política* 38 (2015): 100.

57. Gabriel Vommaro, "Horizontal Coordination and Vertical Aggregation Mechanisms of the PRO in Argentina and its Subnational Variations," in *Diminished Parties: Democratic Representation in Contemporary Latin America*, ed. Juan Pablo Luna, Rafael Piñeiro Rodríguez, Fernando Rosenblatt, and Gabriel Vommaro (New York: Cambridge University Press, 2022), 64.

58. Rottinghaus and Alberro, "Rivaling the PRI," 148.

59. Bruhn, "Chronicle of a Victory."

60. Boas, *Presidential Campaigns*, 48.

61. Boas, "Promoting the Personal Connection," 19.

62. Rubén Aguilar Valenzuela, "La Campaña Presidencial del 2012 en México: La Estrategia y el Discurso de los Candidatos," in *Campañas Electorales en México y Una Visión a Centroamérica*, ed. María Antonia Martínez and Rubén Aguilar Valenzuela (Ciudad de México: Miguel Angel Porrúa/Instituto Federal Electoral/Asociación Latinoamericana de Investigadores en Campañas Electorales/Fundación José Ortega y Gasset-Gregorio Marañón, 2013), 16.

63. Boas, *Presidential Campaigns*, 101.

64. Ibid., 160.

65. Jímenez Alvarado and Salas Narango, "Los Partidos Oficialistas."

66. Natalia Aruguete and Mario Riorda, "An Image Is Worth a Thousand Policies: The Discursive Strategy of Electoral Campaigns of Winning Candidates in Latin America," *Communication & Society* 29, no. 2 (2016): 181, http://dx.doi.org/10.15581/003.29.2.145-159.

67. Heras Gómez and Díaz Jiménez, "Las Redes Sociales."

68. Boas, *Presidential Campaigns*, 87.

69. Porto, "Framing Controversies."

70. Boas, *Presidential Campaigns*, 88.

71. García-Sánchez and Arciniegas, "Political Advertising in Colombia," 333.

72. Pallister, "Digital Caudillos."

73. Pallister and Fitzpatrick, "Medium and the Message."

74. Orlando J. Pérez, "The Impact of Crime on Voter Choice in Latin America," in *The Latin American Voter: Pursuing Representation and Accountability in Challenging Contexts*, ed. Ryan E. Carlin, Matthew M. Singer, and Elizabeth J. Zechmeister (Ann Arbor: University of Michigan Press, 2015), 327.

75. Randy Sunwin Uang, "Campaigning on Public Security in Latin America: Obstacles to Success," *Latin American Politics and Society* 55, no. 2 (2013), doi:10.1111/j.1548-2456.2013.00192.x. See also Alisha C. Holland, "Right on

Crime? Conservative Party Politics and Mano Dura Policies in El Salvador," *Latin American Research Review* 48, no. 1 (2013), doi:10.1353/lar.2013.0009.

76. Todd L. Belt, "Negative Advertising," in *Routledge Handbook of Political Advertising*, ed. Christina Holtz-Bacha and Marion R. Just (New York: Routledge, 2017), 50.

77. Alessandro Nai, "Going Negative, Worldwide: Towards a General Understanding of Determinants and Targets of Negative Campaigning," *Government and Opposition* 55, no. 3 (2020), doi:10.1017/gov.2018.32.

78. Belt, "Negative Advertising," 50; Richard R. Lau and Ivy Brown Rovner, "Negative Campaigning," *Annual Review of Political Science* 12 (2009): 293, https://doi.org/10.1146/annurev.polisci.10.071905.101448.

79. Boas, *Presidential Campaigns*, 39–40.

80. D'Alessandro, "Political Advertising," 80; García-Sánchez and Arciniegas, "Political Advertising in Colombia," 333; Pallister, "Digital Caudillos."

81. Felipe Borba, "Measuring Negative Campaigning on TV, Radio, Debates, Press and Facebook: The Case of 2014 Brazilian Presidential Elections," *Intercom-RBCC (Revista Brasileira de Ciências da Comunicação)* 42, no. 1 (2019), https://doi.org/10.1590/1809-5844201912.

82. Bruhn, "Chronicle of a Victory," 43.

83. Juárez-Gámiz and Arellano-Toledo, "The Lousy Avalanche," 185.

84. Oniel Francisco Díaz Jiménez and Miguel Eduardo Alva Rivera, "El Uso Estratégico de la Publicidad Política de Ataque en la Elección Federal Intermedia de 2015 en México," *Revista Mexicana de Opinión Pública*, July-December (2016): 42, https://doi.org/10.1016/j.rmop.2016.07.002.

85. Chihu Amparán, "El Framing Audiovisual," 145–46.

86. Nai, "Going Negative," 6.

87. Pallister and Fitzpatrick, "Medium and the Message."

88. Juárez-Gámiz and Arellano-Toledo, "The Lousy Avalanche," 185.

Chapter 7

Campaign Finance

Running for office is expensive. Candidates and political parties need to pay campaign staff, conduct polling, print campaign materials, pay for television advertising, employ social media teams, provide transportation to campaign events, rent campaign offices, and so on. Total campaign spending for a general election ranges from tens of millions of dollars in small countries like Costa Rica and Uruguay to several billion dollars in Brazil,[1] where a winning Chamber of Deputies candidate spends on average well over US$100,000–$200,000 on their campaign.[2] While some candidates run shoestring campaigns that rely heavily on social media and avoid buying expensive TV time, most candidates and their political parties need to raise substantial sums of money to fund their campaigns.

Campaign funding inevitably raises normative concerns for democracy. Unequal access to campaign funding can tilt the electoral playing field, advantaging candidates and parties with more money to spend than others. Economic inequality can produce political inequality as wealthy donors have an outsized impact on who wins elections. Perhaps most concerning of all in Latin America, campaign finance can generate corruption, with campaign donors—wealthy individuals, businesses, and criminal interests such as drug trafficking organizations—expecting favors from politicians whose campaigns they fund. The funding of campaigns by criminal groups is particularly harmful, as it weakens the state and subverts the rule of law.[3]

While campaign finance raises similar normative concerns for all democracies, countries vary drastically in how campaign funds are raised and how the state regulates political finance. In some Latin American countries, such as Brazil, candidates mostly raise their own campaign funds, while in others only political parties officially raise money—although candidates and their personal fundraisers may play a central role in soliciting donations to their parties. Countries also vary in the types of legal regulations they have adopted to control the funding of campaigns.

This chapter examines campaign financing in the region, beginning with an overview of scandals involving illicit campaign funding and then analyzing the legal regulations that Latin American countries have established to try to control campaign finance. The chapter concludes with a case study of Guatemala, where campaign finance has been intertwined with government corruption and the problem of illicit funding has proven difficult to resolve. The chapter speaks to an enduring dilemma in all democracies: How can campaign finance be regulated to balance the values of political equality, fairness, integrity, and free speech?

THE PROBLEM OF ILLICIT CAMPAIGN FINANCE

Since the third wave of democratization, Latin America has seen countless corruption scandals. Presidents, legislators, and political parties have been accused—and in some cases convicted in court—of accepting bribes and embezzling staggering sums of money. In the 2010s large anti-corruption protests erupted in many countries in the region, as citizens fed up with government malfeasance took to the streets demanding the ouster of corrupt politicians.

While corruption takes many forms throughout the region, a common arena for corrupt transactions is the financing of election campaigns. Candidates and political parties across Latin America have been involved in illegal campaign financing. In some cases, illicit funding has come from large corporations that secretly channel funds to campaigns in exchange for government contracts and favorable government policy. In other cases, criminal groups fund campaigns for the same purpose: to win favorable government policy that protects their interests. No Latin American country has avoided campaign finance scandals.

In Peru, one of the country's most powerful politicians, Keiko Fujimori, spent more than a year in pre-trial detention when facing accusations of receiving illegal campaign donations from the Brazilian construction company Odebrecht, which spent hundreds of millions of dollars bribing officials throughout Latin America in exchange for government contracts. Former president Ollanta Humala (2011–2016) likewise was under investigation for taking bribes from Odebrecht to fund his campaign. Similarly in Ecuador, former president Rafael Correa's Alianza PAIS party received over $11 million in illegal campaign donations between 2012 and 2016, with donors expecting "repayment through lucrative government contracts."[4] After his presidency, Correa fled the country and was convicted in absentia in 2020 for illegal campaign finance. Even Chile, with its relatively low level of corruption, has experienced scandals involving corporations illegally channeling millions of dollars to political parties.[5]

In some countries drug money makes its way into campaigns. The notorious Mexican drug lord El Chapo allegedly gave $1 million to the brother of Honduran president Juan Orlando Hernández to help finance his presidential campaign in exchange for Hernández protecting drug trafficking operations in the country. The corruption continued after the election. During Hernández's two terms in office he allegedly received millions of dollars in bribes in exchange for providing drug traffickers with protection.[6] Hernández's National Party was also accused of receiving financing from companies involved in a corruption scheme that stole millions of dollars from the country's social security agency[7] and from the embezzlement of state development funds.[8] After leaving office in 2022, Hernández was extradited to the United States to stand trial for drug trafficking and money laundering.

Drug money funds campaigns in other countries as well. Perhaps the most famous such scandal involved the successful presidential campaign of Ernesto Samper in Colombia in 1994, which was financed with millions of dollars from the Cali cartel. Several Samper aides were convicted in the scandal, although Samper himself avoided prosecution. Since then, dozens of Colombian politicians at the national and local levels have been shown to have ties to organized crime groups involved in drug trafficking.[9] Beyond Colombia, it is widely believed that drug money makes its way into election campaigns in many countries in the region, especially in local races.[10]

There remains much that is unknown about who donates money to election campaigns in the region and what donors get in return for their contributions. But the available evidence shows that campaign contributions overwhelmingly come from wealthy business interests.[11] Recent campaign finance scandals show that breaking campaign finance laws is common, even in countries where broader forms of corruption are not widespread. To rein in illicit campaign funding and the influence trafficking that it generates, Latin American countries have adopted a wide range of campaign finance regulations, which have had varying degrees of success.

CAMPAIGN FINANCE REGULATIONS

Countries around the world use a variety of policy tools to regulate campaign finance.[12] These tools can be categorized as relating to campaign contributions, campaign spending, reporting of campaign funding, and the provision of public funding.

Contribution limits can include bans on campaign donations from certain sources, such as foreign entities, as well as limits on how much any individual donor can contribute to a campaign. Contribution limits aim to prevent wealthy donors from wielding excessive political influence, but they are difficult to enforce, as donors may be able to channel contributions through other people.[13] Limits on how much a campaign can spend are also intended to level the playing field by preventing wealthy candidates or parties from overwhelming their opponents through massive campaign spending.

Reporting (or disclosure) requirements aim to expose and deter undue influence over politicians. When candidates and parties must submit detailed reports on their donors and their expenditures, journalists and watchdog groups can track whether campaign donors benefit from subsequent government contracts or regulations. Campaign finance reporting can also allow voters to make more informed decisions by revealing what interest groups are financing each campaign. One type of contribution limit—on anonymous donations to campaigns—complements financial reporting requirements by increasing the transparency of each campaign's funding sources.

Finally, public funding aims to promote equality and limit corruption. Ideally, public funding to political parties for campaigning ensures that all relevant political forces have enough resources to reach the electorate with their views and limits the advantages of parties or candidates with access to overwhelming wealth. It might also "insulate parties and politicians from the undue pressures of wealthy donors, thus permitting them to be more responsive to the broader (nonwealthy) electorate."[14] Public funding can also be used to help enforce other campaign finance regulations, as the threat of withholding public funds if parties violate other rules (such as spending limits or reporting requirements) "can prove a highly effective incentive to obey the rules" if the amount of public funding is significant.[15] Public funding can be provided to all registered political parties, although funds are usually awarded to parties at least in part on a proportional basis, with each party's vote share determining its share of public funding. Such proportional funding avoids spending taxpayer money on marginal parties with little popular following, but it does help perpetuate an advantage for the most powerful parties as they receive the most funding.[16]

Latin American countries make extensive use of all these policy tools (see table 7.1), each of which is explored in more detail in the following sections.

Contribution Limits

Campaign contributions from some sources are widely prohibited in the region. The most commonly banned sources of contributions are those from foreign entities (banned in every country), religious organizations, and

Table 7.1   Campaign Finance Regulations

	Ban on Anonymous Contributions	Limits on Donor Contributions to Party or Candidate	Limits on Party or Candidate Spending	Campaign Finance Reporting Requirement	Public Funding for Parties
Argentina	✓	✓	✓	✓	✓
Bolivia	✓	✓		✓	✓
Brazil	✓	✓	✓	✓	✓
Chile		✓	✓	✓	✓
Colombia	✓	✓	✓	✓	✓
Costa Rica	✓			✓	✓
Dominican Republic	✓	✓	✓	✓	✓
Ecuador	✓	✓	✓	✓	✓
El Salvador	✓	✓		✓	✓
Guatemala	✓	✓	✓	✓	✓
Honduras	✓	✓	✓	✓	✓
Mexico	✓	✓	✓	✓	✓
Nicaragua				✓	✓
Panama	✓	✓	✓	✓	✓
Paraguay	✓	✓	✓	✓	✓
Peru	✓	✓		✓	✓
Uruguay		✓		✓	✓
Venezuela	✓				

Source: International IDEA, Political Finance Database, https://www.idea.int/data-tools/data/political-finance-database, with corrections by the author.

businesses that have contracts with the government.[17] In several scandals, Latin American presidents have been accused of receiving campaign funding from foreign governments, including at least two former presidents of Nicaragua accused of receiving funding from Taiwan[18] and a number of left-wing candidates throughout the region that received funding from Venezuela under President Hugo Chávez.[19] Several countries—including Argentina, Brazil, Chile, and Mexico—ban all corporate donations to campaigns, and many countries also prohibit contributions from trade unions.[20]

To promote transparency in campaign funding, every country in Latin America regulates anonymous campaign donations. Nearly all countries prohibit anonymous donations, with the two exceptions—Chile and Uruguay—both setting limits on the amount that can be donated anonymously. Chile requires that anonymous contributions go to the Electoral Service (the country's electoral management body), which then forwards the money to the political party while maintaining the donor's anonymity. Thus, "the Electoral Service becomes a de facto middleman between the recipient and donor, contributions can be monitored and potentially corrupt exchanges can be stifled—while respecting anonymity."[21]

Nearly all countries in the region also set limits on how much a donor can contribute to a political party or candidate for an electoral period. The contribution limit varies from country to country. In Colombia, the contribution limit in presidential races is 2 percent of the campaign spending limit.[22] In Ecuador, a donor cannot contribute more than 5 percent of the campaign spending limit, while in Bolivia, the cap is 10 percent of the annual budget of the political party.[23] In Paraguay, the contribution limit for the 2018 elections was approximately US$98,000.[24] Mexico limits the total amount that a party can receive from all private donors to 10 percent of the campaign spending limit, which aims to make parties rely primarily on public funding.[25]

Contribution limits seek to promote equality by limiting the political influence of any single wealthy donor. They are difficult to enforce, however. One challenge is tracking and placing a value on in-kind contributions, such as donors allowing parties to use vehicles and facilities for campaign events. Such contributions are not always recorded, and often serve as a way of circumventing contribution limits.[26] They also do not address favorable media coverage that media owners could provide candidates. In Guatemala, for instance, most major broadcast television stations have been owned by one Mexican businessman, allowing him to exercise significant influence over election campaigns without directly contributing money.[27]

Another complicating factor is candidate self-financing. About half of Latin American countries set limits on the amount that candidates can contribute to their own campaigns. In Ecuador, for example, a candidate cannot contribute more than 10 percent of the campaign spending limit.[28] But where candidates are not limited in how much they can contribute (beyond overall campaign spending limits), wealthy individuals can self-finance their own campaigns. This is most commonly the case in local elections and raises concerns about an unlevel playing field. As one report puts it, "[t]his is a problem not only for electoral equality but also for the participation of certain groups in politics, particularly women, whose access to large amounts of money is often more limited."[29]

Spending Limits

A slight majority of Latin American countries impose campaign spending limits. The spending limit varies with the office, with presidential campaigns allowed to spend the most, and limits are typically set as a function of the number of registered voters. In Colombia, presidential campaigns could spend nearly US$27.5 million for the first round of the 2022 election.[30] In smaller Paraguay, campaign spending was limited in 2018 to approximately US$6 million.[31] A few countries impose limits on how much campaigns may spend on media advertising. In Bolivia, for instance, there is no overall campaign spending limit, but parties are limited in how much they may spend on media airtime.[32]

The overall sums of money spent on national campaigns in Latin America tend to be modest. In Mexico's 2018 election, for instance, all five presidential candidates combined spent just under US$45 million on their campaigns.[33] Contrast that with the United States, where spending by the two major candidates and affiliated outside groups can easily top US$1 billion. Spending limits are one factor helping to keep campaign spending down.

However, spending limits can be difficult to enforce if electoral authorities cannot adequately track campaign expenditures. To be effective, spending limits cannot be set too high. However, if set too low, parties will surpass the limits—which has been the case in Colombia, for instance.[34] In some ways, the most effective spending limit may be to simply limit the campaigning period, which almost all Latin American countries do. Campaigning itself is "more easily monitored than the intricacies of gas money and leaflet distribution,"[35] but even determining what counts as "campaigning" and what is simply ordinary political party activities and political speech can be tricky. Consider the presidential campaign of Zury Ríos in Guatemala in 2023. Before the official campaign period had started, Ríos posted photos on social media showing herself meeting with supporters at community events organized by her political party. While the posts were clearly part of her campaign, she made sure to include text on the posts that indicated that the photos showed party affiliation activities and not campaigning, and thus were consistent with the electoral law. (The electoral tribunal did not sanction her—although some other candidates were sanctioned for similar activities.)

In addition to challenges with enforcement, spending limits might be thought to benefit incumbents running for reelection. Incumbents typically benefit from name recognition and thus need less money for publicity than do challengers. However, at least in the case of Brazil, campaign spending has been found to benefit incumbents and challengers equally,[36] suggesting that spending limits may not necessarily disadvantage challengers.

In addition to setting spending limits for parties and candidates, some countries set limits for how much outside actors can spend on campaigning activity. A few countries, including Argentina, Ecuador, and Mexico, ban outside spending altogether. Where such spending is not prohibited, groups such as religious organizations have sometimes spent money to influence elections,[37] much as outside groups like super PACs do in the United States.

Reporting Requirements

Every Latin American country requires political parties or candidates to report their campaign donations and spending. These reports are typically submitted to the electoral management body, which is tasked with reviewing the reports and investigating anomalies. While reporting requirements are intended to ensure transparency of campaign funding, in practice the effectiveness of reporting requirements is limited.

In part this is because the information in finance reports is often limited or incomplete, and in a few cases reports are not made public.[38] In most countries, information on campaign donors is not readily available from the websites of electoral management bodies.[39] Often there is little follow-up investigation into campaign finance reports to identify violations.[40] In Mexico, the National Electoral Institute has used its authority "to conduct on-site, random audits or verification visits during official campaign periods,"[41] but few electoral management bodies are so proactive in monitoring compliance with campaign finance laws. Bolivia illustrates these weaknesses in reporting requirements. While parties must submit to electoral authorities detailed reports on their budgets, including funding sources and expenditures, those reports are not made public, and the electoral management body lacks the power to adequately investigate campaign financing.[42]

Given the limited efficacy of official campaign finance reports, civil society organizations often provide the most helpful data on campaign spending. Groups like Citizen Action (Acción Ciudadana) in Guatemala have developed methodologies such as media advertisement monitoring that estimate how much parties spend on campaigns. Such efforts sometimes reveal that campaigns spend more money than they report to election authorities.[43]

The Challenges of Enforcement

As the preceding sections show, Latin American countries have no shortage of campaign finance regulations. Enforcement of those regulations, however, has often been lacking. One of the biggest challenges in enforcing campaign finance rules and applying sanctions has been the institutional weakness of the agencies that are responsible for monitoring campaign finance. This task is typically the responsibility of the electoral management body or electoral court, but these institutions sometimes lack the resources and technical capacity to effectively monitor campaign fundraising and expenditures.[44] Typical examples are El Salvador, where election observers have reported that the Supreme Electoral Tribunal "lacks the capability to undertake a timely verification" of campaign funding sources, and Paraguay, with its "absence of an effective monitoring and sanctioning mechanism."[45] In Honduras a new campaign finance auditing unit was created in 2016, but by the time of elections the following year, it had just forty-two staff members and was led by three commissioners who were selected by the three largest political parties.[46]

Compounding the problem of inadequate monitoring—which lowers the odds of punishment for violations—is the fact that penalties can be lenient. Penalties for violating financing rules can include fines (which are most common), loss of public funding for political parties that have broken the rules, suspension of political party registration, loss of public office, and, in rare cases, imprisonment.[47] In some cases the fines for finance violations are minuscule relative to the sums spent on campaigns—as has been the case in El Salvador, Guatemala, and Panama.[48] Such minor penalties do little to deter illegal campaign fundraising and spending.

Mexico illustrates the challenges of effective enforcement even with its proactive electoral management body. The country employs each type of campaign finance regulation. Officially, campaigns are financed overwhelmingly through public funding. However, parties routinely receive unreported private donations from companies seeking government contracts and other favorable treatment. Campaign spending limits are in place—a presidential candidate could spend nearly US$22 million in the 2018 election. Yet campaigns routinely spend far more than the law allows. According to a nongovernmental watchdog group, the vast majority of campaign spending goes unreported. The problem, as in many other countries, is that election authorities have lacked the capacity to effectively monitor campaign contributions and spending.[49]

Public Funding

Public funding can help reduce the role of private campaign finance, with all of its potential for inequality and corruption. It can also help political parties institutionalize and function effectively as institutions that mediate between state and society. However, such funding also risks making parties dependent on the state rather than their rank-and-file members, and it can strengthen large parties to the point of disadvantaging newcomers if public funding is distributed largely according to parties' vote shares.

Every Latin American country except for Venezuela provides some degree of direct public funding for parties.[50] Nearly every country also provides subsidized media access to parties during campaign periods. To qualify for public funding, parties generally must participate in every election and in most cases win a minimum share of the vote or seats in office. These thresholds can be lenient (as in Peru, where any party with a seat in Congress is eligible for funding) or strict (as in Brazil, where parties must win fifteen seats in the lower house of Congress to be eligible).

In every country with public funding, at least some portion of public funding is distributed to parties proportionally based on their share of the vote in the previous election. Argentina allocates half of public funding equally to all parties and half according to the share of votes obtained in the previous election. Several countries use a variation on this formula. Bolivia allocates 60 percent equally to all parties and 40 percent according to vote share, while Mexico distributes 30 percent equally and 70 percent proportionally. Many countries distribute all public funding on a proportional basis according to how many votes each party received in the previous election.

Public funding can be quite generous. In Mexico, public funding to parties in 2015 (a midterm election year) amounted to US$37 million.[51] Brazil's public funding in the same year amounted to more than US$200 million.[52] The level of public funding ranges from over US$10 per voter in Costa Rica, where upward of 90 percent of party expenses are covered by public funding, to less than US$1 per voter in several countries.[53] However, even with ample public funding, the high costs of campaigning mean that parties are often reliant to some degree on private funding.

Despite its limitations, public funding is an important tool in containing the worst pathologies of unfettered private campaign financing. Public funding can also help stabilize party systems. Some research finds that less strict thresholds for public funding for parties are associated with less electoral volatility (changes in vote shares across parties from one election to the next), as access to public funding helps established parties survive rather than being replaced by newcomers.[54] Public funding can also be used to promote other goals, such as gender equality. Some Latin American countries use public funding to provide incentives for gender equality within parties. For example, in Chile parties receive additional public funding for each female candidate from the party that is elected.[55] A few countries, including Colombia and Mexico, require parties to earmark a portion of their public funding to efforts to promote the inclusion of, and leadership roles for, women. However, such initiatives remain rare in the region.

CASE STUDY: CRIMINALITY AND CORRUPTION IN GUATEMALA

The challenges of regulating campaign finance, and the pathologies that result from failing to effectively do so, are seen in full force in Guatemala. One of the perennial weaknesses of the country's elections is weak oversight over campaign finance, which allows candidates to circumvent the law and permits criminal groups to corrupt the electoral process—which in turn fuels government corruption between elections. This is despite the fact that Guatemala has in place all of the legal regulations of campaign finance discussed in this chapter.

Guatemala's election law includes a wide range of campaign finance rules, many of which have become stricter since the 2000s in response to persistent campaign finance scandals. Public funding is provided to all parties that received at least 5 percent of the vote in the previous general election or that win at least one seat in Congress. Public funding is provided at a flat rate of US$2 per vote received in the previous election. Anonymous contributions are banned, as are contributions from foreign individuals or entities and people who have been convicted of crimes such as money laundering. The maximum that campaigns are legally allowed to spend is equivalent to US$0.50 for every registered voter. Contributions must be made to political parties rather than individual candidates, and no single donor can contribute more than 10 percent of the campaign spending limit.[56]

Parties must regularly report their donations and expenditures to the Supreme Electoral Tribunal (TSE), which is responsible for monitoring compliance with campaign finance rules. The TSE is required to publish records of campaign contributions to each party. Political parties can be fined between US$50,000 and US$250,000 and lose public campaign funding if they violate financing regulations and can lose their legal registration.[57] Individuals can also face criminal sanctions, including prison time, for campaign finance crimes.

Yet despite ample legal regulations, illicit campaign finance continues to bedevil Guatemalan elections. Large off-the-books contributions flow to campaigns from large business interests, state contractors (especially construction companies seeking public works contracts), and criminal groups.[58] Audits by the TSE and nongovernmental organizations reveal that the leading political parties routinely spend well in excess of their reported income and of legal campaign spending limits.[59] The records of several recent Guatemalan presidents illustrate the pervasiveness of illegal campaign funding.

In 2011, former military officer Otto Pérez Molina of the Patriot Party was elected president. Four years later, Pérez and his party faced the largest popular protests in Guatemala in decades after anti-corruption investigators revealed a massive graft scheme. The prosecutor's office, supported by a United Nations–backed commission against impunity (known by its Spanish acronym CICIG), showed that the Patriot Party was little more than a criminal organization that embezzled state funds and accepted bribes in exchange for government contracts and tax breaks. The party's corruption included campaign financing: the party "financed its rise to power through a series of shell companies that took dark money from a wide range of donors, laundered it and then injected it into the electoral campaign without reporting it to the country's Supreme Electoral Tribunal."[60] Investigators found that the party accepted some US$65 million in unreported donations in exchange for government favors.[61]

Pérez Molina resigned shortly before the 2015 general election, and he and his vice president, Roxana Baldetti, along with many other officials, were arrested and subsequently convicted and sentenced to prison. In 2015, the television comedian Jimmy Morales ran for president as an outsider, using the campaign slogan "not corrupt, nor a thief." But Morales failed to live up to his slogan. His campaign spent millions of dollars that went unreported to the TSE, and the party failed to report basic information about its income. Donations reportedly came from Evangelical churches, ex-military officers seeking protection from prosecution for atrocities committed during the country's civil war, and various businesspeople. Prosecutors ultimately charged his political party with failing to report US$2 million in revenue.[62]

The winner of the 2019 presidential race, Alejandro Giammattei, was also implicated in illegal campaign finance when a witness testified that Giammattei arranged US$2.6 million in campaign donations from construction companies in exchange for government contracts.[63] The runner-up candidate in both the 2015 and 2019 presidential races, Sandra Torres, was arrested for reportedly failing to report over US$2 million in donations to her 2015 campaign. The case was dismissed in 2022 amid a deterioration in judicial independence in the country.[64]

Many of these cases of illegal funding of presidential campaigns involve businesses seeking favorable government treatment. But organized crime groups also contribute to campaigns to protect their interests. In 2007, for instance, the Zetas drug cartel allegedly contributed over US$10 million to the campaign of the UNE party, which won that year's presidential election.[65] In 2019, presidential candidate Mario Estrada pleaded guilty in U.S. court to offering Mexico's Sinaloa cartel access to drug trafficking through Guatemala in exchange for millions of dollars to fund his presidential campaign. Less is known about campaign funding at the local level, but money from organized crime no doubt finds its way into many municipal campaigns.

Guatemala's experience with campaign finance points to the challenges posed by inadequate enforcement of the law. While political parties must report their revenue and expenses, the financial reports that they submit are often incomplete or misleading. Fundraising is also largely conducted by individual political figures rather than political party organizations, which generally lack the organization and resources to adequately monitor the sources of candidate funding.[66] The penalties applied for infractions have often been insufficient to deter campaign finance crimes. In particular, relatively small fines imposed by the TSE are offset by the millions of dollars in secretive funds that campaigns raise. In a context of generalized corruption and weak rule of law, campaign finance rules written into the electoral code—even when occasionally enforced by zealous prosecutors— have been inadequate to rein in the pernicious influence of illegal campaign funding.

NOTES

1. International IDEA, *Funding of Political Parties and Election Campaigns: A Handbook on Political Finance* (Stockholm: International IDEA, 2014), 147.

2. David Samuels, "When Does Every Penny Count? Intra-Party Competition and Campaign Finance in Brazil," *Party Politics* 7, no. 1 (2001): 92, https://doi.org /10.1177/1354068801007001005; Taylor C. Boas, F. Daniel Hidalgo, and Neal P. Richardson, "The Spoils of Victory: Campaign Donations and Government Contracts in Brazil," Kellogg Institute Working Paper #379 (2011), https://kellogg.nd.edu/sites/ default/files/old_files/documents/379_0.pdf.

3. Kevin Casas-Zamora, "On Organized Crime and Political Finance: Why Does the Connection Matter?" in *Dangerous Liaisons: Organized Crime and Political Finance in Latin America and Beyond*, ed. Kevin Casas-Zamora (Washington, DC: The Brookings Institution, 2013), 8.

4. Catherine M. Conaghan, "Diminished by Design: Ecuador's Alianza PAIS," in *Diminished Parties: Democratic Representation in Contemporary Latin America*, eds. Juan Pablo Luna, Rafael Piñeiro Rodríguez, Fernando Rosenblatt, and Gabriel Vommaro (New York: Cambridge University Press, 2022), 212.

5. Pacale Bonnefoy, "Executives Are Jailed in Chile Finance Scandal," *New York Times*, March 8, 2015, https://www.nytimes.com/2015/03/08/world/americas/ executives-are-jailed-in-chile-finance-scandal.html; Kevin Casas-Zamora and Miguel Carter, *Beyond the Scandals: The Changing Context of Corruption in Latin America* (Washington, DC: Inter-American Dialogue, 2017), 20, https://www.thedialogue.org /wp-content/uploads/2017/02/Corruption-in-Latin-America_ROL_Report_FINAL _web-PDF.pdf.

6. Vanessa Buschschlüter, "Juan Orlando Hernández: Honduran Ex-Leader Pleads Not Guilty," BBC News, May 10, 2022, https://www.bbc.com/news/world -latin-america-61393266.

7. Casas-Zamora and Carter, *Beyond the Scandals*, 21.

8. Héctor Silva Ávalos and Victoria Dittmar, "One Party, Many Crimes: The Case of Honduras' National Party," *Insight Crime*, February 16, 2021, https:// insightcrime.org/investigations/one-party-many-crimes-honduras-national-party/.

9. These criminal connections came to light in the mid-2000s during the "parapolitics" scandal. Sibylla Brodzinsky, "Colombia's 'Parapolitics' Scandal Casts Shadow over President," *The Guardian*, April 23, 2008, https://www.theguardian .com/world/2008/apr/23/colombia.

10. Kathleen Bruhn, "Party Finance in Latin America," *Oxford Research Encyclopedias* (2019), 1.

11. Ibid., 1, 9.

12. In addition to sources cited in the text, data on campaign finance regulations in Latin America comes from International IDEA's Political Finance Database, https://www .idea.int/data-tools/data/political-finance-database, last accessed December 15, 2022. I have corrected some of the data by consulting other sources, including the Carter Center, *Financiamiento Político y Regulación de Campañas Electorales en América Latina*.

13. International IDEA, *Funding of Political Parties*, 22.

14. Susan E. Scarrow, "Political Finance in Comparative Perspective," *Annual Review of Political Science* 10 (2007): 205, https://doi.org/10.1146/annurev.polisci .10.080505.100115.

15. International IDEA, *Funding of Political Parties*, 22–23.

16. Ibid., 24.

17. Rossana Andía and Yukihiko Hamada, "The Integrity of Political Finance Systems in Latin America: Tackling Political Corruption," International IDEA Policy Paper No. 21 (Stockholm: International IDEA, 2019).

18. International IDEA, *Funding of Political Parties*, 132.

19. For one such case, involving Venezuelan money sent to Argentina, see Alexei Barrionuevo and Carmen Gentile, "Conviction in Spy Case over Cash-Filled Suitcase," *New York Times*, November 3, 2008, https://www.nytimes.com/2008/11/04/ world/americas/04suitcase.html.

20. Maria Page and Julia Pomares, "The Move toward State-Run Mass Media Electoral Campaigns in Latin America: An Evaluation of the First Implementation in the 2011 Argentine Presidential Elections," *Election Law Journal* 11, no. 4 (2012): 534, https://doi.org/10.1089/elj.2012.1145. Argentina banned corporate donations in 2009, while Chile adopted the ban in 2014 and Brazil in 2016. Most donations in Brazil before the ban took effect came from corporations. David Samuels, "Money, Elections, and Democracy in Brazil," *Latin American Politics and Society* 43, no. 2 (2001): 35, doi:10.1111/j.1548-2456.2001.tb00398.x.

21. International IDEA, *Funding of Political Parties*, 133.

22. Ley No. 1475, Article 23.

23. Ley Orgánica Electoral y de Organizaciones Políticas de la República del Ecuador, Código de la Democracia, Article 221; Bolivia's Ley de Partidos Políticos, Article 51.

24. European Union Election Observation Mission, Republic of Paraguay, Final Report, General Elections, April 22, 2018, 16.

25. Bruhn, "Party Finance," 10.

26. Ibid., 9; International IDEA, *Funding of Political Parties*, 139.

27. International IDEA, *Funding of Political Parties*, 144.

28. Andía and Hamada, "Integrity of Political Finance," 16–17.

29. International IDEA, *Funding of Political Parties*, 138.

30. International IDEA's Political Finance Database, https://www.idea.int/data-tools/data/political-finance-database.

31. European Union Election Observation Mission, Republic of Paraguay, Final Report, General Elections, April 22, 2018, 16.

32. European Union Election Expert Mission, Bolivia 2019, Final Report, 18–19.

33. Octael Nieto-Vazquez, "Political Finance in the Digital Age: A Case Study of Mexico," International IDEA, January 2023, 13.

34. International IDEA, *Funding of Political Parties*, 146.

35. Bruhn, "Party Finance," 16.

36. David Samuels, "Incumbents and Challengers on a Level Playing Field: Assessing the Impact of Campaign Finance in Brazil," *Journal of Politics* 63, no. 2 (2001), https://doi.org/10.1111/0022-3816.00079.

37. Andía and Hamada, "Integrity of Political Finance," 19.

38. International IDEA, *Funding of Political Parties*, 149; Andía and Hamada, "Integrity of Political Finance," 20.

39. Bruhn, "Party Finance," 11.

40. International IDEA, *Funding of Political Parties*, 148.

41. Kevin Casas-Zamora and Daniel Zovatto, "The Cost of Democracy: Campaign Finance Regulation in Latin America," Latin America Initiative, Foreign Policy at Brookings, July 2015, 14.

42. European Union Election Expert Mission, Bolivia 2019, Final Report, 19.

43. International IDEA, *Funding of Political Parties*, 149.

44. Andía and Hamada, "Integrity of Political Finance," 22.

45. European Union Election Observation Mission, El Salvador 2019 Final Report, 2; European Union Election Observation Mission, Republic of Paraguay, Final Report, General Elections, April 22, 2018, 16.

46. Daniel M. Sabet, "When Corruption Funds the Political System: A Case Study of Honduras," Wilson Center Latin American Program, 2020, https://www.wilsoncenter.org/sites/default/files/media/uploads/documents/When%20Corruption%20Funds%20the%20Political%20System_Final.pdf, 34–35.

47. Andía and Hamada, "Integrity of Political Finance," 20–21; Casas-Zamora and Zovatto, "The Cost of Democracy," 15.

48. International IDEA, *Funding of Political Parties*, 151; European Union Election Observation Mission, El Salvador 2019 Final Report, 16.

49. Christine Murray and Stefanie Eschenbacher, "Anti-Corruption Watchdogs Wonder: 'Who Is Funding Mexico's Presidential Candidates?'" Reuters (June 29, 2018), https://www.reuters.com/article/us-mexico-election-financing/anti-corruption-watchdogs-wonder-who-is-funding-mexicos-presidential-candidates-idUSKBN1JP0GG.

50. Venezuela previously had public funding but eliminated it in the 1999 constitution. Uruguay was the first country in the region to adopt public funding, in 1928.

51. Carter Center, *Financiamiento Político*, 263.

52. Scott Mainwaring, Timothy J. Power, and Fernando Bizzarro, "The Uneven Institutionalization of a Party System: Brazil," in *Party Systems in Latin America: Institutionalization, Decay, and Collapse*, ed. Scott Mainwaring (New York: Cambridge University Press, 2018), 192.

53. Bruhn, "Party Finance," 4–5; Kevin Casas-Zamora, "Costa Rica: Four Decades of Campaign Finance Scandals," in *Dangerous Liaisons: Organized Crime and Political Finance in Latin America and Beyond*, ed. Kevin Casas-Zamora (Washington, DC: The Brookings Institution, 2013), 123.

54. Yen-Pin Su, "Rules for Party Subsidies and Electoral Volatility in Latin America," *Latin American Research Review* 57, no. 1 (2022), doi:10.1017/lar.2022.9.

55. Andía and Hamada, "Integrity of Political Finance," 18.

56. Ley Electoral y de Partidos Políticos, Art. 21.

57. Ibid., Art. 21, 90, 90-Bis.

58. Comisión Internacional contra la Impunidad en Guatemala (CICIG), *Financiamiento de la Política en Guatemala* (Guatemala City: CICIG, 2015), 40.

59. Ibid., 32, 38.

60. Felipe Puerta and Steven Dudley, "Guatemala Politics and the Patriotic Party's Theory of 'Eternal Return,'" *Insight Crime*, August 16, 2018, https://www.insightcrime.org/investigations/guatemala-politics-patriotic-partys-theory-eternal-return/.

61. Carlos Álvarez, "Estructura del PP Recibió al Menos q500 Millones en Sobornos," *Prensa Libre*, June 2, 2016, http://www.prensalibre.com/guatemala/justicia/justicia-mp-y-cicig-revelan-detalles-de-operativos; Mike LaSusa, "Ex-President of Guatemala Facing More Corruption Charges," *Insight Crime*, June 3, 2016, http://www.insightcrime.org/news-briefs/guatemala-authorities-allege-ex-president-led-illegal-campaign-finance-network.

62. Héctor Silva Ávalos and Steven Dudley, "President Jimmy Morales' (and Guatemala's) 'Original Sin,'" *Insight Crime*, August 23, 2018, https://www.insightcrime.org/investigations/president-jimmy-morales-guatemalas-original-sin/.

63. José Luis Sanz, "Witness Accuses Guatemalan President of Funding Campaign with Construction Bribes," *El Faro*, February 14, 2022, https://elfaro.net/en/202202/centroamerica/26008/Witness-Accuses-Guatemalan-President-of-Funding-Campaign-with-Construction-Bribes.htm.

64. Sara Solórzano, "Sandra Torres: Un Camino de 36 Meses para Conseguir su Sobreseimiento," *Prensa Libre*, November 29, 2022, https://www.prensalibre.com/guatemala/justicia/sandra-torres-un-camino-de-36-meses-para-conseguir-su-sobreseimiento/.

65. Steven Dudley, "The Zetas, Drug Money and the Colom Campaign in Guatemala," *Insight Crime*, August 9, 2018, https://www.insightcrime.org/investigations/the-zetas-drug-money-colom-campaign-guatemala/.

66. CICIG, *Financiamiento de la Política*, 21, 39, 45, 47.

Chapter 8

Voter Participation

If elections are at the heart of democracy, then voter participation is a core component of democratic citizenship. Elections are a central way in which citizens can select leaders that share their values and interests, and the primary mechanism available to hold politicians accountable for their performance in office. But for elections to serve these functions, citizens must vote. The level of voter participation in an election can determine who controls government and serves as an indicator of the legitimacy of elected officials and the broader political system. When voter turnout is low, it is likely that some segments of society—often the poor, young, and marginalized—are voting at lower rates than older and more affluent citizens. This can contribute to the interests of some groups being given much more weight by elected officials than the interests of groups that tend to abstain from voting.

Because of its importance for democracy, political equality, and government accountability, voter turnout is one of the most extensively studied topics in political science. Researchers generally seek to answer two related questions: Why do some people vote while others don't? And why is voter turnout consistently higher in some countries than in others?

Political scientists' answers to these questions have traditionally relied on research on voter participation in the United States and the long-standing democracies of Western Europe. But over the past few decades many researchers have investigated turnout in other parts of the world, including Latin America. This chapter discusses that research, distinguishing between explanations of voter turnout at the aggregate (national) level and those at the individual level. First, however, the chapter presents a brief overview of voter turnout levels in the region.

VOTER TURNOUT IN LATIN AMERICA

Latin American elections generally see robust levels of voter participation. In presidential elections in the 1980s and 1990s, voter turnout as a percentage of the voting-age population averaged over 64 percent. The average went up in the 2000s–2010s, to nearly 69 percent.[1] By contrast, turnout for presidential elections in the United States averaged just 53.7 percent from 1980 to 2016.[2] Turnout in Latin American legislative elections hasn't been much lower, in part because most countries hold concurrent elections where the president and the legislature are elected at the same time.

While regional averages show a modestly high level of voter turnout, the regional average masks substantial variation across countries. Figure 8.1 shows the wide range of turnout levels in the region, with Uruguay having an average turnout of 95 percent for presidential elections from 1990 to 2019, while at the other end Guatemala's average turnout was only 45 percent. Latin America is thus home to countries with some of the highest and lowest voter turnout in the world.

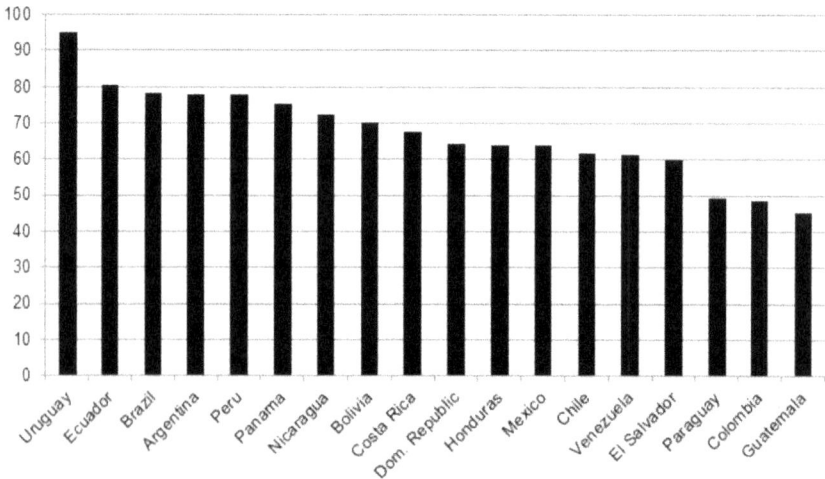

Figure 8.1 Voter Turnout in Presidential Elections, 1990–2019. *Source*: Author's calculations based on data from International IDEA, Voter Turnout Database, https://www.idea.int/data-tools/data/voter-turnout. *Note*: Bars represent average voter turnout for each country.

EXPLAINING VOTER TURNOUT:
THE AGGREGATE LEVEL

A tremendous amount of research has been devoted to explaining such cross-national differences in voter turnout in order to understand why more people vote in some countries than in others. Levels of socioeconomic development, differences in political culture, and especially institutional factors have been proposed to explain differing levels of participation. Some factors that affect the level of voter participation are idiosyncratic to specific elections—such as the appeal of particular candidates, the salience of key issues at a given point in time, and how upset voters are with the government. Yet quantitative studies search for regularities underlying the particularities of any given election.

Perhaps surprising are the factors that don't seem to affect voter turnout in Latin America. Around the world, close elections in which the outcome is uncertain tend to produce higher turnout.[3] Yet several studies of turnout in Latin America find that the closeness of the election has no effect on turnout when controlling for other variables.[4] Socioeconomic development is also linked to voter turnout around the world. It is theorized that socioeconomic development produces the education, wealth, and leisure time that facilitate political involvement and voting. Yet Latin America bucks this trend as well, with level of development showing no relationship to level of voter turnout.[5]

Electoral Systems

While development levels and closeness of races don't explain variation in turnout levels, differences in electoral institutions do. Much of the research on voter turnout has addressed the effects of different types of legislative electoral systems, in particular how proportional representation and single-member districts affect turnout. One of the consistent findings from research on turnout in established democracies is that proportional representation boosts voter turnout.[6] Proportional systems are thought to produce higher turnout compared to single-member districts because under proportional representation votes for small parties are not "wasted"—voters feel like casting a ballot for a small party still might affect the election results—and parties campaign hard in all districts because they have a chance to win seats with just a small share of the vote. In contrast, in single-member districts, voting for a small party can feel pointless because the party has little chance of winning a plurality of votes needed for winning the one seat that is up for grabs. Likewise, political parties are likely to concentrate their campaign resources on swing districts that they have a realistic chance of winning.

Latin America doesn't fit this generalization, however. One study found that proportional representation is correlated with lower turnout in Latin America.[7] This likely has something to do with the fact that all Latin American countries use some degree of proportional representation in electing their legislatures, so studies of turnout in the region only compare varying degrees of proportional representation rather than contrasting PR with pure single-member district systems. Proportional representation also matters primarily for legislative elections. But in Latin America, presidential elections are more important than legislative elections because presidents have so much power and because presidential elections get much more media coverage than legislative and local elections. And a slight majority of legislative elections in the region are held concurrently with presidential elections.[8] In these circumstances, we would expect features of the presidential electoral system to matter more than institutions for electing the legislature.

The major institutional variation in electing presidents in Latin America is the difference between plurality and runoff systems, as seen in chapter 3. In countries with majority-runoff systems, voter turnout tends to be higher in the first round of voting than in the second (runoff) round. In the first round there are more candidates competing, and the first round of presidential voting is typically held at the same time as voting for legislative and local offices. Studies find that concurrent presidential and legislative elections are associated with higher turnout than are elections where only one branch of government is elected.[9] Guatemala offers an example: in its 2019 general election, when the first round of presidential voting was held at the same time as elections for the Congress and municipal governments, 62 percent of registered voters turned out to vote. When the runoff election was held for the presidency two months later, only 40 percent of registered voters turned out.[10]

Even among concurrent elections, turnout is higher in countries with majority-runoff systems for electing presidents than for plurality countries, while controlling for other factors.[11] Another way of putting it is that more people will vote in legislative elections when those elections are concurrent with the first round of a majority-runoff presidential race. Miguel Carreras suggests that this finding results from the same logic linking proportional representation to increased turnout for legislative elections: "First, voters who support minor or mid-sized parties and realize that their vote will be 'lost' may prefer to abstain in plurality systems. Second, under majority-runoff systems, minor parties have more incentives to activate their bases so as to obtain a large share of votes that could be used as an exchange value in the second round."[12]

Number of Political Parties

Many researchers have also investigated the effects of the number of political parties on voter turnout. Here there are countervailing expectations. On the one hand, more political parties should mean higher turnout, because citizens have more options to choose from and are therefore likely to find at least one party that suits their interests.[13] On the other hand, as the number of parties goes up, voters may have more difficulty making up their minds. More importantly, as more parties compete for seats in the legislature, it becomes more likely that no one party will be able to form a legislative majority. In parliamentary systems in particular, more parties competing means that the election might produce a coalition government where different parties make deals to divide up cabinet positions. In these circumstances, elections are seen to be less decisive because they don't produce a clear-cut winning party; as a result, more people are likely to abstain from voting.[14]

Indeed, some research from around the world finds that a higher number of political parties is correlated with lower turnout.[15] However, Latin America is again distinct: some studies find no relationship between the number of political parties and voter turnout in the region.[16] This is likely because of the region's presidential systems, where the issue of coalition government being formed in the legislature—which happens in parliamentary systems—doesn't apply.[17] However, one study finds that a larger number of presidential candidates is associated with lower turnout in Latin America's concurrent elections,[18] suggesting that some would-be voters are turned off by a large field of candidates who may seem indistinguishable from one another.

While the number of political parties may not have clear effects on voter turnout, the ideological distance between major parties—in other words, party polarization—does appear to have a substantial effect. One study finds that higher levels of polarization are associated with higher levels of voter turnout.[19] This is likely because polarization clarifies choices for voters and raises the stakes of election outcomes: when parties are ideologically far apart, which party wins control of government can have enormous consequences for policy.

Compulsory Voting

One of the most distinctive features of Latin American electoral systems that affects participation levels is the fact that voting is mandatory in some countries. This institution, known as compulsory voting, involves a legal requirement for citizens to vote in every election. In some countries the constitution or the electoral law states that voting is a duty of all eligible citizens but doesn't specify any penalties for not voting. But in six countries—Argentina, Bolivia, Brazil, Ecuador, Peru, and Uruguay—voting is mandatory and penalties for not voting are enforced, if imperfectly.

The penalties for not voting vary by country, but typically include a small fine. The maximum fine in Argentina is about US$7; in Uruguay, the fine for a first offense can range from US$11 to $46; in Ecuador, the fine equals 10 percent of the monthly minimum wage. Peru applies a sliding scale so that the fine is lower for people living in poorer districts. Penalties also sometimes include restrictions on one's ability to receive services from the state if he or she has not voted or paid the fine. In Bolivia, for instance, the penalty includes not being able to obtain a passport or engage in banking transactions. In Brazil, penalties include becoming ineligible to enroll in public schools or universities. All countries with compulsory voting include some exemptions from the requirement for citizens over the age of seventy, those who are out of the country on election day, and those with a documented legitimate reason for not voting (such as a medical condition).

Not surprisingly, compulsory voting boosts voter turnout when penalties for non-voting are applied. The five Latin American countries that enforce compulsory voting have the highest average turnout in presidential elections since 1990. As table 8.1 shows, for presidential elections held between 1990 and 2019, those with compulsory voting had an average turnout of 78.9 percent, while elections with voluntary voting had an average turnout of 60.5 percent. The difference in average turnout for legislative elections is even starker: 77.4 percent compared to 55.6 percent. These comparisons don't control for other variables that affect turnout, but multivariate analyses find that when penalties for not voting are applied, compulsory voting indeed increases turnout in Latin America[20] and in elections around the world more generally.[21]

The Latin American countries with compulsory voting adopted it in the early to mid-twentieth century. Argentina adopted it in 1914, followed by Chile in 1925, Brazil in 1932, Peru in 1933, and Uruguay in 1934. Ecuador adopted compulsory voting for men in 1947 and in 1968 for both men and women. But no country has adopted it since then, and some countries have gotten rid of compulsory voting (Venezuela in 1993 and Chile in 2012).[22] Venezuela abolished fines for non-voting in 1993 and fully rescinded compulsory voting in 1999.[23] Voter turnout plummeted in 1993 with the elimination of penalties for non-voting.

Compulsory voting is premised on the concept that voting is not only a right but also a civic duty. This idea is controversial, and scholars and pundits offer an array of arguments in favor of, and against, compulsory voting. One benefit of compulsory voting is reduced class bias in voting: if almost

Table 8.1 Voter Turnout and Compulsory Voting, 1990–2019

	Presidential Elections	*Legislative Elections*
Compulsory Voting	78.9%	77.4%
Voluntary Voting	60.5%	55.6%

Source: Author's calculations based on data from International IDEA, Voter Turnout Database, https://www.idea.int/data-tools/data/voter-turnout.

everyone votes, then the well-off won't disproportionately participate, as tends to be the case under voluntary voting. Relatedly, as a consequence of higher turnout, the government will be incentivized to be more responsive to the needs of all citizens, not just groups that participate at high levels under voluntary voting. Elected officials would also enjoy more legitimacy since they would be chosen by an electorate comprising the large majority of citizens. Finally, mandatory voting might also increase people's broader interest in politics and sense of civic mindedness, thereby stimulating other forms of participation beyond voting.

Of course, opponents of compulsory voting offer their own arguments. Compulsory voting may very well force people with little interest in, or knowledge of, politics to make uninformed choices on their ballot, or to randomly select candidates on the ballot. (Proponents counter that compulsory voting may stimulate people to become better informed about their choices because they know they will need to cast a ballot.) Penalties for not voting like fines will fall hardest on the poor, who may face structural barriers to participation; compulsory voting thus would be a burden on society's most vulnerable. Finally, and perhaps most forcefully, opponents emphasize the coercive nature of compulsory voting, limiting a person's freedom to not vote. Proponents counter that even under compulsory voting, voters can cast a blank ballot—they are not required to vote for anyone—and that the duty of voting should be seen as comparable to jury duty, paying taxes, and other civic requirements. Nevertheless, compulsory voting does impose some loss of liberty on citizens, even if it is minor.[24]

The effects of compulsory voting are debated by scholars. Some evidence supports the claim that people will seek out more political information under compulsory voting but does not show that compulsory voting increases other forms of political participation.[25] A large-scale study of compulsory voting in Brazil found that compulsory voting actually increases the class bias in turnout because the non-monetary penalties for not voting disproportionately push upper-class Brazilians to vote.[26] Both the normative and empirical debates about compulsory voting will no doubt continue, and whether Latin American–style compulsory voting should be a model for democracies elsewhere will remain an open question.

TEXT BOX 8.1: METHODS EXPLAINER: STUDYING VOTER TURNOUT

Studying the effects of different variables on voter turnout requires statistical techniques that allow the researcher to measure the effect of each variable while holding all of the other variables constant. For voter turnout studies, the outcome being explained—the *dependent variable*—is voter turnout. This is usually measured as the percentage of the voting-age population that casts a vote in any given election. (Using the percentage of the voting-eligible population would be preferable, as some people of voting age are not eligible to vote because they lack citizenship, are incarcerated, or for some other reason. However, data on the size of the voting-eligible population is often scarce.)

There are many *independent variables*, or causal factors, that may affect the level of voter turnout. If a researcher were simply to calculate the correlation between level of voter turnout and level of economic development, this would omit the influence of other variables that might be related to both turnout and development. Perhaps countries at higher levels of development tend to have higher levels of turnout, but it could be that more developed countries also disproportionately have certain electoral systems that boost turnout. What initially looks like a correlation between development and turnout could turn out to be spurious.

To assess the influence of each independent variable while controlling for the influences of all other variables, researchers rely on a technique known as *multivariate regression*. As a practical matter, the researcher collects data on all of the relevant variables for each observation. When comparing turnout across different national elections, the researcher would create a dataset with a large number of elections, with data on any number of different variables (the country's level of economic development, its type of electoral system, etc.) corresponding to each individual election. Multivariate regression then uses all of the available data to estimate the effects of each independent variable on voter turnout while accounting for the influence of all the other variables that the researcher includes in the model. The results might show that the presence of a particular variable increases turnout by about 4 percentage points, while increasing the level of another variable from its minimum to maximum value decreases turnout by an estimated 10 points, and so on.

When studying voting at the individual level, researchers use a variation of this technique, known as *logistic regression* (or logit). This technique is used when the dependent variable is binary: an individual person either votes or does not vote in a given election. To measure the dependent variable, researchers must use reliable surveys of national populations that ask respondents whether they voted in the most recent election. For Latin America, researchers most commonly use the AmericasBarometer survey data produced by the Latin American Public Opinion Project (https://www .vanderbilt.edu/lapop/).

Using survey data has its limitations, however. In particular, people have a tendency to over-report voting—a polite way of saying that some people tell the person conducting the survey that they voted even though they did not. It is almost always the case that the percentage of survey respondents reporting that they voted is higher than the actual level of turnout calculated by counting the number of votes cast. This is one instance of social desirability bias, where people tend to give answers on surveys that are considered to be socially acceptable and avoid giving answers that reveal undesirable behavior (such as not voting).[a] Researchers always need to be attentive of this problem and attempt to minimize its effects on their research findings.

[a] Social desirability bias is discussed further in chapter 2.

EXPLAINING VOTER TURNOUT:
THE INDIVIDUAL LEVEL

While a large body of research has investigated the factors affecting voter turnout at the aggregate level, a related area of research focuses on the individual level. Why do some individuals vote regularly, while others vote rarely or not at all? Are there certain characteristics that distinguish voters from non-voters? And if so, how well does the electorate represent the interests of the broader citizenry?

U.S.-focused research on voting at the individual level focuses on the influence of social and demographic attributes (socioeconomic status and resources, age, gender, marital status), psychological investment in politics (such as party identification and interest in politics), and involvement in voluntary associations that can mobilize people to participate in politics.[27] Scholars who study voting in Latin America have found that many of these same factors help explain voting and non-voting in the region. In particular, sociodemographic attributes help explain who votes and who doesn't. Those who vote in Latin America tend to be older, more educated, and interested in politics.

A well-known demographic trait associated with voting is age: older people tend to vote more than younger people. As people transition from early adulthood into middle age, they are likely to become settled into a career and family, and consequently become more invested in their communities and in public affairs. They may also acquire more familiarity with politics. Their motivation to participate in politics therefore increases.

Research bears this out. In multivariate analyses of voting, age is often the strongest predictor of whether an individual votes.[28] This effect is curvilinear: voting becomes more likely as people age, until reaching later years, when voting begins to drop off as people become elderly. Research also suggests that being married increases voting in Latin America,[29] as research on voting in the United States has also found. Because marriage "marks a significant step toward stabilizing one's personal life and establishing roots in the community,"[30] it likely increases forms of political engagement such as voting.

Another well-established finding in research on voting in the United States is that people with higher socioeconomic status and resources (especially education) are more likely to vote than people lacking such resources. The underlying theory is that people with more education are likely to be better informed about, and interested in, politics. People with higher socioeconomic status are also more likely to have free time to participate in politics. The relationship between education and voting also exists in Latin America: individuals with more education are much more likely to vote than those with less education.[31]

This class bias in turnout, where the rich and well-educated vote at higher rates than the poor, has normative implications. It suggests that government will be chosen by an electorate that is not truly representative of the country's population. It is reasonable to assume that the rich and the poor have different and often conflicting interests on at least some policy issues like taxation and social welfare. If the well-off have more political influence by voting at higher rates (not to mention through funding campaigns and lobbying), then the government will be more responsive to the interests of elites than to those of the poor.

Gender has a less clear relationship with voting. Using data from surveys conducted in 2010, one study finds that when controlling for other variables, women vote more than men, and this is because of higher turnout among women in countries with strong gender quotas.[32] However, using a larger set of surveys, another study finds that men are slightly more likely than women to vote when controlling for other variables.[33] These different findings could be the result of different patterns over time and across countries, as well as across age groups. Indeed, one study of Chile has found that among younger cohorts, women vote at higher rates than men, but this pattern is reversed among the oldest cohorts—suggesting generational change in women's voting participation.[34]

Psychological attitudes are also important in accounting for differences in voting. A psychological or emotional attachment to a political party can make an individual more concerned about an election's outcome and raise the expressive value of voting. Party identification can also serve as a decision-making shortcut, making it easier for a voter to choose which candidates to vote for—and thus reducing the cognitive demands of making voting choices. In these ways, party identification can raise the benefits and reduce the costs of voting. Not surprisingly, research finds that partisan identification, as well as broader interest in politics, are associated with a higher probability of voting—although these correlations aren't evident in every Latin American country.[35]

Involvement in voluntary associations also seems to encourage voting, as does being employed.[36] In both cases, being embedded in social networks—with fellow employees, churchgoers, union members, and so on—makes individuals more likely to engage in politics through voting, perhaps through social pressures and encouragement to participate.

The relationships in Latin America between factors like age, education, party identification, and civic activism, on the one hand, and voting on the other, are similar to those found in the United States. However, research on voter turnout in Latin America also considers some factors that are unique to the region. One is citizens' trust in the fairness of the electoral process. Considering the region's history with authoritarian regimes and less-than-fair electoral contests, as well as many contemporary problems with electoral integrity (see chapter 2), many voters have little confidence in the electoral process. This lack of trust could make individuals less likely to vote. After all, why bother going to vote if you believe the election is rigged? Indeed, statistical studies—both for specific countries like Mexico and for the region more broadly—have found that lack of confidence in the integrity of the electoral process reduces the chances that an individual will vote.[37]

Another factor to consider in Latin America is the prevalence of crime. The region is home to some of the countries with the highest homicide rates in the world, and some research suggests that crime lowers voter turnout. A study of Mexican elections in the 2000s found that higher homicide rates at the municipal level were correlated with lower voter turnout in those municipalities, and that individuals who live in the most violent Mexican states and who think violence is the most important issue facing the country are less likely to report that they intend to vote in the next election.[38] Other studies also find that criminal violence decreases turnout in Mexico.[39]

It's not clear why violence should lower voter turnout. One possibility is that high levels of crime cause citizens to become disenchanted with government, and therefore they choose not to participate in elections. Another possibility is that prevalent violent crime makes some voters fearful of going to the polling place to vote on election day. As one interview respondent in Ciudad Juarez, Mexico, put it, "If I cannot go out with my family to a restaurant because of fear, of course I will not vote tomorrow."[40] Widespread violence may also make candidates and political parties less likely to campaign in dangerous areas, thus failing to mobilize some voters.[41] It is not clear which of these mechanisms best explain the relationship between violence and (non) voting, or whether violence has similar effects on voting in other countries. This remains an area for future research.

Despite all of these generalizations about how individual-level factors affect voting, there are significant variations by country. For instance, wealth is associated with higher rates of voting in some countries but not in others. The influence of individual-level variables depends on context. In particular, compulsory voting dampens the effects of individual-level variables because it incentivizes everyone to vote. Polarization between political parties also reduces the explanatory power of some individual factors like education and motivation, since party polarization reduces the amount of political information a citizen needs to distinguish one party from another and choose their preferred option.[42] In understanding voter participation, both individual-level and systemic contextual factors matter.

NOTES

1. Author's calculations based on data from International IDEA, "Voter Turnout Database," https://www.idea.int/data-tools/data/voter-turnout. By a slightly different measure—taking the average of each country's mean turnout rather than the average of turnout for all elections—turnout was 66.3 percent for the 1980s and 1990s and 69.4 percent for the 2000s–2010s.

2. Calculated from data from the American Presidency Project, "Voter Turnout in Presidential Elections," https://www.presidency.ucsb.edu/statistics/data/voter-turnout-in-presidential-elections.

3. André Blais, "What Affects Voter Turnout?" *Annual Review of Political Science* 9 (2006); Benny Geys, "Explaining Voter Turnout: A Review of Aggregate-Level Research," *Electoral Studies* 25, no. 4 (2006).

4. Carolina A. Fornos, Timothy J. Power, and James C. Garand, "Explaining Voter Turnout in Latin America, 1980 to 2000," *Comparative Political Studies* 37, no. 8 (2004); Miguel Carreras, "Presidential Institutions and Electoral Participation in Concurrent Elections in Latin America," *Political Studies* 66, no. 3 (2018); Tatiana Kostadinova and Timothy J. Power, "Does Democratization Depress Participation? Voter Turnout in the Latin American and Eastern European Transitional Democracies," *Political Research Quarterly* 60, no. 3 (2007).

5. Ibid.

6. Blais, "What Affects," 113–16.

7. Fornos, Power, and Garand, "Explaining Voter Turnout."

8. Carreras, "Presidential Institutions."

9. Fornos, Power, and Garand, "Explaining Voter Turnout"; Kostadinova and Power, "Does Democratization Depress Participation?"

10. IFES, "Election Guide: Republic of Guatemala," http://www.electionguide.org/countries/id/90/. This rule of thumb doesn't always apply, however. For example, in Peru in 2016, voter turnout was slightly higher in the second round of presidential voting than in the first round, even though congressional elections were held concurrently with the first round of presidential voting.

11. Carreras, "Presidential Institutions."

12. Ibid., 546.

13. Blais, "What Affects," 118.

14. André Blais and Agnieszka Dobrzynska, "Turnout in Electoral Democracies," *European Journal of Political Research* 33 (1998): 248–49.

15. Blais and Dobrzynska, "Turnout in Electoral Democracies."

16. Aníbal Pérez-Liñan, "Neoinstitutional Accounts of Voter Turnout: Moving beyond Industrial Democracies," *Electoral Studies* 20, no. 2 (2001); Fornos, Power, and Garand, "Explaining Voter Turnout."

17. Pérez-Liñan, "Neoinstitutional Accounts," 285.

18. Carreras, "Presidential Institutions."

19. Sergio Béjar, Juan A. Moraes, and Santiago López-Cariboni, "Elite Polarization and Voting Turnout in Latin America, 1993–2010," *Journal of Elections, Public Opinion and Parties* 30, no. 1 (2020).

20. Carreras, "Presidential Institutions"; Fornos, Power, and Garand, "Explaining Voter Turnout."

21. Blais, "What Affects."

22. International IDEA, "What Is Compulsory Voting?" https://www.idea.int/data-tools/data/voter-turnout/compulsory-voting.

23. Timothy J. Power, "Compulsory for Whom? Mandatory Voting and Electoral Participation in Brazil, 1986–2006," *Journal of Politics in Latin America* 1, no. 1 (2009): 98, note 2.

24. These arguments about the pros and cons of compulsory voting are discussed in Arend Lijphart, "Unequal Participation: Democracy's Unresolved Dilemma," *American Political Science Review* 91, no. 1 (1997); and Jason Brennan and Lisa Hill, *Compulsory Voting: For and Against* (New York: Cambridge University Press, 2014).

25. Miguel Carreras, "Compulsory Voting and Political Engagement (Beyond the Ballot Box): A Multilevel Analysis," *Electoral Studies* 43 (2016).

26. Gabriel Cepaluni and F. Daniel Hidalgo, "Compulsory Voting Can Increase Political Inequality: Evidence from Brazil," *Political Analysis* 24, no. 2 (2016).

27. Sidney Verba, Kay Lehman Schlozman, and Henry E. Brady, *Voice and Equality: Civic Voluntarism in American Politics* (Cambridge, MA: Harvard University Press, 1995).

28. Ryan E. Carlin and Gregory J. Love, "Who Is the Latin American Voter?" in *The Latin American Voter: Pursuing Representation and Accountability in Challenging Contexts*, ed. Ryan E. Carlin, Matthew M. Singer, and Elizabeth J. Zechmeister (Ann Arbor: University of Michigan Press, 2015); Miguel Carreras and Nestor Castañeda-Angarita, "Who Votes in Latin America? A Test of Three Theoretical Perspectives," *Comparative Political Studies* 47, no. 8 (2014).

29. Carlin and Love, "Latin American Voter."

30. Ibid., 36.

31. Carlin and Love, "Latin American Voter"; Carreras and Castañeda-Angarita, "Who Votes"; Agustina Haime, "What Explains Voter Turnout in Latin America? A Test of the Effect of Citizens' Attitudes towards the Electoral Process," *Revista de Ciencia Política* 37, no. 1 (2017).

32. Carreras and Castañeda-Angarita, "Who Votes."

33. Carlin and Love, "Latin American Voter."

34. Paulo Cox and Mauricio Morales, "The Chilean Turnout Gender Gap: Evidence from Administrative Census Data," *Acta Politica* 58, no. 2 (2023).

35. Carreras and Castañeda-Angarita, "Who Votes"; Carlin and Love, "Latin American Voter." Interestingly, while research on voting at the individual level often addresses the effect of partisan identification, research that investigates voter turnout across Latin American countries often doesn't consider the level of party identification as an explanatory variable.

36. Carreras and Castañeda-Angarita, "Who Votes"; Carlin and Love, "Latin American Voter."

37. James McCann and Jorge Domínguez, "Mexicans React to Electoral Fraud and Political Corruption: An Assessment of Public Opinion and Voting Behavior," *Electoral Studies* 17, no. 4 (1998); Miguel Carreras and Yasemin Irepoglu, "Trust in Elections, Vote Buying, and Turnout in Latin America," *Electoral Studies* 32, no. 4 (2013); Haime, "What Explains Voter Turnout."

38. Alejandro Trelles and Miguel Carreras, "Bullets and Votes: Violence and Electoral Participation in Mexico," *Journal of Politics in Latin America* 4, no. 2 (2012).

39. Sandra Ley, "To Vote or Not to Vote: How Criminal Violence Shapes Electoral Participation," *Journal of Conflict Resolution* 62, no. 9 (2018).

40. Quoted in Trelles and Carreras, "Bullets and Votes," 90.

41. Ibid., 99, 102.

42. Carlin and Love, "Latin American Voter," 51.

Chapter 9

Voter Behavior

Election outcomes determine which individuals and groups will govern, which programs or platforms will shape government policy, which road a country will take. But what determines election outcomes? More specifically, what explains the choices that voters make when they cast their ballots? How do myriad influences—from the characteristics of voters themselves to the campaign messages that they receive—affect voter decisions? And how well does voter behavior in Latin America conform to ideals of democratic accountability? These are perennial questions in the field of political behavior and the questions that we take up in this chapter.

The democratic ideal is that voters pay attention to public affairs and follow election campaigns closely, weigh the platforms of competing candidates, and make well-reasoned decisions in casting their ballots. Reality falls far short of this ideal, of course. Most people don't pay close attention to politics, so they often rely on decision-making shortcuts or heuristics (rules of thumb) in making their voting decisions. One goal of this chapter is to sort through the heuristics that voters use.

The chapter is organized around a set of factors that influence vote choice. It begins by examining the demographic features and group memberships that shape voting behavior. Voters may vote for the party with which they identify, which is often the party aligned with the social groups to which the voter belongs. The chapter then examines ideology and issue positions. To the extent that parties provide coherent and distinct ideologies or packages of policies to the electorate (and this varies greatly from country to country, as seen in chapter 5), voters can select the option that most closely corresponds with their own issue positions or ideology.

The chapter then explores the extent to which voters use their ballots to reward or punish the incumbent party based on how the country is doing, and especially how the economy is doing. This kind of retrospective economic voting represents a kind of heuristic for voters: if the country seems to be doing well, vote to reelect the people already in office; if the country isn't doing well, kick the bums out and elect someone new. We also consider how the messages from campaigns can influence voters, as well as the influence of the traits of individual candidates. Finally, we look at why some voters show up to the polls and decide to cast a blank or spoiled ballot rather than selecting a candidate or political party.[1]

Some heuristics on which voters rely suggest that democratic reality is far from the democratic ideal of reasoned deliberation. But as the most definitive study of voting behavior in Latin America concludes, "Latin American voters, on average, tend to vote for candidates they believe will best advocate for and represent their social group; vote for candidates with whom they share similar issue positions, party identities, and left-right orientations; and use their votes in an attempt to hold leaders accountable for their actions."[2]

VOTER IDENTITY: THE IMPACT OF DEMOGRAPHICS

A long tradition of political science research argues that voters identify with political parties and make voting decisions based on their membership in particular social groups, such as those of social class, religion, race, and so on. The most relevant political divides (or cleavages) in a country are often based around identity groups, such as the divide between Catholics and Protestants or between the upper classes and lower classes. As such, members of each group are likely to vote for the party that best represents their group.

Overall, demographic characteristics like ethnicity, gender, and social class have only modest effects on voting in Latin America. But the effects of demographic variables vary a lot by country. For example, while controlling for other variables, age is not correlated with vote choice in many countries, but older age is associated with voting for more left-wing candidates in some countries and with voting for more right-wing candidates in others.[3] Precisely because some demographic features have different effects in different countries, the overall effect looks small when analyzing data for Latin America as a whole. With this country-to-country variation in mind, across Latin America, there is a tendency for voters who are older, white, female, Catholic, and frequent churchgoers to be more likely to vote for conservative candidates.[4] This section takes a closer look at these and other factors.

Social Class

One demographic feature we would expect to affect voting decisions is social class, a concept that incorporates indicators such as income, wealth, and education. Well-off citizens might be expected to support candidates attuned to middle- and upper-class interests, while the working class and poor would prefer candidates that speak to their concerns. There is a relationship between household wealth and vote choice in some Latin American countries, including Argentina, Bolivia, and Venezuela, where those with less wealth tend to vote for left-of-center parties. This is to be expected: other things being equal, those less well-off tend to support candidates most likely to redistribute resources from the haves to the have-nots. Argentina's 2007 presidential election provides an example. In that contest, the leftist incumbent Cristina Fernández de Kirchner faced off against a more conservative opponent, Roberto Lavagna. The wealthiest voters were fifty-seven percentage points less likely to vote for Kirchner than the poorest voters.[5]

Yet in many other countries social class doesn't seem to influence vote choice at all. The reason for the difference seems to be the political-party system, and in particular whether there are viable left-wing parties or candidates that have a chance of winning. In countries like Venezuela and Bolivia that have been governed by left-wing populist presidents, there are strong class patterns to voting. But in many other countries electoral competition has not presented clear left-wing versus right-wing options, and social class has therefore been less salient to voters.[6]

Even in the case of Venezuela, class voting can take complex forms. One would expect that a candidate like Hugo Chávez, espousing rhetoric that denounced the corrupt oligarchy and presenting himself as the embodiment of poor and working-class Venezuelans, would be strongly supported by the poor and strongly opposed by the middle and upper classes. The reality was more complicated: Chávez voters were disproportionately poor in the 1998 election that won Chávez the presidency, but in subsequent elections Chávez won significant support from the middle classes while the very wealthiest Venezuelans most strongly opposed Chávez.[7] In sum, social class helps predict voting behavior in only some contexts in Latin America.

Gender

While the wealthy tend to vote for conservative parties in at least some Latin American countries, the same is true for women. Public opinion data shows that women are on average slightly more right-leaning than men in the region, and women with children and those who do not work outside the home tend to vote for conservative candidates at slightly higher rates. Women are also more likely to vote for female presidential candidates (as are younger voters).[8]

It is important to note that there is no relationship between gender and vote choice in many countries in the region.[9] Where women vote to the right of men, this is the opposite of the pattern found in the United States, where women lean to the left compared to men. One prevailing theory of the gender-ideology relationship focuses on changes in women's roles in postindustrial societies. As women increasingly enter the workforce and gain education, these experiences lead to changes in values, and women tend to become more liberal.[10] An implication of this theory is that as countries develop economically, the traditional difference in voting will disappear, and may actually reverse, with women on average becoming more progressive than men. For now, gender is not strongly related to voting for particular types of parties, but that may change over time as broader gender roles shift.

Religion

Religion also plays a modest role in voting in at least a handful of Latin American countries. There are two main religious cleavages in the region: between the devout and secular, and between Catholics and Protestants. While a majority of Latin Americans are Catholic, about 20 percent of Latin Americans were mainline Protestants or Evangelicals by 2014,[11] and that number has been growing. There are reasons to expect the relationship between religion and voting in the region to be complex. The Catholic Church has historically supported right-wing governments and conservative social values, including opposition to abortion and same-sex marriage, while at times advocating for policies and structural changes to help the poor, sometimes aligning with left-wing movements. The increasing prevalence of Protestantism and particularly Pentecostalism in recent decades further complicates the region's politico-religious landscape.

In one study on the topic, Taylor Boas and Amy Erica Smith find that non-religious persons are more likely to vote for leftist candidates, while frequent churchgoers are more likely to vote to the right—though the size of these effects depends on how programmatic and polarized political parties are in a given country. Non-religious voters are also more likely to vote for secular candidates than are religious voters. (Voters who are younger, more educated, and live in urban areas are also more likely to vote for secular candidates.) While Catholics and Protestants don't differ ideologically along a left-right spectrum, Protestants are more likely to vote for non-Catholic candidates than are Catholics.[12]

The relevance of evangelicalism to political behavior has risen in recent years as issues of same-sex marriage, gender identity, and the treatment of sexual orientation in school curricula have come onto the political agenda in some countries. For example, in Chile after same-sex civil unions were legalized, abortion was permitted under some circumstances, and bills related to transgender rights were introduced, evangelicals organized for the general election in 2017, with thirty-two evangelical candidates running for Congress (up from ten in the previous election).[13] In Costa Rica the following year, evangelical Christian singer Fabricio Alvarado led the first round of the presidential election. Alvarado won support from devout conservative Costa Ricans who were opposed to a recent ruling from the Inter-American Court of Human Rights declaring that Costa Rica was obligated to permit same-sex marriages, an issue that came to dominate the election. Post-election surveys indicated "that evangelicals were significantly more likely than those of other faiths to vote for Fabricio Alvarado."[14]

TEXT BOX 9.1: EVANGELICALS FOR BOLSONARO

Perhaps in no other Latin American country has evangelical political mobilization been as intense as in Brazil. Protestants and evangelicals make up as much as 30 percent of Brazil's population. In 1985 the leaders of the Pentecostal Assembly of God endorsed candidates running for the country's constituent assembly, using the slogan "Brother votes for Brother" (a message to church members to vote for their fellow co-religionists).[a] As a result, 33 evangelicals were elected to the constituent assembly, 14 of them from the Assembly of God. The influence of religion has been felt in electoral competition since then. In the 2010 and 2014 presidential elections, evangelical voters were more likely to support candidate Marina Silva, herself an evangelical, than were voters of other faiths.[b]

Brazil's 2018 presidential election highlighted the role of religious identity in the country's electoral politics. Right-wing populist candidate Jair Bolsonaro drew endorsements from evangelical and Pentecostal leaders, including Brazil's major televangelists.[c] Bolsonaro, a former army officer, is himself a Catholic, but his wife is evangelical and he had for years courted the support of the country's evangelical leaders. On a trip to the Middle East before the election, Bolsonaro was baptized in the Jordan River by a prominent Brazilian Pentecostal leader.[d]

His campaign discourse promoted traditional religious values. Bolsonaro gave voice to conservative evangelical hostility towards so-called gender ideology. During the campaign, "fallacious viral rumors circulated through WhatsApp messages in evangelical communities, accusing Bolsonaro's opponent Fernando Haddad of supporting sexual education programs that would manipulate young children to become gay or transgender."[e]

Bolsonaro himself has a history of making incendiary remarks against gays and lesbians, once declaring that he would rather have a dead son than a gay son.

Bolsonaro won the election with strong support from evangelicals. Religion and social values were not Bolsonaro's only appeal, as many voters hoped he would improve the country's economy and public security.[f] But polling and statistical analyses show that evangelicals supported Bolsonaro at a substantially higher rate than did Catholics,[g] highlighting the relevance of religious identity to voting behavior in contemporary Brazil.

[a] Chayenne Polimédio, "The Rise of the Brazilian Evangelicals," *The Atlantic*, January 24, 2018, https://www.theatlantic.com/international/archive/2018/01/the-evangelical-takeover-of-brazilian-politics/551423/.
[b] Boas, "Electoral Representation of Evangelicals."
[c] Catherine Osborn, "The Christian Coalition That Helped Elect Bolsonaro Has Started to Crumble," *Foreign Policy*, April 6, 2019, https://foreignpolicy.com/2019/04/06/the-christian-coalition-that-helped-elect-bolsonaro-has-started-to-crumble/.
[d] Polimédio, "Rise of the Brazilian Evangelicals."
[e] Amy Erica Smith, "For Latin America's Evangelicals, Bolsonaro Is Just the Start," *Americas Quarterly*, November 9, 2018, https://www.americasquarterly.org/article/for-latin-americas-evangelicals-bolsonaro-is-just-the-start/.
[f] Osborn, "The Christian Coalition."
[g] Smith, "Latin America's Evangelicals"; Oswaldo E. do Amaral, "The Victory of Jair Bolsonaro According to the Brazilian Electoral Study of 2018," *Brazilian Political Science Review* 14, no. 1 (2020), https://doi.org/10.1590/1981-3821202000010004.

Ethnicity

A final demographic factor that must be considered is ethnicity or race. Around the world ethnicity is often associated with party loyalties and voting behavior, and one might expect that in Latin America's diverse societies, ethnic identity would map onto political identity and behavior. The region has a large population of indigenous peoples holding distinct identities, along with large populations identifying as white or mestizo (mixed ancestry). Indigenous peoples make up a majority of the population in Bolivia and large minorities in Guatemala, Ecuador, Mexico, and Peru. Some Latin American countries also have large black or Afrodescendant populations, especially the Dominican Republic and Brazil.

Historically the main cleavages in Latin American politics were thought to be based around social class rather than race or ethnicity, despite the fact that indigenous and black Latin Americans have faced discrimination and marginalization both politically and economically. But in the 1990s and 2000s, a number of influential movements of indigenous peoples mobilized politically, bringing ethnic identity to the forefront of politics in some countries in the region. This was most visible in the creation of an indigenous-based political party in Ecuador and the election of Evo Morales as Bolivia's first indigenous president. Brazil has also seen the emergence of a black identity movement since the 1980s that has sought to address racial discrimination.

Does this mean that indigenous and black Latin Americans tend to have voting patterns that are distinct from white and mestizo voters? The evidence is mixed. One study has found that race (broadly defined) has a substantial effect on vote choice in nearly half the countries in the region, and its relationship with voting is strongest in countries with large non-white populations such as Bolivia, Brazil, and Guatemala.[15] Another study finds that ethnic identity has little relationship with voting for left-wing or right-wing parties, except in Bolivia, where indigenous people were much more likely than non-indigenous to vote for (leftist) Evo Morales.[16] This evidence suggests that in most countries ethnicity is not a particularly salient political identity that helps predict voting behavior; the biggest exception is Bolivia, where an indigenous candidate came to power leading a predominantly indigenous social movement.

Race also appears to have some effect on voting in Brazil, a country with a historical myth of being a "racial democracy" free of racial discrimination but a reality of deep racial inequalities.[17] Racial identity in Brazil, as elsewhere, is fluid rather than being a fixed attribute based strictly on skin color. A majority of Brazilians has some African ancestry, and a slight majority self-identify as mixed-race or black.[18] Yet elected officials are disproportionately white. At least some Afro-Brazilian candidates for Congress employ racial cues and black cultural symbols in their campaign messages to target Afro-Brazilian voters.[19] Experimental evidence shows that self-identified black Brazilians tend to prefer black candidates, while white Brazilians tend to prefer white candidates when faced with a long ballot with many candidates (seemingly using race as a decision-making shortcut when presented with many options).[20] This evidence shows that under some conditions, ethnic and racial identity influences vote choice in Latin America.

PARTISANSHIP

Perhaps the most obvious factor affecting vote choice is partisan identification. A voter who identifies with a particular political party will almost always vote for that party's candidates. Moreover, core supporters of a party are unlikely to be persuaded by new information or evidence that their preferred party has performed poorly in office. This is because a psychological attachment to a party can be an important part of a person's social identity. It is often acquired by early adulthood through a process of socialization and is thus difficult to change.

Yet there is reason to doubt that partisanship operates the same way in Latin America or other regions as it does in the older democracies in Europe and the United States. In newer democracies, electoral competition may be slow to produce institutionalized political parties with clear platforms and governing track records. While in some countries old political parties emerged after periods of authoritarianism, and some voters retained their old party loyalties, this did not happen everywhere.[21] Also, as democracy emerged or reemerged in Latin American countries in the late twentieth century, politicians could appeal to voters directly via television rather than through building political party organizations or emphasizing their party ties. Thus voters might be more prone to make vote choices based on the personal characteristics of candidates rather than party labels.

Despite the fluidity of many political party systems in the region, there is indeed a strong association between partisanship and voting in Latin America. Examining survey data, Noam Lupu finds that an average of 69 percent of people in the region who identify with a party report having voted for that party in the most recent election.[22] A multivariate analysis of elections across Latin America shows that party identification is the single strongest predictor of how an individual votes.[23] Importantly though, the strength of the relationship between partisan identification and vote choice varies a lot by country, with the influence of partisanship being reduced in countries with highly fragmented party systems (i.e., countries with a large number of political parties). In sum, Latin Americans who strongly identify with a political party usually vote for that party, as expected. But the prevalence and strength of partisan identification varies across countries, as does the strength of the relationship between partisanship and voting behavior.

ISSUES AND IDEOLOGY

In some models of vote choice, voters choose candidates that are closest to their views on prominent policy issues. The most salient issues to voters might include the economy, crime, corruption, social policy, or social and moral issues like abortion and same-sex marriage. In casting their ballots, voters would take into account where candidates stand on the issues most important to them. But for this to occur, voters must hold clear opinions on at least some issues and be able to discern where candidates stand on those issues. This requires voters to be at least somewhat attentive to politics. It is made more difficult by the fact that candidates are often ambiguous on where they stand on the issues. (In a context of strong party identification, that identification also influences people's issue positions: people tend to adopt the issue positions of their preferred party.)

Related to issue positions is ideology. Even if most voters don't have the time or inclination to research where all of the candidates stand on the issues, and if campaigns don't offer clear policy proposals, voters can rely on their general ideological leanings to choose candidates and parties that are most likely to implement policies that the voter likes. Ideological labels like "left" and "right" (or "progressive" and "conservative") can serve as markers for voters. "Rather than communicate a profuse number of policy stances to the partially tuned in average citizen, a politician can efficiently convey her or his stance in the political space by claiming to be 'on the left' or 'on the right.'"[24] Thus voters who think of themselves as more left-wing might vote for leftist parties, right-wing voters will vote for parties on the right, and moderates will opt for centrist parties. That is, at least if candidates and parties are sufficiently distinct to be placed on an ideological spectrum.

Some observers of Latin American politics have doubted that voters in the region base their vote choice on ideology or policy issues, given the region's unstable party systems and the failure of parties to espouse clear ideological positions or governing programs. Instead, in this view, voters choose candidates based on their personal characteristics and on clientelism—candidates offering material incentives to voters in exchange for their support.[25] So, do voters in Latin America take policy issue positions into account when making their vote choice? Does ideology influence vote choice?

The answer is a qualified "yes." Andy Baker and Kenneth Greene find that voters' positions on economic issues are correlated with their vote choice in most countries in the region.[26] (Less is known about issue voting regarding other policy areas.) A number of studies also find that voters' self-placement on a left–right spectrum tends to correspond to their vote choice.[27] This might seem obvious: conservative voters will tend to vote for conservative candidates, while liberals and progressives will vote for left-leaning candidates. But several big caveats apply: there is variation across Latin American countries in how many people identify themselves on a left–right scale, how those placements relate to people's policy stances, and how strongly ideological placement predicts vote choice. In many countries in the region, left–right identification doesn't correspond to individuals' views on economic issues. For example, someone who considers herself right-of-center doesn't necessarily hold economic views that correspond to the typical conservative free-market views. The relationship between a voter's self-identified ideology and the ideology of the candidate that person votes for also varies drastically by country; in some cases, such as Ecuador, ideological self-placement doesn't predict vote choice at all.

This points to the conclusion that context matters a lot for understanding the role of ideology and issues. Both issue positions and ideology are more strongly associated with vote choice in countries in the region where political parties are more programmatic and polarized.[28] In other words, where parties and candidates stake out clearly distinct positions on issues, and the gap between those positions is large, voters' ideology and opinions on policy issues more strongly influence their vote choice. Thus in countries where the major parties are polarized, as in El Salvador in the years after democratic transition, or where a leftist populist leader is in power, as in Venezuela and Bolivia during the 2000s–2010s, ideology provides voters a stronger signal of where they stand. The same is true in Brazil, where Jair Bolsonaro's candidacy in 2018 polarized the electorate. Studies find that voters' ideology—particularly conservativism, illiberal attitudes, and authoritarian inclinations—was strongly correlated with support for Bolsonaro.[29]

Polarization has many downsides, such as conflict, gridlock, and the potential for wild swings in policy following each election. But the complete absence of polarization has costs as well. Where competing parties don't offer voters distinct policy options, voters are left without a meaningful choice, and elected governments have no clear mandate from the people to implement a specific set of policies.[30] In these circumstances, the best voters can do is to judge the performance of previous governments when making their choice.

RETROSPECTIVE VOTING

Aside from demographics, ideology, and partisan identification, voters also rely on the past performance of the person or party in power when deciding whether or not to support them for reelection. Such retrospective voting allows voters to "throw the bums out" if the country is not doing well, enabling a degree of democratic accountability. In this view, as political scientist V. O. Key famously put it, the electorate acts as a "rational god of vengeance and of reward."[31]

Economic Voting

The issue on which voters most commonly judge incumbents is the economy, rewarding incumbents when the economy is doing well and punishing them when economic conditions are poor. Studies from voting around the world find strong evidence for such retrospective economic voting. One need not look far to find examples in Latin America. In Peru, President Alberto Fujimori was reelected in 1995 after the country experienced rapid economic growth during his first term. Similarly, President Carlos Menem in Argentina won a second term after bringing high inflation under control during his first term. In Brazil, Fernando Henrique Cardoso was chosen as his party's presidential candidate in 1994 because of his success in taming inflation during his tenure as finance minister.[32] In contrast, Argentina's president Mauricio Macri lost his bid for reelection in 2019 after the country experienced a recession during his first term.

The economy is just one area that voters might focus on in evaluating the performance of incumbents. They might also consider the quality of schools and hospitals, foreign relations, and any corruption scandals that have emerged during the incumbent's time in office. While these other issues matter, the economy is an important issue to almost all voters, and they tend to hold the government responsible for economic performance. Survey data from Latin America has shown that economic issues rank at the top of issues that people consider the biggest problem facing their country almost 90 percent of the time.[33] Thus retrospective voting often takes the form of economic voting, using economic conditions to inform one's vote for or against the incumbent party.

Economic voting and other forms of retrospective voting can take two forms: a voter can base their vote on their assessment of the country's economy (sociotropic voting) or on their personal economic situation (egotropic, or pocketbook voting). Sociotropic economic voting is thought to be more common, although there is evidence of pocketbook voting in Latin America as well.

Evidence for economic voting comes from analyses at both the aggregate and individual levels. At the aggregate level, incumbents lose votes when they oversee a deteriorating economic situation. The primary economic condition that affected voters' decisions in the 1980s and 1990s was inflation, as many countries in the region grappled with soaring inflation that devastated people's incomes and economic stability.[34] Incumbent presidents that reduced inflation, like Carlos Menem in Argentina, won reelection, while incumbent presidents who failed to control inflation (e.g., in Bolivia and Venezuela) lost public support. From the late 1990s onward, as Latin American countries had lowered inflation but struggled to jump-start economic growth and rising incomes, growth became associated with incumbent performance. In the 2000s, economic growth was correlated with incumbent gains, while inflation had receded as a concern for voters.[35]

These aggregate patterns are supported by evidence at the individual level. Analyses of survey data find that Latin Americans who have positive perceptions of the state of the economy are much more likely to support the incumbent party.[36] By one estimate, individuals with a positive view of the economy are 13 percent more likely to vote for the incumbent than are those with a negative view of the economy, even when controlling for other factors.[37] Some research also finds evidence of pocketbook voting: among voters who voted for the incumbent in the previous election, those who report that their household income decreased in the last two years are more likely to say that they intend to vote for someone other than the incumbent in the next election.[38]

Some contextual factors affect the prevalence of retrospective economic voting. The effect of economic perceptions on vote choice is stronger when the president's party holds more seats in the legislature and when party polarization is higher.[39] Under these circumstances, voters seem to hold the president more accountable for the economy. It also appears that incumbents are rewarded more for good economic performance (and punished more severely for bad performance) when they break their campaign promises on economic policy. Especially in the 1980s and 1990s, some prominent Latin American presidents campaigned on anti-neoliberal platforms—promising not to implement free-market reforms that were ascendant throughout the region—only to renege on those promises once in office. Those who subsequently governed over good economic times (like Menem in Argentina) were rewarded by voters despite breaking their campaign promises; those who subsequently governed over a crumbling economy, like President Carlos Andrés Pérez in Venezuela after his 1988 election, saw their popularity plummet.[40] Finally, while incumbent presidents running for reelection benefit from a good economy, their political parties don't seem to benefit electorally from economic growth when the incumbent president leaves office because of term limits.[41] It seems that Latin American voters reward individual incumbents but not necessarily their political parties.

The Electoral Effects of Conditional Cash Transfer Programs

Beginning in the 1990s and accelerating in the 2000s, most Latin American countries introduced conditional cash transfer (CCT) programs. CCTs are a type of welfare program that disburses cash payments to poor households that meet certain conditions, including keeping their children in school and taking them for regular health checkups. Since their early introduction in Mexico and Brazil, CCTs have become a popular anti-poverty tool around the world and have been praised for raising the incomes of poor families, boosting school attendance, and reducing child labor.[42]

The electoral effects of CCT programs have been the subject of interest among scholars of voting behavior. CCT programs are sometimes thought of as a form of clientelism, in which officeholders use cash handouts to win political support (and threaten to withdraw benefits from those recipients who don't live up to their end of the bargain). In many countries in Latin America, however, CCTs have strict rules for who is entitled to benefits;

therefore, politicians cannot exclude eligible recipients from benefits if they fail to demonstrate political loyalty. Indeed, this apolitical design of CCT programs is one of their appealing features. Thus in many cases any electoral impact of CCT programs is best thought of in terms of retrospective voting: voters rewarding candidates who have improved their economic conditions.[43]

CCTs might have especially beneficial consequences for the incumbent politicians who oversee the programs because they provide direct benefits to recipients, which are more immediate and connected to government policy than are public goods like economic growth and low inflation.[44] A number of studies of individual countries—Brazil, Mexico, Honduras, and Uruguay—have found that CCT programs benefit incumbents electorally, in some cases showing that CCT beneficiaries vote for incumbents at higher rates than non-recipients.[45]

Brazil is a paradigmatic case. The country has the world's most well-known CCT program, Bolsa Família (renamed Auxilio Brasil in 2021). The program was most strongly associated with President Lula da Silva, who consolidated several preexisting CCT programs into one program and greatly expanded it during his first term in office. In 2006, Lula won reelection with strong support from lower income Brazilians and the poorer north and northeast regions of the country, reversing the pattern of his previous election where his strongest base of support was among more educated Brazilians and in the south and southeast. Lula's approval rate among the affluent declined following corruption scandals that surfaced during his first term in office, whereas among the poor his popularity suffered little. Less economically secure Brazilians may have been more willing to forgive corruption because Lula's government delivered valuable programs to them. Lula's reelection bid benefited from a strong economy, but policies like Bolsa Família also seemed to help him politically, with states with more Bolsa Família recipients tending to swing more strongly in Lula's favor in the 2006 election.[46] Ironically, as Lula ran for election again in 2022, his opponent Jair Bolsonaro, the incumbent president, boosted spending on social programs with an eye to winning over more voters.

Not all research finds that CCT programs increase vote shares for incumbents. Statistical analyses across Latin American countries come to conflicting conclusions about these programs' electoral effects.[47] But the bulk of research on CCTs suggests that incumbents benefit by overseeing CCT programs, not only by winning the support of some beneficiaries (who seem to engage in retrospective voting) but also by mobilizing turnout among program recipients who become more motivated or incentivized to vote as a consequence of receiving CCT benefits.[48]

Crime, Corruption, and Voting

Aside from the economy and social welfare programs, voters might engage in retrospective voting by judging incumbents on their performance in other policy areas as well. One particularly relevant policy area in Latin America is crime. Many countries in the region suffer high homicide rates, and drug trafficking and street gangs are prevalent in many countries, especially Mexico, Colombia, Brazil, and the Northern Triangle countries of Central America (El Salvador, Guatemala, and Honduras).

Some evidence suggests that voters take crime levels into account when casting their ballots. In one analysis of survey data, feeling less secure in one's neighborhood was associated with a lower probability of voting for the incumbent party, but only in a handful of countries in the region. However, being a victim of crime in the previous year had no effect on the likelihood of voting for the incumbent.[49] Another analysis found that voters who more positively evaluate the incumbent's efforts in fighting crime are more likely to vote for the incumbent,[50] although it is important to note that one's evaluation of the incumbent's crime-fighting performance is likely influenced by the person's preexisting support for that incumbent. Despite high levels of crime found in many countries in Latin America, the jury is still out on how much voters weigh the incumbent party's performance in controlling crime when making their voting decision.

Equally murky is the relationship between corruption and voting behavior. Some evidence shows that voters punish incumbents for corruption. Presidential approval and voters' intention to vote for the incumbent president's party are negatively affected by perceptions of corruption, especially when economic conditions are poor.[51] And research shows that the vote share for incumbent mayors in Brazil is affected by information about corruption.[52] Yet voters don't always punish incumbents who engage in corrupt behavior. There are several possible explanations for this. First, voters may be willing to tolerate corruption if an incumbent delivers other goods, such as economic growth— a sentiment captured in the well-known Brazilian saying, "rouba mas faz" (he steals but gets things done). To revisit Brazilian mayors, incumbents facing accusations of corruption routinely get reelected, and evidence shows that while corruption lowers their vote share, this is offset by high public expenditures on public goods for their constituents.[53] Second, voters may lack credible information about corruption, or they may rationalize corrupt behavior of their preferred political party or candidate.[54] Voters seem more willing to punish corruption by voting against corrupt incumbents when there is an alternative party or candidate with which the voter feels ideologically aligned.[55] As with crime, it is still an open question how much (and under what conditions) accusations of corruption affect voting decisions in Latin America.

CAMPAIGN EFFECTS AND CANDIDATE TRAITS

Demographics, partisanship, and retrospective evaluations of the incumbent can all influence a voter's decision. But apart from these individual traits and assessments is a big factor that seeks to sway voters' choices: the election campaign. Campaigns can move voters from being undecided to supporting one candidate or party. In some cases, they can even shift voters from supporting one candidate to supporting a different one.

One way these so-called campaign effects work is through priming, whereby candidates focus their messages on issues or traits on which they have an advantage over their opponents. If a candidate can successfully make those issues or traits the most salient of the election, voters will give them more weight when making their decisions—and the candidate has a better chance of winning. For instance, an incumbent running for reelection in a context of strong economic growth will likely emphasize the economy in their campaign advertising and speeches, hoping that voters will focus on the economy and, engaging in retrospective voting, vote for the incumbent. In contrast, the incumbent's opponents would attempt to prime non-economic issues that are less favorable for the incumbent—perhaps a corruption scandal involving the incumbent's administration.

Campaign effects can also take the form of persuasion, whereby a candidate is able to convince some voters to adopt their positions on particular issues (e.g., to support free trade or a particular health care policy), thereby winning their votes.[56] Persuasion represents a greater degree of campaign influence than priming, as it entails not just prompting people to think about an issue but also shifting what people think about that issue.

But how much do campaigns really matter for voting decisions? Not a lot is known about the magnitude of campaign effects in Latin America, but the few studies on the subject find substantial effects. In Mexico's 2006 presidential election, surveys showed that over one-third of the electorate changed their vote choice at least once during the campaign, and an estimated 20 percent of voters were persuaded by campaign messages, which especially influenced voters' perceptions of the competence of the competing candidates.[57] Studies also find that campaign effects may very well have shifted the outcome of Argentina's 2015 presidential election and the pivotal plebiscite election in Chile in 1988 that began the country's democratic transition.[58] In at least some elections, many voters' decisions have been swayed by campaign messages, highlighting the importance of taking campaign effects into account when explaining voter behavior in the region.

Not only might voters be swayed by candidates' campaigns; they can also be influenced in myriad ways by candidates themselves—their personality, charisma, physical appearance, age, experience, ethnicity, gender, and so on.

Survey experiments in Brazil, for instance, show that voters can be swayed by heuristics like candidate occupation and religion, with voter choice being affected when municipal candidate names on the ballot are preceded by the labels "Doctor" or "Pastor."[59]

It can be difficult to predict how certain candidate traits will influence voters. But one robust research finding from around the world—including Mexico and Brazil—is that physically attractive candidates outperform less attractive opponents. When studies show people photos of unknown candidates from various elections and ask which candidates would make better elected officials, people choose the photos of the actual election winners at a rate that is well above chance. This is consistent with findings in psychology that show that people often make snap judgments of people's character and ability based on their physical appearance. This is especially so in elections in which voters lack information, such as down ballot races for lower offices and races with lots of candidates.[60]

CASTING NULL AND BLANK BALLOTS

The importance of which candidates and political parties people vote for is obvious: those choices determine who holds power. But some voters show up to vote on election day and cast a ballot that doesn't count toward any candidate or party. These so-called invalid votes come in two forms: the voter leaves the ballot blank or spoils the ballot (intentionally or unintentionally) by marking it incorrectly.

Such invalid ballots are far from an anomaly in Latin America. As figure 9.1 shows, a sizable proportion of votes cast in the region are invalid. In legislative elections since 1990, approximately 9 percent of ballots have been invalid on average; in presidential elections invalid ballots account for a bit less than 5 percent of votes. Such ballots often outnumber the votes cast for small political parties, and "the proportion of blank and spoiled ballots was larger than the winning candidate's margin of victory in 70 percent of first- or single-round presidential elections in the region between 2000 and 2014."[61] Some countries in the region even have rules in place to nullify an election if invalid votes make up a majority of all votes cast, although that has not happened in practice.

What causes a voter to take the time to show up at a polling place, wait in line, and then cast an invalid vote? Some invalid votes likely reflect simple mistakes on the voter's part, for instance, by marking several candidates from different political parties in a legislative election when only one candidate selection is allowed. But quite a bit of invalid voting is intentional, as shown by the fact that when asked by pollsters, many Latin Americans report having

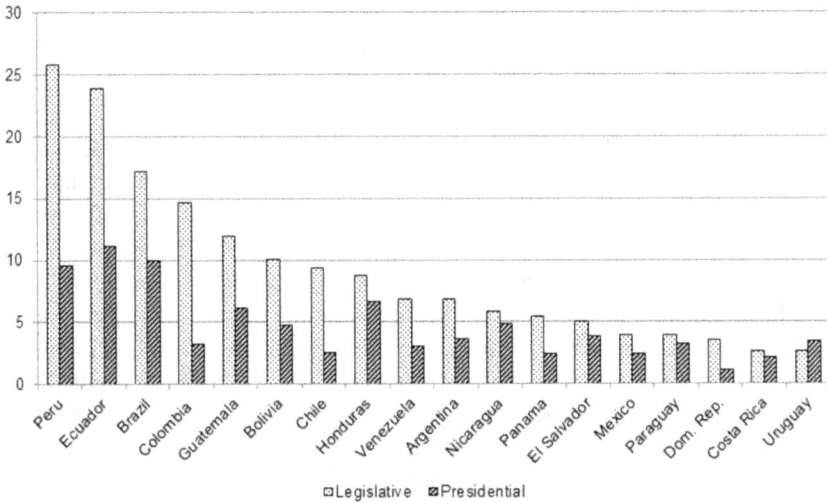

Figure 9.1 **Invalid Votes as Percentage of All Votes, 1990–2020.** *Source*: Based on data from International IDEA, Voter Turnout Database, https://www.idea.int/data-tools/data/voter-turnout. *Note*: Calculated as an unweighted average of invalid votes from all elections.

cast a blank or spoiled ballot.[62] Explanations for intentional blank and null voting include a lack of information about the candidates on the voter's part, disinterest in politics or the election, and a voter's desire to send a signal of protest and their disenchantment with the political system. Disinterest may be an especially strong explanation of invalid voting in countries with compulsory voting, where citizens with little intrinsic motivation to vote are compelled to turn out and cast a ballot.[63]

Relatively little is known about the underlying motivations of voters who intentionally cast blank and spoiled ballots. At the aggregate level, compulsory voting is associated with more invalid voting. In elections for members of a constituent assembly in Chile in 2023, for instance, public interest was low but voting was mandatory. As a consequence, more than 20 percent of ballots cast were spoiled or blank.[64] Where open-list proportional representation is combined with high district magnitude—a circumstance where voters are presented with a complex ballot with many candidates to choose from—invalid voting increases.[65] In Brazil, for example, elections to the Chamber of Deputies (the lower house of Congress) use open-list proportional representation and see high levels of invalid voting, whereas Senate elections use single-member districts and invalid voting is less common.[66]

At the individual level, voters who report casting an invalid ballot tend to have less interest in politics and less satisfaction with the performance of their government, and these attitudes are more strongly associated with invalid voting in countries with compulsory voting. However, those casting invalid ballots are not more likely to reject democracy or their country's political institutions than are voters who cast a valid ballot.[67]

A combination of these influences can be seen in Bolivia's 2011 election of judges, in which a staggering 60 percent of ballots were blank or spoiled. The election was held under compulsory voting in a context of low information for voters. Candidates were not allowed to campaign or to have an affiliation with a political party; instead, the country's electoral management body provided standardized information about the candidates to voters. Supporters of incumbent president Evo Morales and his Movement toward Socialism (MAS) party were much less likely to report casting a blank or spoiled ballot than were voters who didn't support Morales or MAS. Thus a structural explanation—compulsory voting—certainly contributed to the massive level of invalid voting, as did the informational and attitudinal explanations. Being required to vote under compulsory voting, lacking the hype of a presidential or even legislative campaign, and possessing little information about the candidates, most voters chose to cast an invalid ballot. And those with little sympathy for the governing party did so in greater numbers than the party's supporters.[68]

Wherever elections are fair, voters ultimately decide who will govern. Many factors, both personal and contextual, influence how voters decide. And as blank and spoiled ballots show, sometimes voters use their ballot to send the message that they are fed up with the status quo and seek what democracy never ceases to promise: change.

NOTES

1. Another potential influence on voting behavior, vote buying, is covered in chapter 2.

2. Ryan E. Carlin, Matthew M. Singer, and Elizabeth J. Zechmeister, "Conclusion," in *The Latin American Voter: Pursuing Representation and Accountability in Challenging Contexts*, ed. Ryan E. Carlin, Matthew M. Singer, and Elizabeth J. Zechmeister (Ann Arbor: University of Michigan Press, 2015), 351.

3. Richard Nadeau, Éric Bélanger, Michael S. Lewis-Beck, Matthieu Turgeon, and François Gélineau, *Latin American Elections: Choice and Change* (Ann Arbor: University of Michigan Press, 2017), 40.

4. Nadeau et al., *Latin American Elections*.

5. Scott Mainwaring, Mariano Torcal, and Nicolás M. Somma, "The Left and the Mobilization of Class Voting in Latin America," in *The Latin American Voter: Pursuing Representation and Accountability in Challenging Contexts*, ed. Ryan E.

Carlin, Matthew M. Singer, and Elizabeth J. Zechmeister (Ann Arbor: University of Michigan Press, 2015), 78.

6. Mainwaring, Torcal, and Somma, "The Left and the Mobilization"; Nadeau et al., *Latin American Elections*.

7. Noam Lupu, "Who Votes for Chavismo? Class Voting in Hugo Chávez's Venezuela," *Latin American Research Review* 45, no. 1 (2010), doi:10.1353/lar.0.0083.

8. Jana Morgan, "Gender and the Latin American Voter," in *The Latin American Voter: Pursuing Representation and Accountability in Challenging Contexts*, ed. Ryan E. Carlin, Matthew M. Singer, and Elizabeth J. Zechmeister (Ann Arbor: University of Michigan Press, 2015).

9. Nadeau et al., *Latin American Elections*, 41.

10. Ronald Inglehart and Pippa Norris, "The Developmental Theory of the Gender Gap: Women's and Men's Voting Behavior in Global Perspective," *International Political Science Review* 21, no. 4 (2000), https://doi.org/10.1177/0192512100214007.

11. Pew Research Center, "Religion in Latin America: Widespread Change in a Historically Catholic Region," November 13, 2014, https://www.pewforum.org/2014/11/13/religion-in-latin-america/.

12. Taylor Boas and Amy Erica Smith, "Religion and the Latin American Voter," in *The Latin American Voter: Pursuing Representation and Accountability in Challenging Contexts*, ed. Ryan E. Carlin, Matthew M. Singer, and Elizabeth J. Zechmeister (Ann Arbor: University of Michigan Press, 2015).

13. Taylor C. Boas, "The Electoral Representation of Evangelicals in Latin America," *Oxford Research Encyclopedia of Politics* (2020), https://oxfordre.com/politics/view/10.1093/acrefore/9780190228637.001.0001/acrefore-9780190228637-e-1748.

14. Ibid. Alvarado went on to lose the second-round runoff election.

15. Nadeau et al., *Latin American Elections*, 42.

16. Daniel E. Moreno Morales, "Ethnicity and Electoral Preferences in Latin America," in *The Latin American Voter: Pursuing Representation and Accountability in Challenging Contexts*, ed. Ryan E. Carlin, Matthew M. Singer, and Elizabeth J. Zechmeister (Ann Arbor: University of Michigan Press, 2015).

17. Edward E. Telles, *Race in Another America: The Significance of Skin Color in Brazil* (Princeton: Princeton University Press, 2004).

18. BBC News, "Brazil 2010 Census Shows Changing Race Balance," November 17, 2011, https://www.bbc.com/news/world-latin-america-15766840.

19. Gladys Lanier Mitchell, "Campaign Strategies of Afro-Brazilian Politicians: A Preliminary Analysis," *Latin American Politics and Society* 51, no. 3 (2009), https://doi.org/10.1111/j.1548-2456.2009.00058.x.

20. Rosario Aguilar, Saul Cunow, Scott Desposato, and Leonardo Sangali Barone, "Ballot Structure, Candidate Race, and Vote Choice in Brazil," *Latin American Research Review* 50, no. 3 (2015), doi:10.1353/lar.2015.0044.

21. Nadeau et al., *Latin American Elections*, 66.

22. Noam Lupu, "Partisanship in Latin America," in *The Latin American Voter: Pursuing Representation and Accountability in Challenging Contexts*, ed. Ryan E. Carlin, Matthew M. Singer, and Elizabeth J. Zechmeister (Ann Arbor: University of Michigan Press, 2015), 238.

23. Nadeau et al., *Latin American Elections*.

24. Elizabeth Zechmeister, "Left-Right Identifications and the Latin American Voter," in *The Latin American Voter: Pursuing Representation and Accountability in Challenging Contexts*, ed. Ryan E. Carlin, Matthew M. Singer, and Elizabeth J. Zechmeister (Ann Arbor: University of Michigan Press, 2015), 195.

25. See Matthew Singer, "Elite Polarization and the Electoral Impact of Left-Right Placements: Evidence from Latin America, 1995–2009," *Latin American Research Review* 51, no. 2 (2016): 174, doi:10.1353/lar.2016.0022.

26. Andy Baker and Kenneth F. Greene, "Positional Issue Voting in Latin America," in *The Latin American Voter: Pursuing Representation and Accountability in Challenging Contexts*, ed. Ryan E. Carlin, Matthew M. Singer, and Elizabeth J. Zechmeister (Ann Arbor: University of Michigan Press, 2015).

27. Nadeau et al., *Latin American Elections*; Singer, "Elite Polarization"; Zechmeister, "Left-Right Identifications."

28. Baker and Greene, "Positional Issue Voting"; Zechmeister, "Left-Right Identifications"; Nadeau et al., *Latin American Elections*; Singer, "Elite Polarization."

29. Robert Vidigal, "Authoritarianism and Right-Wing Voting in Brazil," *Latin American Research Review* 57, no. 3 (2022), doi:10.1017/lar.2022.32; Lucio R. Rennó, "The Bolsonaro Voter: Issue Positions and Vote Choice in the 2018 Brazilian Presidential Elections," *Latin American Politics and Society* 62, no. 4 (2020), doi:10.1017/lap.2020.13; Bruno Castanho Silva, Mario Fuks, and Eduardo Ryô Tamaki, "So Thin It's Almost Invisible: Populist Attitudes and Voting Behavior in Brazil," *Electoral Studies* 75 (2022), https://doi.org/10.1016/j.electstud.2021.102434.

30. See Singer, "Elite Polarization," 175.

31. V. O. Key Jr., *Politics, Parties, and Pressure Groups*, 5th edition (New York: Thomas Crowell, 1964), 568.

32. Taylor C. Boas, *Presidential Campaigns in Latin America: Electoral Strategies and Success Contagion* (New York: Cambridge University Press, 2016), 98.

33. Matthew M. Singer, "Economic Voting in an Era of Non-Crisis: The Changing Electoral Agenda in Latin America, 1982–2010," *Comparative Politics* 45, no. 2 (2013): 174, https://www.jstor.org/stable/41714181.

34. Karen L. Remmer, "The Political Impact of Economic Crisis in Latin America in the 1980s," *American Political Science Review* 85, no. 3 (1991), doi:10.2307/1963850; Fabián Echegaray, *Economic Crises and Electoral Responses in Latin America* (Lanham: University Press of America, 2005).

35. Singer, "Economic Voting."

36. Francois Gélineau and Matthew M. Singer, "The Economy and Incumbent Support in Latin America," in *The Latin American Voter: Pursuing Representation and Accountability in Challenging Contexts*, ed. Ryan E. Carlin, Matthew M. Singer, and Elizabeth J. Zechmeister (Ann Arbor: University of Michigan Press, 2015); Michael S. Lewis-Beck and Maria Celeste Ratto, "Economic Voting in Latin America: A General Model," *Electoral Studies* 32, no. 3 (2013).

37. Nadeau et al., *Latin American Elections*, 94.

38. M. Victoria Murillo and Giancarlo Visconti, "Economic Performance and Incumbents' Support in Latin America," *Electoral Studies* 45 (2017), https://doi.org/10.1016/j.electstud.2016.10.007.

39. Gélineau and Singer, "The Economy and Incumbent Support."

40. Gregg B. Johnson and Sooh-Rhee Ryu, "Repudiating or Rewarding Neoliberalism? How Broken Campaign Promises Condition Economic Voting in Latin America," *Latin American Politics and Society* 52, no. 4 (2010), doi:10.1111/j.1548-2456.2010.00096.x. In the case of Andrés Pérez, he faced two military coup attempts and was ultimately removed from office through impeachment.

41. Melody E. Valdini and Michael S. Lewis-Beck, "Economic Voting in Latin America: Rules and Responsibility," *American Journal of Political Science* 62, no. 2 (2018), https://doi.org/10.1111/ajps.12339.

42. For a review of CCTs in Latin America, see Alberto Díaz-Cayeros and Beatriz Magaloni, "Aiding Latin America's Poor," *Journal of Democracy* 20, no. 4 (2009), http://doi.org/10.1353/jod.0.0115.

43. Nara Pavão, "Conditional Cash Transfer Programs and Electoral Accountability: Evidence from Latin America," *Latin American Politics and Society* 58, no. 2 (2016): 77, doi:10.1111/j.1548-2456.2016.00311.x.

44. Matthew L. Layton and Amy Erica Smith, "Incorporating Marginal Citizens and Voters: The Conditional Electoral Effects of Targeted Social Assistance in Latin America," *Comparative Political Studies* 48, no. 7 (2015), https://doi.org/10.1177/0010414014565889.

45. Ana L. De la O, "Do Conditional Cash Transfers Affect Electoral Behavior? Evidence from a Randomized Experiment in Mexico," *American Journal of Political Science* 57, no. 1 (2013), https://doi.org/10.1111/j.1540-5907.2012.00617.x; Elizabeth Linos, "Do Conditional Cash Transfer Programs Shift Votes? Evidence from the Honduran PRAF," *Electoral Studies* 32, no. 4 (2013), https://doi.org/10.1016/j.electstud.2013.03.007; Cesar Zucco, "When Payouts Pay Off: Conditional Cash Transfers and Voting Behavior in Brazil 2002–10," *American Journal of Political Science* 57, no. 4 (2013): https://doi.org/10.1111/ajps.12026. In Honduras, Linos finds that incumbent mayors benefited from the CCT program, rather than the incumbent president.

46. Wendy Hunter and Timothy J. Power, "Rewarding Lula: Executive Power, Social Policy, and the Brazilian Elections of 2006," *Latin American Politics and Society* 49, no. 1 (2007), doi:10.1111/j.1548-2456.2007.tb00372.x.

47. Diego Sanches Corrêa, "Conditional Cash Transfer Programs, the Economy, and Presidential Elections in Latin America," *Latin American Research Review* 50, no. 2 (2015), doi:10.1353/lar.2015.0020; Layton and Smith, "Incorporating Marginal Citizens"; Pavão, "Conditional Cash Transfer Programs."

48. Layton and Smith speculate that CCTs might mobilize voters because they provide poor citizens with additional resources that enable them to get to the polls on election day, help ensure that recipients have the requisite ID cards needed to vote, and lead recipients to interact with the state more often (e.g., by meeting with CCT program case workers) and thereby reduce psychological barriers to political participation. See Layton and Smith, "Incorporating Marginal Citizens."

49. Orlando J. Pérez, "The Impact of Crime on Voter Choice in Latin America," in *The Latin American Voter: Pursuing Representation and Accountability in Challenging Contexts*, ed. Ryan E. Carlin, Matthew M. Singer, and Elizabeth J. Zechmeister (Ann Arbor: University of Michigan Press, 2015).

50. Nadeau et al., *Latin American Elections*, chapter 5.

51. Elizabeth J. Zechmeister and Daniel Zizumbo-Colunga, "The Varying Political Toll of Concerns about Corruption in Good Versus Bad Economic Times," *Comparative Political Studies* 46, no. 10 (2013), https://doi.org/10.1177/0010414012472468; Luigi Manzetti and Guillermo Rosas, "Corruption and the Latin American Voter," in *The Latin American Voter: Pursuing Representation and Accountability in Challenging Contexts*, ed. Ryan E.Carlin, Matthew M. Singer, and Elizabeth J. Zechmeister (Ann Arbor: University of Michigan Press, 2015).

52. Claudio Ferraz and Frederico Finan, "Exposing Corrupt Politicians: The Effects of Brazil's Publicly Released Audits on Electoral Outcomes," *Quarterly Journal of Economics* 123, no. 2 (2008), https://doi.org/10.1162/qjec.2008.123.2.703.

53. Carlos Pereira and Marcus André Melo, "Reelecting Corrupt Incumbents in Exchange for Public Goods: Rouba Mas Faz in Brazil," *Latin American Research Review* 50, no. 4 (2015), doi:10.1353/lar.2015.0054.

54. Catherine E. De Vries and Hector Solaz, "The Electoral Consequences of Corruption," *Annual Review of Political Science* 20 (2017), https://doi.org/10.1146/annurev-polisci-052715-111917; Rodrigo Castro Cornejo, "Same Scandal, Different Interpretations: Politics of Corruption, Anger, and Partisan Bias in Mexico," *Journal of Elections, Public Opinion and Parties* 33, no. 3 (2023), https://doi.org/10.1080/17457289.2022.2120487.

55. Emily Elia and Leslie A. Schwindt-Bayer, "Corruption Perceptions, Opposition Parties, and Reelecting Incumbents in Latin America," *Electoral Studies* 80 (2022), https://doi.org/10.1016/j.electstud.2022.102545.

56. Kenneth F. Greene, "Dealigning Campaign Effects in Argentina in Comparative Perspective," in *Campaigns and Voters in Developing Democracies: Argentina in Comparative Perspective*, ed. Noam Lupu, Virginia Oliveros, and Luis Schiumerini (Ann Arbor: University of Michigan Press, 2019), 165.

57. Kenneth Greene, "Campaign Persuasion and Nascent Partisanship in Mexico's New Democracy," *American Journal of Political Science* 55, no. 2 (2011), https://doi.org/10.1111/j.1540-5907.2010.00497.x.

58. Greene, "Dealigning Campaign Effects"; Taylor C. Boas, "Voting for Democracy: Campaign Effects in Chile's Democratic Transition," *Latin American Politics and Society* 57, no. 2 (2015), doi:10.1111/j.1548-2456.2015.00267.x.

59. Taylor C. Boas, "Pastor Paulo vs. Doctor Carlos: Professional Titles as Voting Heuristics in Brazil," *Journal of Politics in Latin America* 6, no. 2 (2014), https://doi.org/10.1177/1866802X1400600202.

60. Chappell Lawson, Gabriel S. Lenz, Andy Baker, and Michael Myers, "Looking Like a Winner: Candidate Appearance and Electoral Success in New Democracies," *World Politics* 62, no. 4 (2010), doi:10.1017/S0043887110000195.

61. Mollie J. Cohen, "Protesting via the Null Ballot: An Assessment of the Decision to Cast an Invalid Vote in Latin America," *Political Behavior* 40, no. 2 (2018): 396, https://doi.org/10.1007/s11109-017-9405-9.

62. Cohen, "Protest via the Null Ballot."

63. Ibid., 401–2.

64. Ana Vergara, "Conservatives Prevail in Key Vote for New Chile Constitution," AP News, May 7, 2023, https://apnews.com/article/chile-constitution-kast-boric-plebiscite-referendum-4a3941e0541a9fee0c1b5976c0c6af40.

65. Timothy J. Power and James C. Garand, "Determinants of Invalid Voting in Latin America," *Electoral Studies* 26, no. 2 (2007), https://doi.org/10.1016/j.electstud.2006.11.001.

66. Ibid., 434.

67. Cohen, "Protest via the Null Ballot."

68. Amanda Driscoll and Michael J. Nelson, "Ignorance or Opposition? Blank and Spoiled Votes in Low-Information, Highly Politicized Environments," *Political Research Quarterly* 67, no. 3 (2014), https://doi.org/10.1177/1065912914524634.

Bibliography

Aguilar, Rosario, Saul Cunow, Scott Desposato, and Leonardo Sangali Barone. "Ballot Structure, Candidate Race, and Vote Choice in Brazil." *Latin American Research Review* 50, no. 3 (2015): 175–202. https://doi:10.1353/lar.2015.0044.

Albarracín, Juan, Laura Gamboa, and Scott Mainwaring. "Deinstitutionalization without Collapse: Colombia's Party System." In *Party Systems in Latin America: Institutionalization, Decay, and Collapse*, edited by Scott Mainwaring, 227–54. New York: Cambridge University Press, 2018.

Aldé, Alessandra, and Felipe Borba. "Prime Time Electoral Propaganda: The Brazilian Model of Free Airtime." In *Routledge Handbook of Political Advertising*, edited by Christina Holtz-Bacha and Marion R. Just, 87–100. New York: Routledge, 2017.

Alfaro-Redondo, Ronald, and Steffan Gómez-Campos. "PLN and PAC: Two Costa Rican Parties with Constituencies Evolving in Opposite Directions." In *Diminished Parties: Democratic Representation in Contemporary Latin America*, edited by Juan Pablo Luna, Rafael Piñeiro Rodríguez, Fernando Rosenblatt, and Gabriel Vommaro, 111–28. New York: Cambridge University Press, 2022.

Alhosaini, Ehab, and Oscar Castorena. "Trust in Elections and Electoral Integrity." In *Pulse of Democracy*, edited by Noam Lupu, Mariana Rodríguez, and Elizabeth J. Zechmeister, 34–49. Nashville, TN: LAPOP, 2021. https://www.vanderbilt.edu/lapop/ab2021/2021_LAPOP_AmericasBarometer_2021_Pulse_of_Democracy.pdf.

Alonso, Paula. "Voting in Buenos Aires (Argentina) before 1912." In *Elections before Democracy: The History of Elections in Europe and Latin America*, edited by Eduardo Posada-Carbó, 181–99. New York: St. Martin's Press, 1996.

Altman, David. "Direct Democracy in Latin America." In *Referendums around the World: The Continued Growth of Direct Democracy*, edited by Matt Qvortrup, 162–85. New York: Palgrave Macmillan, 2014.

———. "Political Recruitment and Candidate Selection in Chile, 1990 to 2006: The Executive Branch." In *Pathways to Power: Political Recruitment and Candidate*

Selection in Latin America, edited by Peter Siavelis and Scott Morgenstern, 241–70. University Park, PA: Penn State University Press, 2008.

Amaral, Oswaldo E. do. "The Victory of Jair Bolsonaro According to the Brazilian Electoral Study of 2018." *Brazilian Political Science Review* 14, no. 1 (2020): 1–13. https://doi.org/10.1590/1981-3821202000010004.

Amaral, Oswaldo E. do, and Timothy J. Power. "The PT at 35: Revisiting Scholarly Interpretations of the Brazilian Workers' Party." *Journal of Latin American Studies* 48, no. 1 (2016): 147–71. https://doi:10.1017/S0022216X15001200.

Amparán, Aquiles Chihu. "El Framing Audiovisual del Discurso de Reparación de Imagen: Elecciones Federales, México 2009." In *Campañas Electorales en México y Una Visión a Centroamérica*, edited by María Antonia Martínez and Rubén Aguilar Valenzuela, 131–54. Ciudad de México: Miguel Angel Porrúa/Instituto Federal Electoral/Asociación Latinoamericana de Investigadores en Campañas Electorales/Fundación José Ortega y Gasset-Gregorio Marañón, 2013.

Andía, Rossana, and Yukihiko Hamada. "The Integrity of Political Finance Systems in Latin America: Tackling Political Corruption." International IDEA Policy Paper No. 21. Stockholm: International IDEA, 2019. https://www.idea.int/sites/default/files/publications/integrity-of-political-finance-systems-in-latin-america.pdf.

Angell, Alan, and Benny Pollack. "The Chilean Elections of 1989 and the Politics of the Transition to Democracy." *Bulletin of Latin American Research* 9, no. 1 (1990): 1–23. https://doi.org/10.2307/3338214.

Angell, Alan, Maria D'Alva Kinzo, and Diego Urbaneja. "Latin America." In *Electioneering: A Comparative Study of Continuity and Change*, edited by David Butler and Austin Ranney, 43–69. Oxford: Clarendon Press, 1992.

Aruguete, Natalia, and Mario Riorda. "An Image Is Worth a Thousand Policies: The Discursive Strategy of Electoral Campaigns of Winning Candidates in Latin America." *Communication & Society* 29, no. 2 (2016): 173–91. http://dx.doi.org/10.15581/003.29.2.145-159.

Ascencio, Sergio J. "Party Influence in Presidential Primaries: Evidence from Mexico." *Party Politics* 27, no. 6 (2021): 1229–42. https://doi.org/10.1177/1354068820946424.

Avellaneda, Claudia N., and María C. Escobar-Lemmon. "All by Myself: Personal Qualifications versus Party Affiliation in Colombian Mayoral Elections." *Latin American Politics and Society* 54, no. 2 (2012): 109–32. https://doi.org/10.1111/j.1548-2456.2012.00155.x.

Azpuru, Dinorah. "The Salience of Ideology: Fifteen Years of Presidential Elections in El Salvador." *Latin American Politics and Society* 52, no. 2 (2010): 103–38. https://doi:10.1111/j.1548-2456.2010.00083.x.

Baker, Andy, and Kenneth F. Greene. 2015. "Positional Issue Voting in Latin America." In *The Latin American Voter: Pursuing Representation and Accountability in Challenging Contexts*, edited by Ryan E. Carlin, Matthew M. Singer, and Elizabeth J. Zechmeister, 173–94. Ann Arbor: University of Michigan Press.

Bandeira, Luiza, and Roberta Braga. "Disinformation in the 2018 Elections: Brazil." In *Disinformation in Democracies: Strengthening Digital Resilience in Latin America*, edited by Luiza Bandeira, Donara Barojan, Roberta Braga, Jose Luis

Peñarredonda, and Maria Fernanda Pérez Argüello, 6–19. Washington, DC: Atlantic Council, 2019.

Barczak, Monica. 2001. "Representation by Consultation? The Rise of Direct Democracy in Latin America." *Latin American Politics and Society* 43, no. 3 (2001): 37–59. https://doi:10.1111/j.1548-2456.2001.tb00178.x.

Barnes, Tiffany D., and Gregory W. Saxton. "Working-Class Legislators and Perceptions of Representation in Latin America." *Political Research Quarterly* 72, no. 4 (2019): 910–28. https://doi.org/10.1177/1065912919829583.

Becker, Marc. *Pachakutik: Indigenous Movements and Electoral Politics in Ecuador.* Lanham, MD: Rowman & Littlefield Publishers, 2011.

Béjar, Sergio, Juan A. Moraes, and Santiago López-Cariboni. "Elite Polarization and Voting Turnout in Latin America, 1993–2010." *Journal of Elections, Public Opinion and Parties* 30, no. 1 (2020): 1–21. https://doi.org/10.1080/17457289 .2018.1545775.

Belt, Todd L. "Negative Advertising." In *Routledge Handbook of Political Advertising*, edited by Christina Holtz-Bacha and Marion R. Just, 49–60. New York: Routledge, 2017.

Bjornlund, Eric C. *Beyond Free and Fair: Monitoring Elections and Building Democracy.* Baltimore: Johns Hopkins University Press, 2004.

Blais, André. "What Affects Voter Turnout?" *Annual Review of Political Science* 9 (2006): 111–25. https://doi.org/10.1146/annurev.polisci.9.070204.105121.

Blais, André, and Agnieszka Dobrzynska. "Turnout in Electoral Democracies." *European Journal of Political Research* 33, no. 2 (1998): 239–61. https://doi.org /10.1111/1475-6765.00382.

Boas, Taylor. "Chile: Promoting the Personal Connection—The Internet and Presidential Election Campaigns." In *Making a Difference: A Comparative View of the Role of the Internet in Election Politics*, edited by Diana Owen and David Taras, 15–34. Lanham: Lexington Books, 2008.

———. "The Electoral Representation of Evangelicals in Latin America." *Oxford Research Encyclopedia of Politics*, 2020. https://oxfordre.com/politics/view/10 .1093/acrefore/9780190228637.001.0001/acrefore-9780190228637-e-1748.

———. "Mass Media and Politics in Latin America." In *Constructing Democratic Governance in Latin America*, 4th edition, edited by Jorge I. Domínguez and Michael Shifter, 48–77. Baltimore: Johns Hopkins University Press, 2013.

———. "Pastor Paulo vs. Doctor Carlos: Professional Titles as Voting Heuristics in Brazil." *Journal of Politics in Latin America* 6, no. 2 (2014): 39–72. https://doi.org /10.1177/1866802X1400600202.

———. *Presidential Campaigns in Latin America: Electoral Strategies and Success Contagion.* New York: Cambridge University Press, 2016.

———. "Varieties of Electioneering: Success Contagion and Presidential Campaigns in Latin America." *World Politics* 62, no. 4 (2010): 636–75. https://doi:10.1017/ S0043887110000213.

Boas, Taylor C. "Voting for Democracy: Campaign Effects in Chile's Democratic Transition." *Latin American Politics and Society* 57, no. 2 (2015): 67–90. https:// doi:10.1111/j.1548-2456.2015.00267.x.

Boas, Taylor C., F. Daniel Hidalgo, and Neal P. Richardson. "The Spoils of Victory: Campaign Donations and Government Contracts in Brazil." Kellogg Institute Working Paper #379, 2011. https://kellogg.nd.edu/sites/default/files/old_files/documents/379_0.pdf.

Boas, Taylor, and Amy Erica Smith. "Religion and the Latin American Voter." In *The Latin American Voter: Pursuing Representation and Accountability in Challenging Contexts*, edited by Ryan E. Carlin, Matthew M. Singer, and Elizabeth J. Zechmeister, 99–121. Ann Arbor: University of Michigan Press, 2015.

Borba, Felipe. "Measuring Negative Campaigning on TV, Radio, Debates, Press and Facebook: The Case of 2014 Brazilian Presidential Elections." *Intercom-RBCC (Revista Brasileira de Ciências da Comunicação)* 42, no. 1 (2019): 37–54. https://doi.org/10.1590/1809-5844201912.

Brennan, Jason, and Lisa Hill. *Compulsory Voting: For and Against*. New York: Cambridge University Press, 2014.

Breuer, Anita. "The Use of Government-Initiated Referendums in Latin America: Towards a Theory of Referendum Causes." *Revista de Ciencia Política* 29, no. 1 (2009): 23–55. http://dx.doi.org/10.4067/S0718-090X2009000100002.

Bruhn, Kathleen. "Chronicle of a Victory Foretold: Candidates, Parties, and Campaign Strategies in the 2012 Mexican Presidential Election." In *Mexico's Evolving Democracy: A Comparative Study of the 2012 Elections*, edited by Jorge I. Domínguez, Kenneth F. Greene, Chappell H. Lawson, and Alejandro Moreno, 32–62. Baltimore: Johns Hopkins University Press, 2015.

———. "Electing Extremists? Party Primaries and Legislative Candidates in Mexico." *Comparative Politics* 45, no. 4 (2013): 398–417. https://www.jstor.org/stable/43664073.

———. "The Making of the Mexican President, 2000: Parties, Candidates, and Campaign Strategy." In *Mexico's Pivotal Democratic Election: Candidates, Voters, and the Presidential Campaign of 2000*, edited by Jorge I. Dominguez and Chappell Lawson, 123–56. Stanford/La Jolla, CA: Stanford University Press and Center for U.S.-Mexican Studies, University of California at San Diego, 2004.

———. "Party Finance in Latin America." *Oxford Research Encyclopedias*, 2019. https://doi.org/10.1093/acrefore/9780190228637.013.1665.

———. "Too Much Democracy? Primaries and Candidate Success in the 2006 Mexican National Elections." *Latin American Politics and Society* 52, no. 4 (2010): 25–52. https://doi.org/10.1111/j.1548-2456.2010.00097.x.

Brusco, Valeria, Marcelo Nazareno, and Susan Carol Stokes. "Vote Buying in Argentina." *Latin American Research Review* 39, no. 2 (2004): 66–88. http://www.jstor.org/stable/1555401.

Calingaert, Daniel. "Election Rigging and How to Fight It." *Journal of Democracy* 17, no. 3 (2006): 138–51. https://doi:10.1353/jod.2006.0043.

Calvo, Ernesto. "Down to the Wire: Argentina's 2015 Campaign." In *Campaigns and Voters in Developing Democracies: Argentina in Comparative Perspective*, edited by Noam Lupu, Virginia Oliveros, and Luis Schiumerini, 53–71. Ann Arbor: University of Michigan Press, 2019.

Camp, Roderic Ai. "Political Recruitment, Governance, and Leadership in Mexico: How Democracy Has Made a Difference." In *Pathways to Power: Political*

Recruitment and Candidate Selection in Latin America, edited by Peter Siavelis and Scott Morgenstern, 292–315. University Park, PA: Penn State University Press, 2008.

Cantillana Pena, Carlos, Gonzalo Contreras Aguirre, and Mauricio Morales Quiroga. "Elecciones Primarias y Personalización de la Política: El Caso de las Elecciones Locales en Chile 2012." *Revista de Ciencia Política* 35, no. 2 (2015): 273–98. http://dx.doi.org/10.4067/S0718-090X2015000200002.

Carey, John. "The Reelection Debate in Latin America." *Latin American Politics and Society* 45, no. 1 (2003): 119–33. https://doi:10.1111/j.1548-2456.2003.tb00234.x.

Carey, John M., and John Polga-Hecimovich. "Primary Elections and Candidate Strength in Latin America." *Journal of Politics* 68, no. 3 (2006): 530–43. https://doi.org/10.1111/j.1468-2508.2006.00443.x.

Carlin, Ryan E., and Gregory J. Love. "Who Is the Latin American Voter?" In *The Latin American Voter: Pursuing Representation and Accountability in Challenging Contexts*, edited by Ryan E. Carlin, Matthew M. Singer, and Elizabeth J. Zechmeister, 31–59. Ann Arbor: University of Michigan Press, 2015.

Carlin, Ryan E., Matthew M. Singer, and Elizabeth J. Zechmeister. "Introduction to the Latin American Voter." In *The Latin American Voter: Pursuing Representation and Accountability in Challenging Contexts*, edited by Ryan E. Carlin, Matthew M. Singer, and Elizabeth J. Zechmeister, 1–27. Ann Arbor: University of Michigan Press, 2015.

———. "Conclusion." In *The Latin American Voter: Pursuing Representation and Accountability in Challenging Contexts*, edited by Ryan E. Carlin, Matthew M. Singer, and Elizabeth J. Zechmeister, 346–69. Ann Arbor: University of Michigan Press, 2015.

Carnes, Nicholas, and Noam Lupu. "Rethinking the Comparative Perspective on Class and Representation: Evidence from Latin America." *American Journal of Political Science* 59, no. 1 (2015): 1–18. https://doi.org/10.1111/ajps.12112.

Carreras, Miguel. "Compulsory Voting and Political Engagement (Beyond the Ballot Box): A Multilevel Analysis." *Electoral Studies* 43 (2016): 158–68. https://doi.org/10.1016/j.electstud.2016.04.005.

———. "Presidential Institutions and Electoral Participation in Concurrent Elections in Latin America." *Political Studies* 66, no. 3 (2018): 541–59. https://doi.org/10.1177/0032321717723502.

———. "The Rise of Outsiders in Latin America, 1980–2010: An Institutionalist Perspective." *Comparative Political Studies* 45, no. 12 (2012): 1451–82. https://doi.org/10.1177/0010414012445753.

Carreras, Miguel, and Nestor Castañeda-Angarita. "Who Votes in Latin America? A Test of Three Theoretical Perspectives." *Comparative Political Studies* 47, no. 8 (2014): 1079–1104. https://doi.org/10.1177/0010414013488558.

Carreras, Miguel, and Yasemin Irepoglu. "Trust in Elections, Vote Buying, and Turnout in Latin America." *Electoral Studies* 32, no. 4 (2013): 609–19. https://doi.org/10.1016/j.electstud.2013.07.012.

Carter Center. *Las Elecciones de 2011 en Nicaragua: Informe de una Misión de Estudio*. Atlanta: Carter Center, n.d.

———. *Financiamiento Político y Regulación de Campañas Electorales en América Latina*. Atlanta: Carter Center, n.d.

————. *Observing Nicaragua's Elections, 1989–1990*. Atlanta: Carter Center, 1990.

————. *Observing the Venezuela Presidential Recall Referendum, Comprehensive Report*. Atlanta: Carter Center, 2005.

————. *Study Mission of The Carter Center 2013 Presidential Elections in Venezuela, Final Report*. Atlanta: Carter Center, 2013.

————. *Study Mission to the October 7, 2012, Presidential Election in Venezuela*. Atlanta: Carter Center, n.d.

Casas, Kevin, and Tomás Quesada. *Legislative Candidate Vetting Mechanisms in Latin American Political Parties*. National Democratic Institute and National Endowment for Democracy, 2019.

Casas-Zamora, Kevin. "Costa Rica: Four Decades of Campaign Finance Scandals." In *Dangerous Liaisons: Organized Crime and Political Finance in Latin America and Beyond*, edited by Kevin Casas-Zamora, 107–35. Washington, DC: The Brookings Institution, 2013.

————. "On Organized Crime and Political Finance: Why Does the Connection Matter?" In *Dangerous Liaisons: Organized Crime and Political Finance in Latin America and Beyond*, edited by Kevin Casas-Zamora, 1–21. Washington, DC: The Brookings Institution, 2013.

Casas-Zamora, Kevin, and Miguel Carter. *Beyond the Scandals: The Changing Context of Corruption in Latin America*. Washington, DC: Inter-American Dialogue, 2017. https://www.thedialogue.org/wp-content/uploads/2017/02/Corruption-in-Latin-America_ROL_Report_FINAL_web-PDF.pdf.

Casas-Zamora, Kevin, and Daniel Zovatto. *The Cost of Democracy: Campaign Finance Regulation in Latin America*. Latin America Initiative, Foreign Policy at Brookings, 2015.

Castanho Silva, Bruno, Mario Fuks, and Eduardo Ryô Tamaki. "So Thin It's Almost Invisible: Populist Attitudes and Voting Behavior in Brazil." *Electoral Studies* 75 (2022): 102434. https://doi.org/10.1016/j.electstud.2021.102434.

Castro Cornejo, Rodrigo. "Same Scandal, Different Interpretations: Politics of Corruption, Anger, and Partisan Bias in Mexico." *Journal of Elections, Public Opinion and Parties* 33, no. 3 (2023): 497–518. https://doi.org/10.1080/17457289.2022.2120487.

Castro Cornejo, Rodrigo, and Ulises Beltrán. "List Experiments, Political Sophistication, and Vote Buying: Experimental Evidence from Mexico." *Journal of Politics in Latin America* 12, no. 2 (2020): 219–34. https://doi.org/10.1177/1866802X20937713.

Cepaluni, Gabriel, and F. Daniel Hidalgo. "Compulsory Voting Can Increase Political Inequality: Evidence from Brazil." *Political Analysis* 24, no. 2 (2016): 273–80. https://doi:10.1093/pan/mpw004.

Chalker, Cynthia H. "Elections and Democracy in Costa Rica." In *Elections and Democracy in Central America Revisited*, edited by Mitchell A. Seligson and John A. Booth, 103–122. Chapel Hill: University of North Carolina Press, 1995.

Chasteen, John Charles. *Americanos: Latin America's Struggle for Independence*. New York: Oxford University Press, 2008.

Cheibub, José Antonio, and Alejandro Medina. "The Politics of Presidential Term Limits in Latin America: From Re-democratization to Today." In *The Politics of*

Presidential Term Limits, edited by Alexander Baturo and Robert Elgie, 517–34. New York: Oxford University Press, 2019.

Clayton, Amanda. "How Do Electoral Gender Quotas Affect Policy?" *Annual Review of Political Science* 24 (2021): 235–52. https://doi.org/10.1146/annurev-polisci-041719-102019.

Cohen, Mollie J. "Protesting via the Null Ballot: An Assessment of the Decision to Cast an Invalid Vote in Latin America." *Political Behavior* 40, no. 2 (2018): 395–414. https://doi.org/10.1007/s11109-017-9405-9.

Cohen, Mollie J., Facundo E. Salles Kobilanski, and Elizabeth Zechmeister. "Electoral Volatility in Latin America." *Journal of Politics* 80, no. 3 (2018): 1017–22. https://doi.org/10.1086/697464.

Colburn, Forrest D., and Arturo Cruz S. "The Fading of Costa Rica's Old Parties." *Journal of Democracy* 29, no. 4 (2018): 43–53. https://doi:10.1353/jod.2018.0061.

Comisión Internacional contra la Impunidad en Guatemala (CICIG). *Financiamiento de la Política en Guatemala*. Guatemala City: CICIG, 2015.

Conaghan, Catherine M. "Diminished by Design: Ecuador's Alianza PAIS." In *Diminished Parties: Democratic Representation in Contemporary Latin America*, edited by Juan Pablo Luna, Rafael Piñeiro Rodríguez, Fernando Rosenblatt, and Gabriel Vommaro, 197–219. New York: Cambridge University Press, 2022.

Constable, Pamela, and Arturo Valenzuela. *A Nation of Enemies: Chile under Pinochet*. New York: W.W. Norton, 1991.

Cornelius, Wayne A. "Mobilized Voting in the 2000 Elections: The Changing Efficacy of Vote Buying and Coercion in Mexican Electoral Politics." In *Mexico's Pivotal Democratic Election: Candidates, Voters, and the Presidential Campaign of 2000*, edited by Jorge I. Dominguez and Chappell Lawson, 47–65. Stanford/La Jolla, CA: Stanford University Press and Center for U.S.-Mexican Studies, University of California at San Diego, 2004.

Corrales, Javier. *Fixing Democracy: Why Constitutional Change Often Fails to Enhance Democracy in Latin America*. New York: Oxford University Press, 2018.

———. "Latin America's Neocaudillismo: Ex-presidents and Newcomers Running for President . . . and Winning." *Latin American Politics and Society* 50, no. 3 (2008): 1–35. https://doi:10.1111/j.1548-2456.2008.00020.x.

Corrales, Javier, and Michael Penfold. "Manipulating Term Limits in Latin America." *Journal of Democracy* 25, no. 4 (2014): 157–68. https://doi:10.1353/jod.2014.0066.

Corrêa, Diego Sanches. "Conditional Cash Transfer Programs, the Economy, and Presidential Elections in Latin America." *Latin American Research Review* 50, no. 2 (2015): 63–85. https://doi:10.1353/lar.2015.0020.

Cortés, Juve. "Self-Governance in Latin America: To What Extent Can Citizens Make Policy via Direct Democracy?" *Latin American Policy* 9, no. 1 (2018): 5–26. https://doi.org/10.1111/lamp.12139.

Cox, Paulo, and Mauricio Morales. "The Chilean Turnout Gender Gap: Evidence from Administrative Census Data." *Acta Politica* 58, no. 2 (2023): 306–36. https://doi.org/10.1057/s41269-022-00245-8.

D'Alessandro, Martin. "Political Advertising in Argentina." In *Routledge Handbook of Political Advertising*, edited by Christina Holtz-Bacha and Marion R. Just, 75–86. New York: Routledge, 2017.

Dargent, Eduardo, and Paula Muñoz. "Democracy against Parties? Party System De-Institutionalization in Colombia." *Journal of Politics in Latin America* 3, no. 2 (2011): 43–71. https://doi.org/10.1177/1866802X1100300202.

Della Costa Stuenkel, Oliver, and Andreas E. Feldman. "The Unchecked Demise of Nicaraguan Democracy." *Carnegie Endowment for International Peace*, November 26, 2017. https://carnegieendowment.org/2017/11/16/unchecked-demise-of -nicaraguan-democracy-pub-74761.

De la O, Ana L. "Do Conditional Cash Transfers Affect Electoral Behavior? Evidence from a Randomized Experiment in Mexico." *American Journal of Political Science* 57, no. 1 (2013): 1–14. https://doi.org/10.1111/j.1540-5907.2012.00617.x.

De la Torre, Carlos. "Technocratic Populism in Ecuador." *Journal of Democracy* 24, no. 3 (2013): 33–46. https://doi:10.1353/jod.2013.0047.

De la Torre, Carlos, and Catherine Conaghan. "The Hybrid Campaign: Tradition and Modernity in Ecuador's 2006 Presidential Election." *International Journal of Press/Politics* 14, no. 3 (2009): 335–52. https://doi.org/10.1177 /1940161209334523.

De Luca, Miguel. "Political Recruitment and Candidate Selection in Argentina: Presidents and Governors, 1983 to 2006." In *Pathways to Power: Political Recruitment and Candidate Selection in Latin America*, edited by Peter Siavelis and Scott Morgenstern, 189–217. University Park, PA: Penn State University Press, 2008.

De Vries, Catherine E., and Hector Solaz. "The Electoral Consequences of Corruption." *Annual Review of Political Science* 20 (2017): 391–408. https://doi.org/10 .1146/annurev-polisci-052715-111917.

Desposato, Scott W. "Parties for Rent? Ambition, Ideology, and Party Switching in Brazil's Chamber of Deputies." *American Journal of Political Science* 50, no. 1 (2006): 62–80. https://doi.org/10.1111/j.1540-5907.2006.00170.x.

Díaz-Cayeros, Alberto, and Beatriz Magaloni. "Aiding Latin America's Poor." *Journal of Democracy* 20, no. 4 (2009): 36–49. http://doi.org/10.1353/jod.0.0115.

Díaz Jiménez, Oniel Francisco. "Marketing Político y Profesionalización de las Campañas Electorales del Partido Acción Nacional y el Partido de la Revolución Democrática." *Polis: Investigación y Análisis Sociopolítico y Psicosocial* 11, no. 1 (2015): 119–67. https://www.scielo.org.mx/scielo.php?script=sci_arttext&pid =S1870-23332015000100119.

Díaz Jiménez, Oniel Francisco, and Miguel Eduardo Alva Rivera. "El Uso Estratégico de la Publicidad Política de Ataque en la Elección Federal Intermedia de 2015 en México." *Revista Mexicana de Opinión Pública* (July–December 2016): 33–49. https://doi.org/10.1016/j.rmop.2016.07.002.

Dickinson, Elizabeth. "Local Polls in Colombia Put Peace to the Test." International Crisis Group, October 25, 2019. https://www.crisisgroup.org/fa-AF/node/11762.

Domínguez, Jorge I. "Mexico's Campaigns and the Benchmark Elections of 2000 and 2006." In *The Oxford Handbook of Mexican Politics*, edited by Roderic Ai Camp, 523–44. New York: Oxford University Press, 2012.

Dosek, Tomás. "El Clientelismo en Paraguay: Compra de Votos o Compra de Participación Electoral?" *Latin American Research Review* 58, no. 3 (2023): 612–30. https://doi:10.1017/lar.2023.8.

Drake, Paul W. *Between Tyranny and Anarchy: A History of Democracy in Latin America, 1800–2006*. Stanford: Stanford University Press, 2009.

Driscoll, Amanda, and Michael J. Nelson. "Ignorance or Opposition? Blank and Spoiled Votes in Low-Information, Highly Politicized Environments." *Political Research Quarterly* 67, no. 3 (2014): 547–61. https://doi.org/10.1177 /1065912914524634.

Duverger, Maurice. *Political Parties: Their Organization and Activity in the Modern State*. New York: Wiley, 1954.

Echegaray, Fabián. *Economic Crises and Electoral Responses in Latin America*. Lanham: University Press of America, 2005.

Elia, Emily, and Leslie A. Schwindt-Bayer. "Corruption Perceptions, Opposition Parties, and Reelecting Incumbents in Latin America." *Electoral Studies* 80 (2022): 102545. https://doi.org/10.1016/j.electstud.2022.102545.

Espíndola, Roberto. "Electoral Campaigning in Latin America's New Democracies: The Southern Cone." In *Mass Media and Political Communication in New Democracies*, edited by Katrin Voltmer, 115–32. New York: Routledge, 2006.

Estévez, Federico, Eric Magar, and Guillermo Rosas. "Partisanship in Non-partisan Electoral Agencies and Democratic Compliance: Evidence from Mexico's Federal Electoral Institute." *Electoral Studies* 27, no. 2 (2008): 257–71. https://doi.org/10 .1016/j.electstud.2007.11.013.

European Union Election Expert Mission, Bolivia 2019. Final Report. European Union, n.d.

European Union Election Observation Mission, El Salvador 2018. "Preliminary Statement." European Union External Action, March 6, 2018. https://eeas.europa .eu/election-observation-missions/eom-el-salvador-2018/40894/node/40894_en.

European Union Election Observation Mission. El Salvador 2019 Final Report. n.d.

———. Honduras Final Report, General Elections 2017. n.d.

———. Honduras Final Report, General Elections 2013. n.d.

———. Nicaragua 2011, Final Report on the General Elections and Parlacen Elections. n.d.

———. Republic of Paraguay, Final Report, General Elections, 22 April 2018. n.d.

Fernández, Carmen Beatriz. "Ciberpolítica 2018: Tendencias en Latinoamérica." In *Nuevas Campañas Electorales en América Latina*, edited by Ángel Arellano, 147–62. Montevideo: Konrad-Adenauer-Stiftung, 2018.

Ferraz, Claudio, and Frederico Finan. "Exposing Corrupt Politicians: The Effects of Brazil's Publicly Released Audits on Electoral Outcomes." *Quarterly Journal of Economics* 123, no. 2 (2008): 703–45. https://doi.org/10.1162/qjec.2008.123.2 .703.

Fornos, Carolina A., Timothy J. Power, and James C. Garand. "Explaining Voter Turnout in Latin America, 1980 to 2000." *Comparative Political Studies* 37, no. 8 (2004): 909–40. https://doi.org/10.1177/0010414004267981.

Franceschet, Susan, and Jennifer M. Piscopo. "Gender and Political Backgrounds in Argentina." In *The Impact of Gender Quotas*, edited by Susan Franceschet, Mona Lena Krook, and Jennifer M. Piscopo, 43–56. New York: Oxford University Press, 2012.

Franceschet, Susan, Mona Lena Krook, and Jennifer M. Piscopo. "Conceptualizing the Impact of Gender Quotas." In *The Impact of Gender Quotas*, edited by Susan Franceschet, Mona Lena Krook, and Jennifer M. Piscopo, 3–24. New York: Oxford University Press, 2012.

Franceschet, Susan, and Gwynn Thomas. "Renegotiating Political Leadership: Michelle Bachelet's Rise to the Chilean Presidency." In *Cracking the Highest Glass Ceiling: A Global Comparison of Women's Campaigns for Executive Office*, edited by Rainbow Murray, 177–95. Santa Barbara, CA: Praeger, 2010.

Freidenberg, Flavia, and Tomáš Došek. "Las Reformas Electorales en América Latina (1978–2015)." In *Reformas Políticas en América Latina, Tendencias y Casos*, edited by Kevin Casas-Zamora, Marian Vidaurri, Betilde Muñoz-Pogossian, and Raquel Chanto, 25–92. Washington, DC: Organization of American States, 2016.

Gamarra, Eduardo A. "Municipal Elections in Bolivia." In *Urban Elections in Democratic Latin America*, edited by Henry A. Dietz and Gil Shidlo, 21–61. Wilmington, DE: Scholarly Resources, 1998.

Gamboa, Ricardo, and Mauricio Morales. "Chile's 2015 Electoral Reform: Changing the Rules of the Game." *Latin American Politics and Society* 58, no. 4 (2016): 126–44. https://doi.org/10.1111/laps.12005.

García-Sánchez, Miguel, and Jair Alberto Arciniegas. "Political Advertising in Colombia: Between the Narratives of War and Peace." In *Routledge Handbook of Political Advertising*, edited by Christina Holtz-Bacha and Marion R. Just, 320–39. New York: Routledge, 2017.

Gélineau, Francois, and Matthew M. Singer. "The Economy and Incumbent Support in Latin America." In *The Latin American Voter: Pursuing Representation and Accountability in Challenging Contexts*, edited by Ryan E. Carlin, Matthew M. Singer, and Elizabeth J. Zechmeister, 281–99. Ann Arbor: University of Michigan Press, 2015.

Gervasoni, Carlos. "Argentina's Declining Party System: Fragmentation, Denationalization, Factionalization, Personalization, and Increasing Fluidity." In *Party Systems in Latin America: Institutionalization, Decay, and Collapse*, edited by Scott Mainwaring, 255–90. New York: Cambridge University Press, 2018.

Gervasoni, Carlos, and María Laura Tagina. "Explaining Support for the Incumbent in Presidential Elections." In *Campaigns and Voters in Developing Democracies: Argentina in Comparative Perspective*, edited by Noam Lupu, Virginia Oliveros, and Luis Schiumerini, 114–35. Ann Arbor: University of Michigan Press, 2019.

Geys, Benny. "Explaining Voter Turnout: A Review of Aggregate-Level Research." *Electoral Studies* 25, no. 4 (2006): 637–63. https://doi.org/10.1016/j.electstud.2005.09.002.

Gillingham, Paul. "Mexican Elections, 1910–1994: Voters, Violence, and Veto Power." In *The Oxford Handbook of Mexican Politics*, edited by Roderic Ai Camp, 53–76. New York: Oxford University Press, 2012.

Gilmore, Jason. "Ditching the Pack: Digital Media in the 2010 Brazilian Congressional Campaigns." *New Media & Society* 14, no. 4 (2012): 617–33. https://doi.org/10.1177/1461444811422429.

Gilmore, Jason, and Philip N. Howard. "Does Social Media Make a Difference in Political Campaigns? Digital Dividends in Brazil's 2010 National Elections." Center for Communication and Civic Engagement, University of Washington, Working Paper 2013-2, 2013. https://papers.ssrn.com/sol3/papers.cfm?abstract_id=2273832.

González-Ocantos, Ezequiel, Chad Kiewiet de Jonge, Carlos Meléndez, David Nickerson, and Javier Osorio. "Carrots and Sticks: Experimental Evidence of Vote-Buying and Voter Intimidation in Guatemala." *Journal of Peace Research* 57, no. 1 (2020): 46–61. https://doi.org/10.1177/0022343319884998.

González-Ocantos, Ezequiel, Chad Kiewiet de Jonge, Carlos Meléndez, Javier Osorio, and David W. Nickerson. "Vote Buying and Social Desirability Bias: Experimental Evidence from Nicaragua." *American Journal of Political Science* 56, no. 1 (2012): 202–17. https://doi.org/10.1111/j.1540-5907.2011.00540.x.

González-Ocantos, Ezequiel, Chad Kiewiet de Jonge, and Covadonga Meseguer. "Remittances and Vote Buying." *Latin American Research Review* 53, no. 4 (2018): 689–707. https://doi:10.25222/larr.396.

Gonzalez Ocantos, Ezequiel, Chad Kiewiet de Jonge, and David W. Nickerson. "The Conditionality of Vote-Buying Norms: Experimental Evidence from Latin America." *American Journal of Political Science* 58, no. 1 (2014): 197–211. https://doi.org/10.1111/ajps.12047.

Graham, Richard. *Patronage and Politics in Nineteenth-Century Brazil.* Stanford: Stanford University Press, 1990.

Greene, Kenneth. "Campaign Persuasion and Nascent Partisanship in Mexico's New Democracy." *American Journal of Political Science* 55, no. 2 (2011): 398–416. https://doi.org/10.1111/j.1540-5907.2010.00497.x.

———. "Dealigning Campaign Effects in Argentina in Comparative Perspective." In *Campaigns and Voters in Developing Democracies: Argentina in Comparative Perspective*, edited by Noam Lupu, Virginia Oliveros, and Luis Schiumerini, 162–86. Ann Arbor: University of Michigan Press, 2019.

Greene, Kenneth F., and Mariano Sánchez-Talanquer. "Authoritarian Legacies and Party System Stability in Mexico." In *Party Systems in Latin America: Institutionalization, Decay, and Collapse*, edited by Scott Mainwaring, 201–226 New York: Cambridge University Press, 2018.

Haime, Agustina. "What Explains Voter Turnout in Latin America? A Test of the Effect of Citizens' Attitudes towards the Electoral Process." *Revista de Ciencia Política* 37, no. 1 (2017): 69–93. http://dx.doi.org/10.4067/S0718-090X2017000100004.

Haime, Agustina, and Francisco Cantú. "Negative Partisanship in Latin America." *Latin American Politics and Society* 64, no. 1 (2022): 72–92. https://doi:10.1017/lap.2021.54.

Hartlyn, Jonathan, Jennifer McCoy, and Thomas M. Mustillo. "Electoral Governance Matters: Explaining the Quality of Elections in Latin America." *Comparative Political Studies* 41, no. 4 (2008): 73–98. https://doi.org/10.1177/0010414007301701.

Heras Gómez, Leticia, and Oniel Francisco Díaz Jiménez. "Las Redes Sociales en las Campañas de los Candidatos a Diputados Locales del PRI, el PAN y el PRD en las Elecciones de 2015 en el Estado de México." *Apuntes Electorales* 16, no. 57 (July–December 2017): 71–108.

Hernández-Huerta, Victor, and Francisco Cantú. "Public Distrust in Disputed Elections: Evidence from Latin America." *British Journal of Political Science* 52, no. 4 (2022): 1923–30. https://doi:10.1017/S0007123421000399.

Hinojosa, Magda. *Selecting Women, Electing Women: Political Representation and Candidate Selection in Latin America*. Philadelphia: Temple University Press, 2012.

Holland, Alisha C. "Right on Crime? Conservative Party Politics and Mano Dura Policies in El Salvador." *Latin American Research Review* 48, no. 1 (2013): 44–67. https://doi:10.1353/lar.2013.0009.

Hoskin, Gary. "Urban Electoral Behavior in Colombia." In *Urban Elections in Democratic Latin America*, edited by Henry A. Dietz and Gil Shidlo, 91–116. Wilmington, DE: Scholarly Resources, 1998.

Htun, Mala. *Inclusion without Representation in Latin America: Gender Quotas and Ethnic Reservations*. New York: Cambridge University Press, 2016.

Human Rights Watch. "Nicaragua: Law Threatens Free, Fair Elections." December 22, 2020. https://www.hrw.org/news/2020/12/22/nicaragua-law-threatens-free-fair-elections#.

———. "Venezuela: Rulings Threaten Free and Fair Elections." July 7, 2020. https://www.hrw.org/news/2020/07/07/venezuela-rulings-threaten-free-and-fair-elections.

Hunter, Wendy, and Timothy J. Power. "Lula's Second Act." *Journal of Democracy* 34, no. 1 (2023): 126–40. http://doi.org/10.1353/jod.2023.0008.

———. "Rewarding Lula: Executive Power, Social Policy, and the Brazilian Elections of 2006." *Latin American Politics and Society* 49, no. 1 (2007): 1–30. https://doi:10.1111/j.1548-2456.2007.tb00372.x.

Huntington, Samuel P. *The Third Wave: Democratization in the Late Twentieth Century*. Norman: University of Oklahoma Press, 1991.

Hyde, Susan. *The Pseudo-Democrat's Dilemma: Why Election Observation Became an International Norm*. Ithaca and London: Cornell University Press, 2011.

Inglehart, Ronald, and Pippa Norris. "The Developmental Theory of the Gender Gap: Women's and Men's Voting Behavior in Global Perspective." *International Political Science Review* 21, no. 4 (2000): 441–63. https://doi.org/10.1177/0192512100214007.

International IDEA. *Funding of Political Parties and Election Campaigns: A Handbook on Political Finance*. Stockholm: International IDEA, 2014.

Jímenez Alvarado, Óscar, and Mariano Salas Narango. "Los Partidos Oficialistas en Centramérica y sus Campañas Electorales en Televisión: Análisis de los *Spots* del PLN (Costa Rica) y el FSLN (Nicaragua)." In *Campañas Electorales en México y Una Visión a Centroamérica*, edited by María Antonia Martínez and Rubén Aguilar Valenzuela, 157–76. Ciudad de México: Miguel Angel Porrúa/Instituto Federal Electoral/Asociación Latinoamericana de Investigadores en Campañas Electorales/Fundación José Ortega y Gasset-Gregorio Marañón, 2013.

Johnson, Gregg B., and Sooh-Rhee Ryu. "Repudiating or Rewarding Neoliberalism? How Broken Campaign Promises Condition Economic Voting in Latin America." *Latin American Politics and Society* 52, no. 4 (2010): 1–24. https://doi:10.1111/j.1548-2456.2010.00096.x.

Johnston, Jack, and David Rosnick. *Observing the Observers: The OAS in the 2019 Bolivian Elections*. Washington, DC: Center for Economic and Policy Research, 2020. https://www.cepr.net/wp-content/uploads/2020/03/bolivia-2020-3.pdf.

Jones, Mark P. "Gender Quotas, Electoral Laws, and the Election of Women: Evidence from the Latin American Vanguard." *Comparative Political Studies* 42, no. 1 (2009): 56–81. https://doi.org/10.1177/0010414008324993.

———. "Quota Legislation and the Election of Women: Learning from the Costa Rican Experience." *Journal of Politics* 66, no. 4 (2004): 1203–23. https://doi.org/10.1111/j.0022-3816.2004.00296.x.

———. "The Recruitment and Selection of Legislative Candidates in Argentina." In *Pathways to Power: Political Recruitment and Candidate Selection in Latin America*, edited by Peter Siavelis and Scott Morgenstern, 41–75. University Park, PA: Penn State University Press, 2008.

Juárez- Gámiz, Julio, and Marco Arellano-Toledo. "The Lousy Avalanche: Political Advertising in Mexico." In *Routledge Handbook of Political Advertising*, edited by Christina Holtz-Bacha and Marion R. Just, 179–89. New York: Routledge, 2017.

Katz, Friederich. "Mexico: Restored Republic and Porfiriato, 1867–1910." In *The Cambridge History of Latin America*, v. 5, edited by Leslie Bethell, 3–78. New York: Cambridge University Press, 1986.

Kelley, Judith G. *Monitoring Democracy: When International Election Observation Works, and Why It Often Fails*. Princeton: Princeton University Press, 2012.

Kemahlioglu, Ozge, Rebecca Weitz-Shapiro, and Shigeo Hirano. "Why Primaries in Latin American Presidential Elections?" *Journal of Politics* 71, no. 1 (2009): 339–52. https://doi.org/10.1017/S0022381608090221.

Key Jr., V. O. *Politics, Parties, and Pressure Groups*, 5th edition. New York: Thomas Crowell, 1964.

Kiewiet de Jonge, Chad P. "Who Lies about Electoral Gifts? Experimental Evidence from Latin America." *Public Opinion Quarterly* 79, no. 3 (2015): 710–30. https://doi.org/10.1093/poq/nfv024.

Kinsbruner, Jay. *Independence in Spanish America*. Albuquerque: University of New Mexico Press, 1994.

Kitschelt, Herbert, and Melina Altamirano. "Clientelism in Latin America: Effort and Effectiveness." In *The Latin American Voter: Pursuing Representation and Accountability in Challenging Contexts*, edited by Ryan E. Carlin, Matthew M. Singer, and Elizabeth J. Zechmeister, 246–73. Ann Arbor: University of Michigan Press, 2015.

Kitschelt, Herbert, Kirk A. Hawkins, Juan Pablo Luna, Guillermo Rosas, and Elizabeth J. Zechmeister. *Latin American Party Systems*. New York: Cambridge University Press, 2010.

Klein, Herbert S. "Bolivia from the War of the Pacific to the Chaco War, 1880–1932." In *The Cambridge History of Latin America*, v. 5, edited by Leslie Bethell, 553–86. New York: Cambridge University Press, 1986.

Klesner, Joseph L. "The Structure of the Mexican Electorate: Social, Attitudinal, and Partisan Bases of Vicente Fox's Victory." In *Mexico's Pivotal Democratic Election: Candidates, Voters, and the Presidential Campaign of 2000*, edited by Jorge I. Dominguez and Chappell Lawson, 91–122. Stanford/La Jolla, CA: Stanford

University Press and Center for U.S.-Mexican Studies, University of California at San Diego, 2004.

Knutsen, Carl Henrik, Håvard Mokleiv Nygård, and Tore Wig. "Autocratic Elections: Stabilizing Tool or Force for Change?" *World Politics* 69, no. 1 (2017): 98–143. https://doi: 10.1017/s0043887116000149.

Kostadinova, Tatiana, and Timothy J. Power. "Does Democratization Depress Participation? Voter Turnout in the Latin American and Eastern European Transitional Democracies." *Political Research Quarterly* 60, no. 3 (2007): 363–77. https://doi .org/10.1177/1065912907304154.

Kouba, Karel, and Jan Pumr. "The Democratic Cost of Consecutive Re-election and Presidential Term-Limit Evasion in Latin America." *Government and Opposition* 58, no. 3 (2023): 360–90. https://doi:10.1017/gov.2021.51.

Lamounier, Bolívar, and Octavio Amorim Neto. "Brazil." In *Elections in the Americas: A Data Handbook, vol. 2 South America*, edited by Dieter Nohlen, 163–252. New York: Oxford University Press, 2005.

Langston, Joy. "Congressional Campaigning in Mexico." CIDE Working Paper 184. Ciudad de México: División de Estudios Políticos-Centro de Investigación y Docencia Económicas, 2006.

Langston, Joy, and Scott Morgenstern. "Campaigning in an Electoral Authoritarian Regime: The Case of Mexico." *Comparative Politics* 41, no. 2 (2009): 165–81. http://www.jstor.org/stable/40599208.

Lau, Richard R., and Ivy Brown Rovner. "Negative Campaigning." *Annual Review of Political Science* 12 (2009): 285–306. https://doi.org/10.1146/annurev.polisci .10.071905.101448.

Lawson, Chappell. "Introduction." In *Mexico's Pivotal Democratic Election: Candidates, Voters, and the Presidential Campaign of 2000*, edited by Jorge I. Dominguez and Chappell Lawson, 1–21. Stanford/La Jolla, CA: Stanford University Press and Center for U.S.-Mexican Studies, University of California at San Diego, 2004.

Lawson, Chappell, and Kenneth F. Greene. "Making Clientelism Work: How Norms of Reciprocity Increase Voter Compliance." *Comparative Politics* 47, no. 1 (2014): 61–77. https://www.jstor.org/stable/43664343.

Lawson, Chappell, Gabriel S. Lenz, Andy Baker, and Michael Myers. "Looking Like a Winner: Candidate Appearance and Electoral Success in New Democracies." *World Politics* 62, no. 4 (2010): 561–93. https://doi: 10.1017/S00438871 10000195.

Layton, Matthew L., and Amy Erica Smith. "Incorporating Marginal Citizens and Voters: The Conditional Electoral Effects of Targeted Social Assistance in Latin America." *Comparative Political Studies* 48, no. 7 (2015): 854–81. https://doi.org /10.1177/0010414014565889.

Lazarte R., Jorge. "Bolivia." In *Elections in the Americas: A Data Handbook, vol. 2 South America*, edited by Dieter Nohlen, 123–61. New York: Oxford University Press, 2005.

Lehoucq, Fabrice E., and Iván Molina. *Stuffing the Ballot Box: Fraud, Electoral Reform, and Democratization in Costa Rica*. Cambridge University Press, 2002.

León-Roesch, Marta, and Richard Ortiz Ortiz. "Paraguay." In *Elections in the Americas: A Data Handbook, vol. 2 South America*, edited by Dieter Nohlen, 411–44. New York: Oxford University Press, 2005.

Levitsky, Steven. "Peru: The Institutionalization of Politics without Parties." In *Party Systems in Latin America: Institutionalization, Decay, and Collapse*, edited by Scott Mainwaring, 326–55. New York: Cambridge University Press, 2018.

Levitsky, Steven, and Mauricio Zavaleta. "Why No Party-Building in Peru?" In *Challenges of Party-Building in Latin America*, edited by Steven Levitsky, James Loxton, Brandon van Dyck, and Jorge Dominguez, 412–39. New York: Cambridge University Press, 2017.

Levitsky, Steven, James Loxton, and Brandon van Dyck. "Introduction: Challenges of Party-Building in Latin America." In *Challenges of Party-Building in Latin America*, edited by Steven Levitsky, James Loxton, Brandon van Dyck, and Jorge Dominguez, 1–48. New York: Cambridge University Press, 2017.

Lewis-Beck, Michael S., and Maria Celeste Ratto. "Economic Voting in Latin America: A General Model." *Electoral Studies* 32, no. 3 (2013): 489–93. https://doi.org/10.1016/j.electstud.2013.05.023.

Ley, Sandra. "To Vote or Not to Vote: How Criminal Violence Shapes Electoral Participation." *Journal of Conflict Resolution* 62, no. 9 (2018): 1963–90. https://doi.org/10.1177/0022002717708600.

Lijphart, Arend. "Unequal Participation: Democracy's Unresolved Dilemma." *American Political Science Review* 91, no. 1 (1997): 1–14. https://doi:10.2307/2952255.

Linos, Elizabeth. "Do Conditional Cash Transfer Programs Shift Votes? Evidence from the Honduran PRAF." *Electoral Studies* 32, no. 4 (2013): 864–74. https://doi.org/10.1016/j.electstud.2013.03.007.

López-Hermida Russo, Alberto Pedro. "Political Advertising in Chile: State of Play in a Period of Changes." In *Routledge Handbook of Political Advertising*, edited by Christina Holtz-Bacha and Marion R. Just, 101–12. New York: Routledge, 2017.

Loxton, James. "Authoritarian Successor Parties and the New Right in Latin America." In *Challenges of Party-Building in Latin America*, edited by Steven Levitsky, James Loxton, Brandon van Dyck, and Jorge Dominguez, 245–72. New York: Cambridge University Press, 2017.

Lucardi, Adrián, Juan Pablo Micozzi, and Agustín Vallejo. "Does the Early Bird Always Get the Worm? First Round Advantages and Second Round Victories in Latin America." *Electoral Studies* 81 (2023): 102570. https://doi.org/10.1016/j.electstud.2022.102570.

Luna, Juan Pablo. *Segmented Representation: Political Party Strategies in Unequal Democracies*. New York: Oxford University Press, 2014.

Luna, Juan Pablo, Cristian Pérez, Sergio Toro, Fernando Rosenblatt, Bárbara Poblete Sebastián Valenzuela, Andrés Cruz, Naim Bro, Daniel Alcatruz, and Andrea Escobar. "Much Ado About Facebook? Evidence from 80 Congressional Campaigns in Chile." *Journal of Information Technology & Politics* 19, no. 2 (2021): 129–39. https://doi.org/10.1080/19331681.2021.1936334.

Lupu, Noam. "The End of the Kirchner Era." *Journal of Democracy* 27, no. 2 (2016): 35–49. https://doi:10.1353/jod.2016.0033.

———. "Partisanship in Latin America." In *The Latin American Voter: Pursuing Representation and Accountability in Challenging Contexts*, edited by Ryan E. Carlin, Matthew M. Singer, and Elizabeth J. Zechmeister, 226–45. Ann Arbor: University of Michigan Press, 2015.

———. *Party Brands in Crisis: Partisanship, Brand Dilution, and the Breakdown of Political Parties in Latin America*. New York: Cambridge University Press, 2016.

———. "Who Votes for Chavismo? Class Voting in Hugo Chávez's Venezuela." *Latin American Research Review* 45, no. 1 (2010): 7–32. https://doi:10.1353/lar.0.0083.

Lupu, Noam, Virginia Oliveros, and Luis Schiumerini. "Toward a Theory of Campaigns and Voters in Developing Democracies." In *Campaigns and Voters in Developing Democracies: Argentina in Comparative Perspective*, edited by Noam Lupu, Virginia Oliveros, and Luis Schiumerini, 1–27. Ann Arbor: University of Michigan Press, 2019.

Madrid, Raúl L. *The Rise of Ethnic Politics in Latin America*. New York: Cambridge University Press, 2012.

Magaloni, Beatriz. *Voting for Autocracy: Hegemonic Party Survival and Its Demise in Mexico*. New York: Cambridge University Press, 2006.

Magaloni, Beatriz, and Alejandor Poiré. "The Issues, the Vote, and the Mandate for Change." In *Mexico's Pivotal Democratic Election: Candidates, Voters, and the Presidential Campaign of 2000*, edited by Jorge I. Dominguez and Chappell Lawson, 293–319. Stanford/La Jolla, CA: Stanford University Press and Center for U.S.-Mexican Studies, University of California at San Diego, 2004.

Mahoney, James. *The Legacies of Liberalism: Path Dependence and Political Regimes in Central America*. Baltimore: Johns Hopkins University Press, 2001.

Mainwaring, Scott (ed.). *Party Systems in Latin America: Institutionalization, Decay, and Collapse*. New York: Cambridge University Press, 2018.

———. "Party System Institutionalization in Contemporary Latin America." In *Party Systems in Latin America: Institutionalization, Decay, and Collapse*, edited by Scott Mainwaring, 34–70. New York: Cambridge University Press, 2018.

———. "Party System Institutionalization, Predictability, and Democracy." In *Party Systems in Latin America: Institutionalization, Decay, and Collapse*, edited by Scott Mainwaring, 71–101. New York: Cambridge University Press, 2018.

Mainwaring, Scott, Timothy J. Power, and Fernando Bizzarro. "The Uneven Institutionalization of a Party System: Brazil." In *Party Systems in Latin America: Institutionalization, Decay, and Collapse*, edited by Scott Mainwaring, 164–97. New York: Cambridge University Press, 2018.

Mainwaring, Scott, Mariano Torcal, and Nicolás M. Somma. "The Left and the Mobilization of Class Voting in Latin America." In *The Latin American Voter: Pursuing Representation and Accountability in Challenging Contexts*, edited by Ryan E. Carlin, Matthew M. Singer, and Elizabeth J. Zechmeister, 69–98. Ann Arbor: University of Michigan Press, 2015.

Mainwaring, Scott, and Yen-Pin Su. "Electoral Volatility in Latin America, 1932–2018." *Studies in Comparative International Development* 56, no. 3 (2021): 271–96. https://doi.org/10.1007/s12116-021-09340-x.

Maltz, Gideon. "The Case for Presidential Term Limits." *Journal of Democracy* 18, no. 1 (2007): 128–42. https://doi:10.1353/jod.2007.0010.

Manzetti, Luigi, and Guillermo Rosas. "Corruption and the Latin American Voter." In *The Latin American Voter: Pursuing Representation and Accountability in*

Challenging Contexts, edited by Ryan E. Carlin, Matthew M. Singer, and Elizabeth J. Zechmeister, 300–23. Ann Arbor: University of Michigan Press, 2015.

Marsteintredet, Leiv. "How the Dominican Republic Successfully Resisted Presidential Term Extension." ConstitutionNet, July 25, 2019. https://constitutionnet.org/news/how-dominican-republic-successfully-resisted-presidential-term-extension.

———. "Presidential Term Limits in Latin America: c.1820–1985." In *The Politics of Presidential Term Limits*, edited by Alexander Baturo and Robert Elgie, 103–122. New York: Oxford University Press, 2019.

Martínez i Coma, Ferran. "Electoral Reform." In *Election Watchdogs: Transparency, Accountability and Integrity*, edited by Pippa Norris and Alessandro Nai, 72–91. New York: Oxford University Press, 2017.

Martz, John. "Electoral Campaigning and Latin American Democratization: The Grancolombian Experience." *Journal of Interamerican Studies and World Affairs* 32, no. 1 (1990): 17–43. https://doi:10.2307/166128.

McCann, James A. "Changing Dimensions of National Elections in Mexico." In *The Oxford Handbook of Mexican Politics*, edited by Roderic Ai Camp, 497–522. New York: Oxford University Press, 2012.

McCann, James, and Jorge Domínguez. "Mexicans React to Electoral Fraud and Political Corruption: An Assessment of Public Opinion and Voting Behavior." *Electoral Studies* 17, no. 4 (1998): 483–503. https://doi.org/10.1016/S0261-3794(98)00026-2.

McClintock, Cynthia. *Electoral Rules and Democracy in Latin America*. New York: Oxford University Press, 2018.

McDonald, Ronald H. *Party Systems and Elections in Latin America*. Chicago: Markham Publishers, 1971.

Meléndez-Sánchez, Manuel. "Latin America Erupts: Millennial Authoritarianism in El Salvador." *Journal of Democracy* 32, no. 3 (2021): 19–32. http://doi.org/10.1353/jod.2021.0031.

Meyer, Peter J. "Honduras: Background and U.S. Relations." *Congressional Research Service*, April 27, 2020. https://fas.org/sgp/crs/row/RL34027.pdf.

Millett, Richard. *Guardians of the Dynasty: A History of the U.S.-Created Guardia Nacional de Nicaragua and the Somoza Family*. Maryknoll, NY: Orbis Books, 1977.

Mitchell, Gladys Lanier. "Campaign Strategies of Afro-Brazilian Politicians: A Preliminary Analysis." *Latin American Politics and Society* 51, no. 3 (2009): 111–42. https://doi.org/10.1111/j.1548-2456.2009.00058.x.

Molina, José, and Bernard Thibaut. "Venezuela." In *Elections in the Americas: A Data Handbook, vol. 2 South America*, edited by Dieter Nohlen, 535–92. New York: Oxford University Press, 2005.

Monsiváis-Carrillo, Alejandro. "Happy Winners, Sore Partisans? Political Trust, Partisanship, and the Populist Assault on Electoral Integrity in Mexico." *Journal of Politics in Latin America* 15, no. 1 (2022): 72–95. https://doi.org/10.1177/1866802X221136147.

Moreno, Alejandro. "The Effects of Negative Campaigns on Mexican Voters." In *Mexico's Pivotal Democratic Election: Candidates, Voters, and the Presidential*

Campaign of 2000, edited by Jorge I. Dominguez and Chappell Lawson, 243–68. Stanford/La Jolla, CA: Stanford University Press and Center for U.S.-Mexican Studies, University of California at San Diego, 2004.

Moreno, Dario. "Respectable Intervention: The United States and the Central American Elections." In *Elections and Democracy in Central America Revisited*, edited by Mitchell A. Seligson and John A. Booth, 224–43. Chapel Hill: University of North Carolina Press, 1995.

Moreno Morales, Daniel E. "Ethnicity and Electoral Preferences in Latin America." In *The Latin American Voter: Pursuing Representation and Accountability in Challenging Contexts*, edited by Ryan E. Carlin, Matthew M. Singer, and Elizabeth J. Zechmeister, 122–42. Ann Arbor: University of Michigan Press, 2015.

Morgan, Jana. *Bankrupt Representation and Party System Collapse*. University Park, PA: Pennsylvania State University Press, 2011.

———. "Deterioration and Polarization of Party Politics in Venezuela." In *Party Systems in Latin America: Institutionalization, Decay, and Collapse*, edited by Scott Mainwaring, 291–325. New York: Cambridge University Press, 2018.

———. "Gender and the Latin American Voter." In *The Latin American Voter: Pursuing Representation and Accountability in Challenging Contexts*, edited by Ryan E. Carlin, Matthew M. Singer, and Elizabeth J. Zechmeister, 143–67. Ann Arbor: University of Michigan Press, 2015.

Morgenstern, Scott, and Javier Vázquez-D'Elía. "Electoral Laws, Parties, and Party Systems in Latin America." *Annual Review of Political Science* 10 (2007): 143–68. https://doi.org/10.1146/annurev.polisci.10.081205.094050.

Müller, Jan-Werner. *What Is Populism?* Philadelphia: University of Pennsylvania Press, 2016.

Muñoz, Paula. *Buying Audiences: Clientelism and Electoral Campaigns When Parties Are Weak*. New York: Oxford University Press, 2020.

Murillo, María Victoria, and Steven Levitsky. "Economic Shocks and Partisan Realignment in Argentina." In *Campaigns and Voters in Developing Democracies: Argentina in Comparative Perspective*, edited by Noam Lupu, Virginia Oliveros, and Luis Schiumerini, 28–52. Ann Arbor: University of Michigan Press, 2019.

Murillo, M. Victoria, and Giancarlo Visconti. "Economic Performance and Incumbents' Support in Latin America." *Electoral Studies* 45 (2017): 180–90. https://doi.org/10.1016/j.electstud.2016.10.007.

Nadeau, Richard, Éric Bélanger, Michael S. Lewis-Beck, Matthieu Turgeon, and François Gélineau. *Latin American Elections: Choice and Change*. Ann Arbor: University of Michigan Press, 2017.

Nai, Alessandro. "Going Negative, Worldwide: Towards a General Understanding of Determinants and Targets of Negative Campaigning." *Government and Opposition* 55, no. 3 (2020): 430–55. https://doi:10.1017/gov.2018.32.

National Democratic Institute. *Interim Report on the May 16, 1994, Elections in the Dominican Republic*. 1994. https://www.ndi.org/sites/default/files/263_do_94elections.pdf.

National Democratic Institute and Carter Center. *Peru Elections 2000: Final Report of the National Democratic Institute/Carter Center Joint Election Monitoring Project*. n.d.

Negretto, Gabriel L. "Choosing How to Choose Presidents: Parties, Military Rulers, and Presidential Elections in Latin America." *Journal of Politics* 68, no. 2 (2006): 421–33. https://doi.org/10.1111/j.1468-2508.2006.00417.x.

———. "Tinkering with Executive Term Limits: Partisan Imbalances and Institutional Legacies in Latin America." *Democratization* 29, no. 1 (2022): 38–56. https://doi.org/10.1080/13510347.2021.1980539.

Negretto, Gabriel L., and Giancarlo Visconti. "Electoral Reform under Limited Party Competition: The Adoption of Proportional Representation in Latin America." *Latin American Politics and Society* 60, no. 1 (2018): 27–51. https://www.jstor.org/stable/44684430.

Nichter, Simeon. "Vote Buying or Turnout Buying? Machine Politics and the Secret Ballot." *American Political Science Review* 102, no. 1 (2008): 19–31. https://doi:10.1017/S0003055408080106.

———. *Votes for Survival: Relational Clientelism in Latin America.* New York: Cambridge University Press, 2018.

Nichter, Simeon, and Brian Palmer-Rubin. "Clientelism, Declared Support, and Mexico's 2012 Campaign." In *Mexico's Evolving Democracy: A Comparative Study of the 2012 Elections,* edited by Jorge I. Domínguez, Kenneth F. Greene, Chappell H. Lawson, and Alejandro Moreno, 200–226. Baltimore: Johns Hopkins University Press, 2015.

Nieto-Vazquez, Octael. "Political Finance in the Digital Age: A Case Study of Mexico." International IDEA, 2023. https://www.idea.int/sites/default/files/political-finance-in-the-digital-age-case-study-mexico.pdf.

Nohlen, Dieter (ed.). *Elections in the Americas: A Data Handbook, vol. 2 South America.* New York: Oxford University Press, 2005.

Norris, Pippa, Richard W. Frank, and Ferran Martínez i Coma. "Assessing the Quality of Elections." *Journal of Democracy* 24, no. 4 (2013): 124–35. http://doi.org/10.1353/jod.2013.0063.

Norris, Pippa, and Max Grömping. Perceptions of Electoral Integrity, (PEI-7.0), version 2. Harvard Dataverse, 2019.

Organization of American States (OAS). Análisis de Integridad Electoral: Elecciones Generales en el Estado Plurinacional de Bolivia. October 20, 2019. http://www.oas.org/documents/spa/press/Informe-Auditoria-Bolivia-2019.pdf.

———. Electoral Observation Mission, Elections of Local Authorities, Republic of Colombia, October 27, 2019, Final Report. n.d.

———. Electoral Observation Mission, General Election, Honduras, November 26, 2017, Final Report. n.d.

———. Electoral Observation Mission, Republic of Guatemala, Final Report. 2020.

———. Final Report of the OAS Mission of Electoral Accompaniment to Nicaragua for the General Elections, November 6, 2011. n.d.

———. Informe Final de la Misión de Observación Electoral de la Organización de los Estados Americanos, Elecciones Generales del 24 de Noviembre de 2013 de la República de Honduras. n.d.

Oliveros, Virginia. "Perceptions of Ballot Integrity and Clientelism." In *Campaigns and Voters in Developing Democracies: Argentina in Comparative Perspective,* edited by Noam Lupu, Virginia Oliveros, and Luis Schiumerini, 213–38. Ann Arbor: University of Michigan Press, 2019.

O'Neil, Shannon. "Mexico: Democratic Advances and Limitations." In *Constructing Democratic Governance in Latin America*, 4th edition, edited by Jorge I. Domínguez and Michael Shifter, 255–81. Baltimore: Johns Hopkins University Press, 2013.

Ortiz Ortiz, Ricardo. "Reforma Electoral 2020 y Sistemas Electorales Nacionales y Locales: Igualdad, Proporcionalidad y Paridad." *Democracias* 8 (August 2020): 51–82. http://institutodemocracia.gob.ec/wp-content/uploads/2020/08/reforma _electoral.pdf.

Page, Maria, and Julia Pomares. "The Move Toward State-Run Mass Media Electoral Campaigns in Latin America: An Evaluation of the First Implementation in the 2011 Argentine Presidential Elections." *Election Law Journal* 11, no. 4 (2012): 532–44. https://doi.org/10.1089/elj.2012.1145.

Pallister, Kevin. "Digital Caudillos: The Use of Social Media in Guatemalan Presidential Campaigns." *Journal of Politics in Latin America* 13, no. 2 (2021): 269–83. https://doi.org/10.1177/1866802X211010319.

———. *Election Administration and the Politics of Voter Access*. New York: Routledge, 2017.

Pallister, Kevin, and Erin Fitzpatrick. "The Medium and the Message in Argentina's Presidential Campaigns." *International Journal of Press/Politics* (2023). https://doi .org/10.1177/19401612221149272.

Pastor, Daniel. "Origins of the Chilean Binominal Election System." *Revista de Ciencia Politica* 24, no. 1 (2004): 38–57. http://dx.doi.org/10.4067/S0718 -090X2004000100002.

Pavão, Nara. "Conditional Cash Transfer Programs and Electoral Accountability: Evidence from Latin America." *Latin American Politics and Society* 58, no. 2 (2016): 74–99. https://doi:10.1111/j.1548-2456.2016.00311.x.

Pereira, Carlos, and Marcus André Melo. "Reelecting Corrupt Incumbents in Exchange for Public Goods: Rouba Mas Faz in Brazil." *Latin American Research Review* 50, no. 4 (2015): 88–115. https://doi:10.1353/lar.2015.0054.

Pérez Argüello, Maria Fernanda, and Donara Barojan. "Disinformation in the 2018 Elections: Mexico." In *Disinformation in Democracies: Strengthening Digital Resilience in Latin America*, edited by Luiza Bandeira, Donara Barojan, Roberta Braga, Jose Luis Peñarredonda, and Maria Fernanda Pérez Argüello, 20–29. Washington, DC: Atlantic Council, 2019.

Pérez, Orlando J. "The Impact of Crime on Voter Choice in Latin America." In *The Latin American Voter: Pursuing Representation and Accountability in Challenging Contexts*, edited by Ryan E. Carlin, Matthew M. Singer, and Elizabeth J. Zechmeister, 324–45. Ann Arbor: University of Michigan Press, 2015.

Pérez-Liñán, Aníbal. "Neoinstitutional Accounts of Voter Turnout: Moving Beyond Industrial Democracies." *Electoral Studies* 20, no. 2 (2001): 281–97. https://doi.org /10.1016/S0261-3794(00)00019-6.

Pitkin, Hanna. *The Concept of Representation*. Berkeley: University of California Press, 1967.

Plasser, Fritz. "American Campaign Techniques Worldwide." *Harvard International Journal of Press/Politics* 5, no. 4 (2000): 33–54. https://doi.org/10.1177/1081180X00005004003.

Porto, Mauro. "Framing Controversies: Television and the 2002 Presidential Election in Brazil." *Political Communication* 24, no. 1 (2007): 19–36. https://doi.org/10.1080/10584600601128705.

Posada-Carbó, Eduardo. "Electoral Juggling: A Comparative History of the Corruption of Suffrage in Latin America, 1830–1930." *Journal of Latin American Studies* 32, no. 3 (2000): 611–44. https://doi:10.1017/S0022216X00005782.

Power, Timothy J. "Compulsory for Whom? Mandatory Voting and Electoral Participation in Brazil, 1986–2006." *Journal of Politics in Latin America* 1, no. 1 (2009): 97–122. https://doi.org/10.1177/1866802X0900100105.

Power, Timothy J., and James C. Garand. "Determinants of Invalid Voting in Latin America." *Electoral Studies* 26, no. 2 (2007): 432–44. https://doi.org/10.1016/j.electstud.2006.11.001.

Przeworski, Adam. *Why Bother with Elections?* Cambridge, UK: Polity, 2018.

Remmer, Karen L. "The Political Impact of Economic Crisis in Latin America in the 1980s." *American Political Science Review* 85, no. 3 (1991): 777–800. https://doi:10.2307/1963850.

Rennó, Lucio R. "The Bolsonaro Voter: Issue Positions and Vote Choice in the 2018 Brazilian Presidential Elections." *Latin American Politics and Society* 62, no. 4 (2020): 1–23. https://doi:10.1017/lap.2020.13.

Repucci, Sarah, and Amy Slipowitz. *Freedom in the World 2022: The Global Expansion of Authoritarian Rule.* Freedom House, 2022. https://freedomhouse.org/report/freedom-world/2022/global-expansion-authoritarian-rule.

Restrepo Echavarría, Néstor J. "La Profesionalización de las Campañas Electorales: Las Elecciones Presidenciales de Colombia 2010." *Revista Española de Ciencia Política* 38 (2015): 85–114.

Reyes-Housholder, Catherine. "Women Mobilizing Women: Candidates' Strategies for Winning the Presidency." *Journal of Politics in Latin America* 10, no. 1 (2018): 69–97. https://doi.org/10.1177/1866802X1801000103.

Rios Tobar, Marcela. "Seizing a Window of Opportunity: The Election of President Bachelet in Chile." *Politics & Gender* 4, no. 3 (2008): 509–19. https://doi:10.1017/S1743923X0800041X.

Roberts, Kenneth. *Changing Course in Latin America: Party Systems in the Neoliberal Era.* New York: Cambridge University Press, 2014.

Rock, David. *Argentina, 1516–1987: From Spanish Colonization to Alfonsín.* Berkeley: University of California Press, 1987.

Rodríguez O., Jaime E. *The Independence of Spanish America.* New York: Cambridge University Press, 1998.

Romero Ballivián, Salvador. *Elecciones en América Latina.* La Paz: Tribunal Supremo Electoral and Instituto Internacional para la Democracia la Asistencia Electoral, 2020.

Rosenblatt, Fernando. *Party Vibrancy and Democracy in Latin America.* New York: Oxford University Press, 2018.

Rottinghaus, Brandon, and Irina Alberro. "Rivaling the PRI: The Image Management of Vicente Fox and the Use of Public Opinion Polling in the 2000 Mexican Election." *Latin American Politics and Society* 47, no. 2 (2005): 143–58. https://doi:10.1111/j.1548-2456.2005.tb00312.x.

Sabet, Daniel M. *When Corruption Funds the Political System: A Case Study of Honduras*. Wilson Center Latin American Program, 2020. https://www.wilsoncenter.org/sites/default/files/media/uploads/documents/When%20Corruption%20Funds%20the%20Political%20System_Final.pdf.

Samuels, David. "Incumbents and Challengers on a Level Playing Field: Assessing the Impact of Campaign Finance in Brazil." *Journal of Politics* 63, no. 2 (2001): 569–84. https://doi.org/10.1111/0022-3816.00079.

———. "Money, Elections, and Democracy in Brazil." *Latin American Politics and Society* 43, no. 2 (2001): 27–48. https://doi:10.1111/j.1548-2456.2001.tb00398.x.

———. "Political Ambition, Candidate Recruitment, and Legislative Politics in Brazil." In *Pathways to Power: Political Recruitment and Candidate Selection in Latin America*, edited by Peter Siavelis and Scott Morgenstern, 76–91. University Park, PA: Penn State University Press, 2008.

———. "When Does Every Penny Count? Intra-Party Competition and Campaign Finance in Brazil." *Party Politics* 7, no. 1 (2001): 89–102. https://doi.org/10.1177/1354068801007001005.

Samuels, David J., and Cesar Zucco. *Partisans, Antipartisans, and Nonpartisans: Voting Behavior in Brazil*. New York: Cambridge University Press, 2018.

Sánchez-Sibony, Omar. "Competitive Authoritarianism in Morales's Bolivia: Skewing Arenas of Competition." *Latin American Politics and Society* 63, no. 1 (2021): 118–44. https://doi:10.1017/lap.2020.35.

Scarrow, Susan E. "Political Finance in Comparative Perspective." *Annual Review of Political Science* 10 (2007): 193–210. https://doi.org/10.1146/annurev.polisci.10.080505.100115.

Schafer, Joby, and Andy Baker. "Clientelism as Persuasion-Buying: Evidence from Latin America." *Comparative Political Studies* 48, no. 9 (2015): 1093–1126. https://doi.org/10.1177/0010414015574881.

Schedler, Andreas. "The Criminal Subversion of Mexican Democracy." *Journal of Democracy* 25, no. 1 (2014): 5–18. http://doi.org/10.1353/jod.2014.0016.

———. "The Menu of Manipulation." *Journal of Democracy* 13, no. 2 (2002): 36–50. http://doi.org/10.1353/jod.2002.0031.

Schiumerini, Luis. "Macri's Mandate: Structural Reform or Better Performance?" In *Campaigns and Voters in Developing Democracies: Argentina in Comparative Perspective*, edited by Noam Lupu, Virginia Oliveros, and Luis Schiumerini, 136–61. Ann Arbor: University of Michigan Press, 2019.

Schwindt-Bayer, Leslie A. *Political Power and Women's Representation in Latin America*. New York: Oxford University Press, 2010.

Seawright, Jason. *Party System Collapse: The Roots of Crisis in Peru and Venezuela*. Stanford: Stanford University Press, 2012.

———. "Roots in Society: Attachment between Citizens and Party Systems in Latin America." In *Party Systems in Latin America: Institutionalization, Decay, and*

Collapse, edited by Scott Mainwaring, 380–407. New York: Cambridge University Press, 2018.

Serra, Gilles. "Vote Buying with Illegal Resources: Manifestation of a Weak Rule of Law in Mexico." *Journal of Politics in Latin America* 8, no. 1 (2016): 129–50. https://doi.org/10.1177/1866802X1600800105.

Serrafero, Mario D. "El Control de la Sucesión: Reelección y Limitaciones de Elección Presidencial por Parentesco en América Latina." *Revista de Estudos e Pesquisas sobre as Américas* 9, no. 1 (2015): 81–103. https://periodicos.unb.br/index.php/repam/article/view/16051.

Siavelis, Peter. "Continuity and Change in the Chilean Party System: On the Transformational Effects of Electoral Reform." *Comparative Political Studies* 30, no. 6 (1997): 651–74. https://doi.org/10.1177/0010414097030006001.

Siavelis, Peter, and Scott Morgenstern (eds.). *Pathways to Power: Political Recruitment and Candidate Selection in Latin America*. University Park, PA: Penn State University Press, 2008.

Simpser, Alberto, and Daniela Donno. "Can International Election Monitoring Harm Governance?" *Journal of Politics* 74, no. 2 (2012): 501–13. https://doi.org/10.1017/S002238161100168X.

Singer, Matthew. "Economic Voting in an Era of Non-Crisis: The Changing Electoral Agenda in Latin America, 1982–2010." *Comparative Politics* 45, no. 2 (2013): 169–85. https://www.jstor.org/stable/41714181.

———. "Elite Polarization and the Electoral Impact of Left-Right Placements: Evidence from Latin America." *Latin American Research Review* 51, no. 2 (2016): 174–94. https://doi:10.1353/lar.2016.0022.

Slimovich, Ana. "La Ruta Digital a la Presidencia Argentina: Un Análisis Político e Hipermediático de los Discursos de Mauricio Macri en las Redes Sociales." *Dixit* 26 (2017): 24–43. https://doi.org/10.22235/d.v0i26.1321.

Snyder, Richard, and David Samuels. "Devaluing the Vote in Latin America." *Journal of Democracy* 12, no. 1 (2001): 146–59. http://doi.org/10.1353/jod.2001.0016.

Stokes, Susan, Thad Dunning, Marcelo Nazareno, and Valeria Brusco. *Brokers, Voters, and Clientelism: The Puzzle of Distributive Politics*. New York: Cambridge University Press, 2013.

Su, Yen-Pin. "Party Registration Rules and Party Systems in Latin America." *Party Politics* 21, no. 2 (2015): 295–309. https://doi.org/10.1177/1354068812472585.

———. "Rules for Party Subsidies and Electoral Volatility in Latin America." *Latin American Research Review* 57, no. 1 (2022): 151–69. https://doi:10.1017/lar.2022.9.

Szwarcberg, Mariela. "Political Parties and Rallies in Latin America." *Party Politics* 20, no. 3 (2014): 456–66. https://doi.org/10.1177/1354068811436049.

Taylor, Steven L., Felipe Botero, and Brian F. Crisp. "Precandidates, Candidates, and Presidents: Paths to the Colombian Presidency." In *Pathways to Power: Political Recruitment and Candidate Selection in Latin America*, edited by Peter Siavelis and Scott Morgenstern, 271–91. University Park, PA: Penn State University Press, 2008.

Telles, Edward E. *Race in Another America: The Significance of Skin Color in Brazil*. Princeton: Princeton University Press, 2004.

Thaler, Kai M. "Nicaragua: A Return to Caudillismo." *Journal of Democracy* 28, no. 2 (2017): 157–69. http://doi.org/10.1353/jod.2017.0032.

Trelles, Alejandro, and Miguel Carreras. "Bullets and Votes: Violence and Electoral Participation in Mexico." *Journal of Politics in Latin America* 4, no. 2 (2012): 89–123. https://doi.org/10.1177/1866802X1200400204.

Tuesta Soldevilla, Fernando. "Peru." In *Elections in the Americas: A Data Handbook, vol. 2 South America*, edited by Dieter Nohlen, 445–86. New York: Oxford University Press, 2005.

Uang, Randy Sunwin. "Campaigning on Public Security in Latin America: Obstacles to Success." *Latin American Politics and Society* 55, no. 2 (2013): 26–51. https://doi:10.1111/j.1548-2456.2013.00192.x.

Valdini, Melody E., and Michael S. Lewis-Beck. "Economic Voting in Latin America: Rules and Responsibility." *American Journal of Political Science* 62, no. 2 (2018): 410–23. https://doi.org/10.1111/ajps.12339.

Valenzuela, J. Samuel. "Building Aspects of Democracy before Democracy: Electoral Practices in Nineteenth Century Chile." In *Elections before Democracy: The History of Elections in Europe and Latin America*, edited by Eduardo Posada-Carbó, 223–57. New York: St. Martin's Press, 1996.

Valenzuela, Rubén Aguilar. "La Campaña Presidencial del 2012 en México: La Estrategia y el Discurso de los Candidatos." In *Campañas Electorales en México y Una Visión a Centroamérica*, edited by María Antonia Martínez and Rubén Aguilar Valenzuela, 11–28. Ciudad de México: Miguel Angel Porrúa/Instituto Federal Electoral/Asociación Latinoamericana de Investigadores en Campañas Electorales/Fundación José Ortega y Gasset-Gregorio Marañón, 2013.

Van Cott, Donna Lee. *From Movements to Parties in Latin America: The Evolution of Ethnic Politics*. New York: Cambridge University Press, 2005.

Venzor Coronado, Alberto. "Análisis de las Estrategias del *Marketing* Político y el Uso de Redes Sociales entre los Candidatos a la Presidencia de México en 2012." In *Campañas Electorales en México y una Visión a Centroamérica*, edited by María Antonia Martínez and Rubén Aguilar Valenzuela, 115–29. Ciudad de México: Miguel Angel Porrúa/Instituto Federal Electoral/Asociación Latinoamericana de Investigadores en Campañas Electorales/Fundación José Ortega y Gasset-Gregorio Marañón, 2013.

Verba, Sidney, Kay Lehman Schlozman, and Henry E. Brady. *Voice and Equality: Civic Voluntarism in American Politics*. Cambridge, MA: Harvard University Press, 1995.

Vidigal, Robert. "Authoritarianism and Right-Wing Voting in Brazil." *Latin American Research Review* 57, no. 3 (2022): 554–72. https://doi:10.1017/lar.2022.32.

Vommaro, Gabriel. "Horizontal Coordination and Vertical Aggregation Mechanisms of the PRO in Argentina and Its Subnational Variations." In *Diminished Parties: Democratic Representation in Contemporary Latin America*, edited by Juan Pablo Luna, Rafael Piñeiro Rodríguez, Fernando Rosenblatt, and Gabriel Vommaro, 48–69. New York: Cambridge University Press, 2022.

Walter, Knut. *The Regime of Anastasio Somoza, 1936–1956*. Chapel Hill: University of North Carolina Press, 1993.

Weitz-Shapiro, Rebecca. "What Wins Votes: Why Some Politicians Opt Out of Clientelism." *American Journal of Political Science* 56, no. 3 (2012): 568–83. https://doi.org/10.1111/j.1540-5907.2011.00578.x.

West, Karleen Jones. *Candidate Matters: A Study of Ethnic Parties, Campaigns, and Elections in Latin America*. New York: Oxford University Press, 2020.

Wills-Otero, Laura, Bibiana Ortega, and Viviana Sarmiento. "The Colombian Liberal Party and Conservative Party: From Political Parties to Diminished Subtypes." In *Diminished Parties: Democratic Representation in Contemporary Latin America*, edited by Juan Pablo Luna, Rafael Piñeiro Rodríguez, Fernando Rosenblatt, and Gabriel Vommaro, 151–72. New York: Cambridge University Press, 2022.

Wilson, Bruce M. "Enforcing Rights and Exercising an Accountability Function: Costa Rica's Constitutional Chamber of the Supreme Court." In *Courts in Latin America*, edited by Gretchen Helmke and Julio Rios-Figueroa, 55–80. New York: Cambridge University Press, 2011.

Wolff, Jonas. "The Turbulent End of an Era in Bolivia: Contested Elections, the Ouster of Evo Morales, and the Beginning of a Transition Towards an Uncertain Future." *Revista de Ciencia Política* 40, no. 2 (2020): 163–86. http://dx.doi.org/10.4067/S0718-090X2020005000105.

Wood, Elisabeth J. "Civil War and the Transformation of Elite Representation in El Salvador." In *Conservative Parties, the Right, and Democracy in Latin America*, edited by Kevin J. Middlebrook, 223–54. Baltimore: The Johns Hopkins University Press, 2000.

Woodward Jr., Ralph Lee. *Central America: A Nation Divided*. New York: Oxford University Press, 1999.

Yashar, Deborah J. *Demanding Democracy: Reform and Reaction in Costa Rica and Guatemala, 1870s–1950s*. Stanford: Stanford University Press, 1997.

Zechmeister, Elizabeth J. "Left-Right Identifications and the Latin American Voter." In *The Latin American Voter: Pursuing Representation and Accountability in Challenging Contexts*, edited by Ryan E. Carlin, Matthew M. Singer, and Elizabeth J. Zechmeister, 195–225. Ann Arbor: University of Michigan Press, 2015.

Zechmeister, Elizabeth J., and Daniel Zizumbo-Colunga. "The Varying Political Toll of Concerns About Corruption in Good Versus Bad Economic Times." *Comparative Political Studies* 46, no. 10 (2013): 1190–218. https://doi.org/10.1177/0010414012472468.

Zetterberg, Pär. "Do Gender Quotas Foster Women's Political Engagement? Lessons from Latin America." *Political Research Quarterly* 62, no. 4 (2009): 715–30. https://doi.org/10.1177/1065912908322411.

Zucco, Cesar. "When Payouts Pay Off: Conditional Cash Transfers and Voting Behavior in Brazil 2002–10." *American Journal of Political Science* 57, no. 4 (2013): 810–22. https://doi.org/10.1111/ajps.12026.

Index

Page references for figures are italicized

www.ingramcontent.com/pod-product-compliance
Lightning Source LLC
Chambersburg PA
CBHW070401270326
41926CB00014B/2650